PERFORMED LITERATURE

Words and Music by Bob Dylan

SECOND EDITION

Betsy Bowden

University Press of America,® Inc.
Lanham · New York · Oxford

Copyright © 2001 by
University Press of America,® Inc.
4720 Boston Way
Lanham, Maryland 20706

12 Hid's Copse Rd.
Cumnor Hill, Oxford OX2 9JJ

Library of Congress Cataloging-in-Publication Data

Bowden, Betsy.
Performed literature : words and music by Bob Dylan /
Betsy Bowden.—2nd ed.
p.   cm
Includes bibliographical references, discography, and index.
1. Dylan, Bob, 1941- Songs. 2. Music and literature. 3. Lyric poetry.
I. Dylan, Bob, 1941- II. Title.
ML420.D98 B7   2001   782.42164'092—dc21   00-068318 CIP

ISBN 0-7618-1947-9 (pbk. : alk. paper)

Contents

Preface to the Second Edition

"Does Dylan know that you wrote that book?" I am very often asked. Therefore, I have long promised to introduce a second edition by quoting his comment on my first edition. Once upon a time, in the roomful of books about him at his music publisher's, he was idly flipping pages in mine. An employee remarked, "That one's different from the others. The author's a Chaucer scholar."

> "Yenh?"
> —Bob Dylan

Reporting here live from the academic front, I have made only cosmetic changes in the text of that 1982 edition, a revision of my 1978 dissertation. The song-by-song commentaries remain based on scholarship as of 7 April 1976, when the heavens opened over Berkeley and a booming voice declared, "The world does not need another Chaucer dissertation." Rather than garble the footnotes and bibliography, therefore, I have added an Appendix D of "Reference Sources on Bob Dylan," almost all published since 1975.

The second edition's Overview still describes the potential for future development of performance analysis by specialists in folklore, literature, theater arts, musicology, linguistics, anthropology, and other fields. During the twenty years of schooling since my doctoral work, no one has produced a definitive study of performance—rightly so, in that compilation and consideration of evidence ought always to precede theoretical generalization about any issue. Instead, however, scholarly writing is sinking further and further into a murky bog of abstract assertion rooted in little or no evidence. Nowadays too many literature professors shrug aside any responsibility to think, before they speak or write theory.

In contrast, during the past two decades, toilers outside of academe have given top priority to collecting and documenting essential evidence. Independent research, chronicled in Appendix D, has produced bibliographies of every word written about Dylan and his work, including the ephemeral and unpublished. Discographies, concert-tour playlists, even a studio "sessionography" account for all performances ever captured on tape. Biographies and chronologies trace where, when, why, how, and with whom each recorded utterance took place. Compilers also document early performances that, to their frustration, disappeared into thin air never to be heard again.

What has impelled the gathering of so much information? At first, like any famous person, Dylan attracted curiosity about his personal life—most intrusively that of A. J. Weberman, who dug through his garbage. At the same time, though, intelligent and responsible fans (notably Sandy Gant and Roger Ford) were laying technological groundwork essential to eventual analysis of Dylan's variant artistic performances. As soon as cassette tape started to displace reel-to-reel, they began preparing and trading copies of unreleased performances: concerts, warm-up sessions, and so on. As soon as computers became available for home use, people exchanging bootleg tapes began also to generate updated lists of information about the recordings. Certain entrepreneurial fans took advantage of tapes so obtained, however, to manufacture and sell vinyl records of unreleased material.

Soon Dylan stopped opposing and started supplying popular demand. With several cuts on *Self Portrait* (June '70) and then the whole of *Before the Flood* (June '74), he began releasing material recorded live in concert rather than in a studio. His record producers began also to release cuts previously rejected or never intended for the public: reputedly against the artist's wishes as *Dylan* (Nov. '73), then with compliance for *The Basement Tapes* (June '75), *Biograph* (Nov. '85), and *The Bootleg Series* (March '91).

As bootlegs crossed the line to commercial availability, book publishers likewise began responding to fans' appetite for facts about performance. In 1980 the publishing giant Macmillan took over Paul Cable's pioneering *Bob Dylan: His Unreleased Recordings*. Similar accounts came from small presses in Scotland (Stuart Hoggard and Jim Shields), Scandinavia (Michael Krogsgaard), and France (Dominique Roques). Ever more detailed discographies now see steady publication. In Appendix D, note especially items done in the 1990s by Clinton Heylin, Patrick Humphries and John Bauldie, Michael Krogsgaard, Greil Marcus, William McKeen, John

Nogowski, Jeff Friedman (in Bob Spitz's book), and Richard Wissolik.

Bob Dylan is not a poet. He is a singer-songwriter, a performing artist. The unit of his art, as collected and documented by his intended audience, is the live performance. A posthumous *Complete Works of Bob Dylan* will have to consist of thousands upon thousands of sound recordings, not words on paper. Right now, no existing technological tool can give researchers ready access to his entire corpus of work. But hey, the technologies they are a-changin'. Meanwhile, posthumousness from natural causes is not imminent: Heylin notes that as of 1995, during which year Dylan did a record 118 concerts worldwide, in his entire career he had postponed exactly two concerts due to illness.

Because of Heylin and other avid data assemblers, how close are we to having *The Complete Works So Far of Bob Dylan*? By Friedman's count, between January 1974 and March 1991 Dylan did 761 concerts (excluding guest appearances). Of that number, recordings exist of 713 entire concerts plus 18 partial ones, each at a precisely known location and date with precisely known backup musicians and other details. More recent events are the best preserved. Between March 1986 and his final entry before publication, March 1991, Friedman notes only two concerts not available on tape: one in São Paulo, Brazil, on 18 Jan. 1990, and one in Oklahoma City on 5 Sept. 1990. Doubtless those two, and all concerts since 1991, have since come into circulation thanks to these published discographies; to "fanzines" such as *On the Tracks*, *Telegraph/Wanted Man*, *Look Back*, and *Isis*; to the international swap-meet at Plankenstein Castle, organized each year by Robert Koehler, Vogtgasse 1/52, A-1140 Vienna, Austria; and to a collectors' service: Rolling Tomes, P. O. Box 1943, Grand Junction, CO 81502, U.S.A. [Two previously active collectors' services did not respond to query letters in summer 1999.]

Singers other than Dylan, to be sure, have engendered interest in their variant oral performances. Analogous material is taped and traded by fans of the Grateful Dead or Beatles, for example. Dylan's case differs in both focus and scope. He as an individual composes almost everything that he performs, either solo or else as lead singer with backup musicians of his choice. And, only for Dylan is the international data exchange now so solidly established that future investigators will have access to just about everything sung or indeed spoken during the artist's entire public adult life—"public" including, for example, a friend's apartment in 1961 with a reel-to-reel recorder running in the background. Such "party tapes" constitute primary evidence, along with concerts and guest appearances on stage, studio recording sessions and outtakes of them, jam sessions, practice sessions, participation (pseudonymous or no) in others' released recordings, interviews, phone messages, and performances on radio, on film, on television, perhaps on media not yet invented.

Given such massive amounts of evidence both extant and potential, what can be concluded about Dylan's or anyone's performing art *qua* art? Nothing, so far. No academic field yet provides methodology adequate to words and music combined in variant oral performances. Musicology, even ethnomusicology, falls far short, as do folklore and related fields; jargon-drenched literary criticism may someday wash back ashore unfit for even its established realms of inquiry. As appropriate methodologies do emerge, though, with help from outside the ivory tower, Dylan's songs will stand firm as the first and the largest lifetime performance corpus ever to be recorded and documented.

In the meantime, analysis must focus on what William Blake would call Minute Particulars. We must listen carefully and ask of each separate performance as recorded, How does it feel? How does it say what we know that it says? How does a song mean in our ears, not in print? Yes 'n' how many times can a man turn his head and pretend that he just doesn't. . . oh, oops, sorry about that. Sometimes The Man just takes over.

Betsy Bowden
Philadelphia
January 1997

P.S. July 2000. Nearly four years have passed since I sent this second edition off to a small press that thereafter collapsed due to computer-related pressures on academic publishing—specifically, due to a technique called "scanning," which creates errors that keep resurfacing despite human attempts at correction. Publication now moves with snaillike majesty. Obviously, by now I could have typed this whole book on a manual typewriter and sent carbon copies. . . nay, indeed, could have carved it in runes on a tree trunk and sent it floating toward the hands of you the readers. I have made no attempt to update Appendix D or E past 1997.

Acknowledgments

This book began as a dissertation in English at the University of California at Berkeley—inspired by folklorist Alan Dundes, encouraged by medievalist Charles Muscatine, directed by poet Ron Loewinsohn, and patiently made more precise by musicologist Bonnie Wade. Donna Holloway helped us all, and Wayne Bernhardson got me through dissertation and book in ways too numerous to enumerate. But the book really began in a smoky Madison apartment, in 1966, when David Dunaway said, "Hear the one with the mustache say 'geez, I can't find my knees'—isn't that a great line?" My parents, Edward and Ruth Bowden, have only recently ceased to regret that they bought me my first Dylan album that Christmas.

For financial support I thank Dean Thomas Magner of Penn State, whose generosity with research funds has enabled me to forgive his once having called me "Betsy Bowden, Girl Scholar." For information and encouragement and support on all kinds of levels, I also thank Borgo Press (*requiescat in pacem*), Janet Cooper, Brian Cotter, Sis Cunningham, Eleanor Ely, Roger Ford, Robert Worth Frank, Jr., Gordon Friesen, Sandy Gant, Mel Greenlee, Marjorie Guthrie, Suzanne Korey, Sonia Krutzke, Greil Marcus, Andrew Mirer, Alice Radin, Christopher Ricks, Jeff Rosen, Wendy Sarvasy, Deborah Shaw, Robert Shelton, R. L. and Sallie Wadsworth, and Cindy Wells.

For permission to reproduce entire song texts I am grateful to Dwarf Music for the words to "Just Like a Woman" (c 1966) and "Sad-Eyed Lady of the Lowlands" (c 1966); Ram's Horn Music for "Idiot Wind" (c 1974, 1975), "Isis" (c 1975, 1976), and "Shelter from the Storm" (c 1974, 1975); Warner Bros. Inc. for "A Hard Rain's A-Gonna Fall" (c 1963), "It Ain't Me, Babe" (c 1964), "Like a Rolling Stone" (c 1965), "Oxford Town" (c

1963), "She Belongs to Me" (c 1965), and "Subterranean Homesick Blues" (c 1965); and Appleseed Music, Inc. for "The Ballad of Oxford, Mississippi" by Phil Ochs (c 1962).

I also wish to thank each publisher specified for permission to quote lines from the following songs: Big Sky Music for "If Dogs Run Free" (c 1970), "Lay, Lady, Lay" (c 1969), and "Is Your Love in Vain?" (c 1978); Dwarf Music for "Absolutely Sweet Marie" (c 1966), "Dear Landlord" (c 1968), "Pledging My Time" (c 1966), "Rainy Day Women #12 & 35" (c 1966), and "Stuck Inside of Mobile with the Memphis Blues Again" (c 1966); Ram's Horn Music for "George Jackson" (c 1971, 1976), "Tangled Up in Blue" (c 1974, 1976), and "You're a Big Girl Now" (c 1974, 1976); Warner Bros. Inc. for "Blowin' in the Wind" (c 1962), "Gates of Eden" (c 1965), "Hero Blues" (c 1963), "If You Gotta Go, Go Now" (c 1965), "It's Alright, Ma (I'm Only Bleeding)" (c 1965, 1966), "Love Minus Zero / No Limit" (c 1965), "Maggie's Farm" (c 1965), "Mr. Tambourine Man" (c 1964), "My Back Pages" (c 1964), "On the Road Again" (c 1965), "Queen Jane Approximately" (c 1965), "Talkin' World War III Blues" (c 1963), and "To Ramona" (c 1964); and Witmark Music for "One Too Many Mornings" (c 1964) and "The Times They Are A-Changin'" (c 1963).

Etiam dissertationes Chaucerianae non
sunt multiplicandae praeter necessitatem.

Overview

Colleges are like old-age homes; except for the fact that more people die in college than in old-age homes.[1]

Bob Dylan would be little concerned to learn that his songs, which guided rock musicians and audiences through the 1960s, present knotty methodological problems to scholars in any university discipline. His performances are distributed on records—which had carried far simpler songs until the early sixties, when stereophonics and other industry inventions began allowing accurate reproduction of complex sounds for an expanding audience. Because Dylan's work shares with cartoons and advertisements the mass-distribution media, some have termed it "popular culture." But the sociological approaches of popular-culture studies barely skim the surface of the best Dylan songs. Nor do musicologists have much to say, for without words most Dylan melodies and chord changes would be boring—and besides, like nearly all musicians outside the Western-European classical tradition, Dylan does not bother to stay on notated pitches.

Some literary critics have allowed that some Dylan lyrics on the printed page, as compared with other "popular songs," resemble poetry. These lyrics, however, are not poems. They are songs: words and music combined for oral performance. And literary critics, like everybody else, have only recently gained access to recording equipment, only recently begun remarking that much literature is meant for oral delivery. A silent reader performs in her imagination such lines as that with which Chaucer's Pardoner, after telling the other Canterbury pilgrims how he convinces gullible churchgoers to buy false relics and pardons, says, "I wol yow nat deceyve." Would the Pardoner here emphasize "yow"—I'd deceive those others, but not you? Would he speak the line comfortingly? Or perhaps smoothly, with shifting eyes and a tight-lipped smile? Or perhaps hesitantly, suddenly unsure of his own future after death, or in the "paroxysm of agonized sincerity" that Professor Kittredge heard?

Usually, each literary critic tries to prove that her interpretation is the right one. Yet I would argue that Chaucer's genius, and that of many another author whose work outlives its times, has much to do with flexibility—with an author's ability to put together words on the page that readers in ensuing centuries, with shifting values, can imagine performed differently.

Literature has been analyzed with an eye to textual ambiguity, but never yet from the hypothesis that unresolved binary oppositions on the page allow flexibility in performance. As I compare several versions of a Dylan song, I will show how different meanings can be given to the same text. On paper, for example, "It Ain't Me, Babe" (1964) expresses a man's harsh rejection of a woman's romantic expectations, using oppositional images: weak/strong, right/wrong, death/life, and so on. But in six performances it becomes variously a happy love song, a statement of political protest, a shout of triumph, a ritualistic commonplace, an escapist reassurance, and a devil-may-care denial of responsibility for the woman's hurt.

A song that could mean only what its printed lyrics say would be, at best, timebound. My analyses show that lyrics malleable in performance tend to include textual ambiguity—often images in clear binary opposition— that a listener can experience as resolved or unresolved because of such performance elements as vocal inflections, instrumentation, tempo, phrasing, sliding pitches, pauses. I show also that oral literature, to be aesthetically effective, need not have a unified structure or linear development; that pronouns and other words that look vague on paper can be vital in performance; and that sound patterns, such as those I term voice-forced rhyme and oral onomatopoeia, can create connections impossible to make on the page.

Thus, an analysis of Dylan's lyrics shows what in a text may allow flexibility in performance. And many Dylan lines can stand alone, in aphoristic glory: Henry Nash Smith's 1969 presidential address to the Modern Language Association, for instance, was entitled "Something Is Happening Here But You Don't Know What It Is, Do You, Mr. Jones?" (from "Ballad of a Thin Man," 1965).

But it was not Dylan's lyrics alone, nor his guitar and harmonica, that sent our parents clutching their ears and climbing their respective suburban walls in the sixties. It was that voice—that whining, grating, snarling voice that can drip scorn or comfort, can stretch or snap off words in disregard of their meaning or in fulfillment of it, can say for the listener what she has not quite yet said for herself. Dylan can't sing, they said. But then neither can I.

How does one describe a sneer in Dylan's voice? Linguists have some interest in analyzing how the voice conveys emotions. But the last major experiments were done in 1940, by Grant Fairbanks; increasingly sophisticated machinery still allows only general formulations. (A voice expressing anger is usually higher pitched than one expressing grief, for example.) Linguists, like sociologists, depend on polls as scientific evidence: a reading is proven "angry" if a majority of listeners hear it as angry.

For purposes of this initial study, as an absolutely typical member of Dylan's white, middle-class audience, I must dispense with polls in support of my listener response. I assume that if I hear a sneer, the sneer exists; and I start at once on the more difficult and promising task of understanding just how his vocal inflections interact with words and music to create aural meaning. My credentials of absolute typicality include Grove City High School, class of '65; Haight-Ashbury, summer of '67; University of Wisconsin at Madison, '66-70; down and out in London, '68; motorcycles and jobs in the early seventies; and then back to graduate school, at Berkeley, eventually emerging as a professor of English who, like the doctors and lawyers and carpenters and cab drivers my fellow students became, listens to rock music as much as to classical, and reads complex modern novels for occasional relaxation but "Doonesbury" daily.

Any line drawn nowadays between high culture and popular culture, between fine art and folk art, is arbitrary. Those who might want to maintain the old distinctions—that fine art has more internal complexity, that it appeals to a more educated audience—have been stunned into silence by American studies, folkloristics, film criticism, and other disciplines bent on showing how complex are the ideas and expressions of ordinary people.

Why were such untenable dichotomies proposed to begin with? The fine-art/popular-art distinction is little more than a century old, born as the British class system was dying. In America, the elite could look down their noses at immigrants, identifiable by accent, and most of all at blacks, identifiable by color. But elitism necessitated more analytic effort in nineteenth-century Britain, where everyone physically resembled the upper classes. Those with higher education—those, that is, with money—set up as many dichotomies as possible to distinguish their own "high" culture from that of the masses, including a dichotomy of written vs. oral literature that is particularly unsound for drama and for medieval manuscripts, which survive as texts but were nearly always performed aloud. The emergence in America and Britain of an educated mass audience—still a white, educated mass audience to be sure—gives the lie to any assumption that oral literature, or folklore, must be studied not as self-contained art but as a symptom of something else.

Performed literature can sustain analysis as precise and as thorough as can texts intended for silent reading. Yet early folklore scholars, trained in literature, themselves tended to assume that if the text of a performed work fell short of established artistic criteria for a silent text, study of it would have to be relegated to an imprecise limbo of quasi-scientific techniques: the Victorian folklorist's search for communal origins, the historic-geographic method, structuralist schemas, formula counting, statistical or sociofunctional or Marxist or psychoanalytic analysis. Artistry and the folklorist's appreciation of the work were too often left out.

But folklorists, for all the shortcomings of scholarship during the decades when their only recording device was words on paper, saw right away the value of each step in advancing technology, and right away began using sound and video equipment to capture all besides words that constitutes a folk performance—the gestures, facial expressions, pauses, vocal inflections, audience response, and so on. Only during recent decades have folklorists begun developing ways to analyze, or even display on paper, what they collect on sound tape and now video as well. Such studies are the most immediate models for my close analyses of Dylan songs.[2]

Most material for my comparative analyses of Dylan songs comes from commercially released records and, significantly, from tapes made by rock-music fans just as eager as folklorists to take advantage of galloping technology. As soon as battery-powered cassette recorders became commercially available, people began secretly making "bulky-sweater recordings" at concerts and then copying them for each other, along with tapes of Dylan playing at private parties, radio broadcasts, and practice sessions. The resulting international network of bootleg-tape exchanges lost some momentum in the mid-seventies, after record companies realized they could make money from live albums that contain concert performances of songs previously released in studio versions.

Dylan's studio sessions, by all accounts, differed only in scope from his live performances: especially in the sixties, he would play for friends and hangers-on who invaded the Columbia studios with cheap wine, smokes, biker boots, long hair, and kids. Until about 1980, Dylan insisted on recording "live in the studio." He seldom rerecorded a cut, and he supervised any adjusting or mixing of sound tracks. Songs released on his studio albums, therefore, are spontaneously created performances that are aesthetically satisfactory to the singer-songwriter.

Hardly anyone, however, smuggled video equipment into concerts or studios. And the early film clips available of Dylan performing—mostly in D. A. Pennebaker's *Don't Look Back* and Dylan's *Renaldo and Clara*—cannot suffice for a study of the total kinetics of performance and audience interaction. On bootleg and other live recordings, the audience can be heard cheering or—in a few mid-sixties concerts, as Dylan supposedly "went electric"—booing their hero. And sound tapes preserve a bit of his stage presence: "It's Halloween," the 23-year-old singer tells a New York City audience in 1964, "and I've got my Bob Dylan mask on." But these are hints, not a corpus for analysis.

Throughout this study, thus, I work with what I have: the words and music of Bob Dylan. I can wish for videotapes of performances, toward a more complete analysis—as I wish Chaucer had lived to finish *The Canterbury Tales* and had left us a cassette of his own reading aloud of, say, the Host's reply to the Pardoner. But here I use what I have to contribute what I can to the analysis of performance—an issue, made possible by technology, that has revitalized a dozen fields besides folklore. Like the blind men interpreting the elephant, these past decades, cultural anthropologists and sociolinguists and ethnomusicologists and others have found much to say about various aspects of performance.

Most studies, so far, are minutely practical. In oral interpretation, for example, a discipline risen phoenixlike from the old schools of elocution, scholars regard texts as potential scripts for performance, considering the aesthetic impact of pauses, vocal inflections, and so on. As exemplified by *Literature in Performance*, a journal begun in 1980, their prescriptive approach meshes neatly with the carefully descriptive concerns of folklorists.

Because performance analysis is of such obvious importance to their discipline, however, some folklorists leapt at once to theoretical statements.[3] Such o'er-hasty abstraction of principles, from studies barely begun, is carried to extremes by philosophers of art and language like those collected in *Performance in Postmodern Culture*.[4] Jargon and Latinate abstraction are such that this entire book never describes an actual performance of anything, nor hints that "postmodern culture" might have something to do with tape recorders.

Those who would brush past a close examination of Dylan's songs as performed to declare What It All Means must forgive my concern with details of evidence. I beg forbearance, as well, from a far larger group— from those listeners who would refrain altogether from analyzing Dylan. His songs are strong: as art, they survive minute analysis and survive being left alone. But each of us has her own special background, interests, ideas....

> *And if you don't underestimate me*
> *I won't underestimate you*
> —*"Dear Landlord,"* *1968*

I

Protests

I write the songs because I need something to sing. It's the difference between the words on paper and the song. The song disappears into the air, the paper stays. They have little in common.[1]

By age twenty-one, Bob Dylan had been declared spokesman for his generation, a generation now suggesting sheepishly that you can't trust anyone under thirty (except concerning computers). He reached his mass audience not on paper that stays, nor with live songs that disappear forever, but on records that put the same performance of a song into the air, time after time. Yet neither he nor his audience, I will show, ever meant to limit a song to that one oral performance as somehow the correct one.

Throughout the sixties Dylan stayed a step ahead of other rock musicians, two steps ahead of his audience, and a city block or country mile ahead of the grown-ups. Other singers followed his lead after 1962, as Dylan released albums of rough-edged impromptu performances rather than the smoothly produced songs then expected of commercial recordings. Other groups followed, in 1965, after Dylan moved from acoustic to electric guitar and added a backup band—moved, that is, from white rural folksong style to black urban folk music, the electric blues. As white groups began playing ever more shrieking "acid rock," then, Dylan reopened the way to calmer country music with his 1967-1969 albums. Other musicians followed toward "soft rock." Through it all, too, he brought poetry into rock lyrics—imagery, replacing the inanity common in the fifties, and allowing room for the even more cerebral lyrics of Simon and Garfunkel or of Jim Morrison, so inspired by William Blake.

Dylan never expected so intense a spotlight, even though he told the other kids in high school in Hibbing, Minnesota, that someday he'd be a famous rock-and-roll star.[2] As Robert Zimmerman, he enlivened his small-town upbringing by identifying with James Dean and Little Richard, and by occasionally taking the bus or his parents' car into Minneapolis to hear black musicians (this in contradiction to the stories of a wild youth he was to tell gullible reporters a few years later). In 1960 he quit college, during his freshman year at the University of Minnesota, and by January 1961 ended up in New York City, having gone there to meet the dying singer whose life story and music had so inspired him—Woody Guthrie. Dylan converged on Greenwich Village with others of the lumber-jacketed "folksong revival," and there—not as the most melodic singer or accomplished guitarist but as brilliant songwriter and powerful personality—he had greatness thrust upon him.

Columbia Records signed him on. He got famous. He got rich. A nationwide audience clung to every word, based major life decisions on single lines, built prophecies on every song, marked eras with Dylan albums. We needed a hero, and a hero we made him. He became more rich, more famous, touring America and Europe, his life going faster and faster. He turned twenty-five.

Then, in 1966, a motorcycle accident sent Dylan into seclusion to heal body and, presumably, soul. He stopped doing concert tours until 1974. His audience's still-high expectations dulled only gradually, as his early-seventies albums became increasingly contented. Dylan was trying out a happy marriage and five children. In 1975 came a new burst of artistic vitality—the sweet and bitter songs of parting on *Blood on the Tracks*—and then a messily public divorce. He experimented for a couple of albums with Middle Eastern music, horns, backup singers; some of the old snarl returned to his lyrics ("Do you need me half as bad as you say, or are you just feeling guilt?"—"Is Your Love in Vain?" 1978). Then Dylan found Jesus and began allowing record producers to mix sound tracks for him. He still performs live.

Despite individual preferences, most Dylan fans would agree that his most powerful and widely influential songs come from three albums released in 1965-1966, when his life was racing full tilt: *Bringing It All Back Home*, *Highway 61 Revisited*, and *Blonde on Blonde*. Yet his earlier love songs and much-heralded "protest songs" contributed substantially to the peak that he would reach in this newly possible artistic merger of words and music.

In his earliest career—while absorbing and catalyzing musical influences from Anglo- and Afro-American traditions, especially the blues—Dylan wrote songs most obviously like those of Woody Guthrie, Pete Seeger, and others who had done union organizing in the thirties and, scarred personally and professionally by the Red-baiting witchhunts of the fifties, were struggling to keep alive the idea of song as vehicle for political protest.[3] By 1962 the political shroud had lifted enough that the young Dylan could compose a satire like "Talkin' John Birch Paranoid Blues" (1970) but not enough that he could sing it on the *Ed Sullivan Show* or record it for his second album, *The Freewheelin' Bob Dylan*.[4]

Some of Dylan's song texts first appeared in *Sing Out!*, a magazine that survived the fifties by shifting its focus from overtly political songs to preserved folksongs, mostly white rural American songs like "Tom Dooley" with which the Kingston Trio set off a wider "folksong revival" in 1959. But far more of Dylan's early songs were first published in the mimeographed periodical *Broadside* (New York). In February 1962, the first issue of *Broadside* featured Dylan's "Talking John Birch Society Blues" and stated the editorial policy: "Many people throughout the country today are writing topical songs, and the only way to find out if a song is good is to give it wide circulation and let singers and listeners decide for themselves."[5] At least fifteen of Dylan's songs appeared in the first two years. Between *Broadside* no. 23 (late March 1963) and no. 57 (10 April 1965), Dylan is listed as a contributing editor on the masthead, along with Pete Seeger and now lesser-known songwriters such as Peter LaFarge, Len Chandler, and Phil Ochs.

Phil Ochs was outstanding among these young writers of topical, or "finger-pointing," songs. After his suicide on 9 April 1976, he was often termed a "child of the sixties" who had been unable to readjust his political goals.[6] Ochs's songs show a skillful craftsman working within the musical and sociological context of Greenwich Village in the early 1960s, a context that Dylan's songs have outlasted and indeed transformed. Thus, a comparison of Phil Ochs's "The Ballad of Oxford, Mississippi" (*Broadside*, no. 15, November 1962) and Dylan's "Oxford Town" (*Broadside*, no. 17, December 1962) can show how Dylan was straining at the bounds of his medium, even while writing about the same topic as did Ochs. (See Appendix A for texts.)[7] Ochs's song is handicapped in the comparison, for all we have of it is a printed text. Still, to look at Ochs's song alongside both text and studio performance of "Oxford Town" will isolate characteristics of Dylan's songwriting style, and suggest how words on paper can acquire more complex meanings and create unresolved tensions in performance.

The best of Dylan's protest songs not only draw the listener into interaction with the song but also can make a responsive listener take action outside the song, to change what is wrong. The songs of political protest that preceded Dylan's usually pose problems and suggest solutions (as in those of Woody Guthrie, Dylan's idol: "I'm sticking to the Union," for example, or "This land was made for you and me").[8] Yet, in his first song to attain and retain international popularity, Dylan asks a series of rhetorical questions and offers no solutions: "the answer, my friend, is blowing in the wind" (1962), there to be grasped at by each listener. Some of Dylan's songs, such as "Only a Pawn in Their Game" (1963), deny outright the possibility of simple answers. Others, such as "[I ain't gonna work on] Maggie's Farm" (1965) or "It Ain't Me, Babe" (1964), give enigmatic answers, like proverbs or slogans, that each listener can take to fit her own experience.

Phil Ochs's "Ballad of Oxford, Mississippi," instead, supplies answers. (See Appendix A.) It is inflammatory journalism, set to music and interwoven with poetic imagery—images of cold and heat, red and yellow, and finally, ironically, the white heat that evil racists will suffer in hell. Ochs's omnipresent narrator knows all the facts behind the violent scene he witnesses. He knows, for example, that the governor backed down on a promise to send troops and that the Confederate flag symbolizes states' rights. The last verse makes an optimistic threat toward specific villains, with an implied solution: "the times are changing mighty fast."

Dylan was to turn Ochs's phrase into "The Times They Are A-Changin'" (1963), which sketches a series of nonspecific situations into which each listener can fit herself.[9] In comparison to Ochs's entire song, similarly, Dylan's "Oxford Town" uses the specific incident, the "topic" as reported in northern newspapers, as a starting point to create a song with which a responsive listener can interact. The narrator of "Oxford Town," confronted by violence he does not understand, simply gives up: "Going back where we come from," he says. "Somebody better investigate soon." Ochs's narrator tells a listener how to respond, and why. A listener to Dylan's song, instead, reacts against the narrator's apathy by, at the least, subconsciously trying to unravel the nonlinear narrative within the song. At the most dramatic, a listener may vow to become a somebody and go investigate.

On the page, the narrator of "Oxford Town" is quite clearly a southerner demonstrating against James Meredith's entering the University of Mississippi. (Ochs's report that "Gas was hurled against the mob after each attack" substantiates this identification.) Yet, when I listen to this song, I still think of "where we come from" as the north and of "I" as a civil-rights activist giving up. Both performer and narrator are "I," addressing the listener as "you… my friend." But because the performer is no southern racist, a listener experiences an unresolved opposition between the cognitive meaning of the lyrics and the performance of them, such that no one knows where "Me and my girl and my girl's son" will go.

And as they go back to wherever, the listener must ask herself not only "What do you think about that, my friend?" but also other questions, like "What happened in Oxford, and why?" The song's narrator sees only in cinematic flashes: Meredith is just "he," followed by guns and clubs, then standing before a door. The narrator knows two facts: the tear-gas bomb and the two men dead. And he tries twice to analyze the violence, repeating "All because…" with comments that provide no causes after all.

The narrator also, more frequently, repeats the phrase "Oxford town," evoking scenes and images that make it a place to avoid. The imagery begins with the sun and ends with the moon, illuminating the two dead men. The opening scene anticipates the closing one, for the first-stanza sun shines only on what is below the ground—graves, apparently, surrounded by bowed heads. Such cyclical imagery disrupts potential indicators of time's orderly passing—"sun," "afternoon," "moon"—to make the sequence of scenes less resemble a linear narrative and even more recreate someone's jumbled impressions while hightailing it out of Oxford.

The tangled negatives of the line "Sun don't shine above the ground" rework one of the most frequent floating lines in the blues tradition, "The sun's gonna shine in my back door someday." The structure of "Oxford Town" evokes black musical tradition also—spirituals, more directly than the blues. Tom Paxton, another songwriter in Dylan and Ochs's immediate circle, describes the difference between the strophic songs they were writing and the songs actually sung by black demonstrators in the South. Songs like Ochs's are musical editorials with verse and refrain—"if you agree with me, you join in the chorus." But civil-rights marchers create "songs to be sung in the thick of it with no need for guitars or microphones… structurally set for mass singing… with only a few words being changed from verse to verse," [10] mostly adapted spirituals, like "We Shall Overcome."

By repeating "Oxford town" and other phrases within stanzas, not during a set-apart refrain, and by varying the melody slightly for each stanza, Dylan suggests black musical tradition without actually reproducing it. Thus the song's structure, as well as its immediate performance by Dylan, sets up unresolved tension with the sense of the lyrics. The confusion of the white southern narrator increases as he tries to articulate his perceptions about Oxford town in the musical style of those whom he came there to (as it were) denigrate.

A responsive listener to Dylan's song thus experiences unresolved oppositions in at least four ways that do not show in the printed text. There is one unresolved tension between "I" the performer, a civil-rights advocate, and "I" the narrator, a southern racist; there is another between white performer/narrator and the black musical structure being adapted. Third, the cheerful musical performance stands in contrast to the despair in the lyrics. In print this cheeriness appears mainly in the tempo indication on the sheet music, "Bright," and in Dylan's comment on the cover of *Freewheelin'* that "Oxford Town" is "a banjo tune I play on the guitar." In performance, the emotional dichotomy between words and tune is obvious.

Intensified by these three dichotomies is the one that makes this a protest song that can incite a listener to action: the unresolved tension leading to opposition between listener and narrator. Each time the album cut is played, the narrator remains apathetic because confused and confused because apathetic. A listener, drawn into the narrator's experience time after time, gradually comes to feel (but not articulate, because aural understanding almost never becomes conscious) that she can avoid the narrator's plight by making herself the opposite of apathetic and the opposite of confused. Thus, a listener may make changes in her own life, outside the song, to become politically active and well informed. The latter is probably easier: someone who wishes to learn what happened in Oxford can find facts in the masses of newsprint always available.

Ochs's "Ballad of Oxford, Mississippi" is partly a functional relic of the pre-twentieth-century broadside ballad, which disseminated information as well as spurred to action. But Dylan, unlike most contributors to *Broadside*, saw that factual information was precisely what his audience did not need and that his audience precisely did not want to be told how to feel or what to do. Most of these listeners, the first generation of white Americans to take a college education for granted, were steadily bombarded with facts flung by grown-ups who pretended to have answers and obviously had none.

Phil Ochs probably never quite realized the anachronistic shortcomings of musical journalism. But he did realize the artistic value of editorial restraint, of a songwriter's suggesting rather than commanding listener response: in *Broadside* no. 48 (20 July 1964), Ochs praises Dylan's "Lonesome Death of Hattie Carroll" (1964) as an exemplary topical song that avoids the "empty cry of shame, or bland pleas for decency." But still, his "Ballad of Oxford, Mississippi" remains solidly within the topical-song tradition, a musical editorial decorated with poetic imagery, whereas Dylan's "Oxford Town" uses topicality as a springboard for artistic complexity in performance and for political effectiveness.

"A Hard Rain's A-Gonna Fall" springs even further, for the incident disappears completely. (See Appendix A for text.) The listener learns neither what happened nor what she ought to feel. Instead, she is led through a series of visual scenes that, as performed on Dylan's 1963 album, build a more and more intense feeling of foreboding, a feeling like that of an American during the Cuban missile crisis of October 1962. To learn what happened during this incident, a listener can go to books or newspapers or personal experience. To learn that this is a topical song, of sorts, one need only read the cover notes to *The Freewheelin' Bob Dylan*. There, Nat Hentoff quotes Dylan calling "Hard Rain" a "desperate kind of song," written during the Cuban missile crisis: "Every line in it is actually the start of a whole song. But when I wrote it, I thought I wouldn't have enough time alive to write all those songs so I put all I could into this one."

Dylan's comments on this song, as elsewhere in interviews, show him fully aware of the traditions he is working with and of the artistic effects he intends. There is no doubting Dylan's sincerity, in that "Hard Rain" expresses his own feelings of impending doom. There is likewise no doubting his growing professionalism, for this song appears in both *Broadside* no. 31 (September 1963) and *Sing Out!* vol. 12 (December 1962-January 1963), copyrighted by Witmark Music instead of, as for previous songs, "author." Dylan himself has considered this a major work: his 1974 concert album is entitled *Before the Flood*, evoking a major pattern of imagery from "Hard Rain," and his 1976 concert album is called *Hard Rain,* although it includes no version of this song.

Dylan has performed many later versions of "Hard Rain," alone or with others (with Leon Russell, George Harrison, and Ringo Starr, for example, on *Concert for Bangladesh,* Apple STCX 3385). To demonstrate the extent to which the same set of lyrics can vary in performance, however, I will compare Dylan's 1963 rendering of the song on *Freewheelin'* to a 1973 performance of it by Bryan Ferry.[11]

A vocabulary and methodology for analysis of performed literature have yet to be established. As I attempt to do so, I begin with two performances whose effects are not just different but, in many articulable ways, opposite. The early Dylan version is pessimistic, the later one by Ferry optimistic.

The single guitar that accompanies Dylan's 1963 voice helps create an atmosphere of foreboding; in 1973, the elaborate instrumentation and backup singers reinforce Ferry's voice in its mood of mocking triumph. Dylan's narrator is a Christlike figure, martyred in the end; Ferry's narrator cackles satanically.[12] The 1963 song ends in defeat, forcing the listener to assume responsibility as the narrator dies. The 1973 version entertains the listener, assuring her at last that none of those gloomy scenes in the lyrics need be taken seriously.

The lyrics alone would demand neither extreme: the words include images of good and evil, hope and despair, death and birth, black and white, gloom and triumph. The potential in these clusters of imagery, unresolved on the page, can be released toward one pole or the other in performance. On paper, for example, the final scene looks possibly optimistic. On paper, the narrator says that he will speak out against the atrocities he has seen and heard and met, stanza by stanza. He says that he will stand on the ocean until he starts sinking and know his song well before he starts singing.

So he says. But in Dylan's 1963 performance, the narrator sinks immediately, with no chance to sing out anything—sinks from four vocal measures into three instrumental measures, all with the same guitar pattern (in rhythm ♩ ♩ ♫♩), during every one of the thirty-seven narrative lines in the song and all but one of the stanza-opening questions as well. And he sinks into a final refrain that Dylan performs with vocal phrasing and inflections quite identical to those of the four previous refrains. The unrelieved oppressiveness of the performance stands in tension with any potential for hope in the lyrics.

The entire song is one of Dylan's more monotonous. Its melody is almost a chant; the vocal range is less than an octave, and only in the penultimate line of each stanza do notes occur more than a third apart. The guitar repeats three chords—D, A, G in *Broadside,* or E♭, B♭, A♭ in later songbooks. By comparison, "Blowin' in the Wind" (1962) requires only four chords and a limited vocal range. But in performance, as recorded on the same side of *Freewheelin' Bob Dylan* as "Hard Rain," Dylan varies his vocal phrasing in relation to the guitar and varies the harmonica breaks between stanzas.

"Hard Rain" has no such variation. The seven measures per line go on and on, line after line—a bit more than four measures of voice and guitar, a bit less than three measures of guitar alone. A listener expects eight musical measures; the incomplete seven-measure structure reinforces the lyrics' warnings that something unknown is about to arrive. Poetic images join with truncated musical lines to file without protest toward headlong destruction. Seven guitar measures open and close the song, and seven come also between sung stanzas. The last three sung lines in each stanza flow together without instrumental breaks. All other lines in the song are performed identically, except for one: the question "And what did you meet, my blue-eyed son?" begins offbeat and slides with a shorter break than elsewhere into "who did you meet, my darling young one?" The following four, rather than three, instrumental measures help set apart the fourth stanza—the shortest and most tightly structured one, which includes the song's most clearly optimistic image, the young girl's rainbow.

The symbolic import of this rainbow is a bit too clear, in fact, to be effective as poetry on the printed page. Similarly, for example, "guns and sharp swords in the hands of young children" is sentimental, pathetic; "thunder that roared out a warning" is foreboding, as is the "black branch with blood that kept dripping" and the implied racism of the "white man who walked a black dog." Some images do make effective poetry. But this song is meant to be performed, not read. A listener experiences each image only while she is hearing it; she has three guitar strums for absorption and evaluation before the next image is tossed onto the heap.

Bryan Ferry's performance, I will show, accentuates the emotional variety of these shifting scenes and images, allows no thinking time at all between lines, and does a listener's responding for her. Dylan's 1963 performance, instead, equates all emotional states. Hope and foreboding and sentimentality, singing and sinking and stumbling and stepping—all are dragged down to the same vocal pitch and drowned in the same three guitar measures. The narrator claims that he believes in his visions and in the extremes of emotion they represent, but he too sinks helplessly. A listener must strain against the monotony of performance to experience, in her own intellectual responses, the emotions aroused by the words. A responsive listener can come to set herself in opposition to the unsuccessful narrator. She can believe in visions and in emotions, and can struggle to speak out, even against odds as overwhelming as seven repeated monotonous measures.

In the opening stanzas, the poetic imagery looks not only unsubtle but also randomly arranged. This too can be characteristic of aurally experienced words, in which line-by-line relationships may take precedence over full-length linear development of imagery. A listener to early stanzas of the 1963 "Hard Rain" makes a visual and emotional leap from one line to the next—from a babe with wild wolves to a highway of diamonds, for instance—but because of voice and guitar is kept from feeling any exhilaration during that leap. But in the third and fourth stanzas the arrangement of lines becomes less random: scenes begin to line up in pairs, pairs that become more and more clearly oppositional until the "wounded in love/wounded in hatred" couplet.

After this fourth stanza the sentimental children/animals imagery drops away, except for the blue-eyed narrator, but the other poetic patterns continue: images of roads, landforms, death, black and white, multitudes of unheard people, and the flood or tidal wave that will follow the ever-threatening hard rain. These images appear earlier in separate scenes. In the last stanza they merge into an extended vision of one spot in the depths of the forest, just before the flood, "Where black is the color and none is the number." It is a swirl into nothingness and infinity, a Blakean vortex from which the narrator emerges just long enough to make his closing vow and pass the torch to the listener.

The mountain from which he tries to reflect his message, at the end, appears in the opening stanza; so does the ocean he stands on and sinks into. Oceans are dead, as the song opens, and the midsong "wave that could drown the whole world" also anticipates his final drowning. And because he stumbles on misty mountains, as the song begins, it will be difficult to reflect a message through that mist, at the end, especially if he has broken his mirrors. Oceans and mountains frame the song, then: the narrator's journey among hordes of people begins and ends with him upon the largest of landforms, alone. At the beginning he is overwhelmed and confused; by the end he is using each landform to try to communicate with the people.

The structures of poetic imagery imitate developments in the narrator's thinking. Oceans and mountains occur randomly in the first stanza, related only by two terms for the same number; by the last stanza oceans and mountains, in juxtaposed lines, have parallel functions in the narrator's world. The song's progressive binary structuring, in this and other features, parallels the movement toward dialectical understanding in the narrator's (and listener's) mind. Early scenes may be paired, but usually not juxtaposed, and the poetic device linking two images may seem strained. In the third and fourth stanzas the poetic connections become more subtle and sophisticated, as the scenes muster themselves into double file and march (as do the members of the conquered race in a 1960 MGM production of H. G. Wells's *Time Machine*) obediently toward extinction.

The simplest poetic links, early in the song, involve repetition of a phrase with slight variation. The twelve mountains and dozen oceans show such "incremental repetition," as does the twice-asked question that opens each stanza. This question—along with the song's overall structure of parent's inquiry and son's response, and some elements of its melody—echoes Child ballad no. 12, "Lord Randal." In one of its innumerable variants, this ballad begins, "O where ha' you been, Lord Randal, my son?/And where ha' you been, my handsome young man?"[13] His answers gradually reveal that he has been off in the woods being fatally poisoned by eels, usually, fed to him by his treacherous true love. A listener who knows "Lord Randal" (thereby not quite a typical listener in 1963) can feel in "Hard Rain" added ominousness: the contrast between modern society and the olden days, when death by poisoning came to one person at a time, when murder was motivated by personal relationships and preventable by precautions (such as eating only Mom's cooking).

Furthermore, the line-by-line scene shifts in "Hard Rain" make it resemble a Child ballad being run through a projector too fast, for a Child ballad characteristically leaps—but stanza by stanza—from scene to scene of dramatic and emotional intensity.[14] Lord Randal could spend hours dying, while telling his mother who was to blame. In October 1962, we would have had only seconds to die blameless.

Lord Randal escapes from the forest and dies in his own bed, but the homeless narrator of "Hard Rain" must explore further. Images of death and geography open the song: manmade highways and graveyards mingle with natural oceans and mountains, and all are misshapen. The alliteration in these lines, like the assigning of human feelings to the landscape, looks overdone on paper; in performance, however, the opening alliteration prepares the listener for the sharp line-by-line contrasts in emotion that will follow. Every scene is uniformly gloomy at the start, though, and most lines contain a prominent *m* sound. In tension with this continuity are the contrasts set up by a different set of initial consonants in each line: first *m*, then *cr,* then *s* (picking up on the "six" just before), then *d*, then *m* and *th*, culminating in "mouth."

The pattern of numbers also begins in the first stanza. First come low numbers with ritualistic associations, then the "ten thousand" that will be repeated in the second and third stanzas, thereby taking on ritualistic overtones appropriate to a society of uncountable numbers of people. Both later references are to ten thousand people struggling but failing to be heard. And their failure, in view of "ten thousand miles in the mouth of a graveyard," leads them not just to close-mouthed silence but back, perhaps, to this yawning grave.

In the second stanza, the penultimate line about "ten thousand talkers" is paired with the scene that follows: those children's weapons ought to be broken toys. The stanza thus ends, as it begins, with an image of children in danger. The first line's "newborn babe with wild wolves" furthermore forms a pair with the child and dead pony in the fourth stanza, which in its turn is paired with the man/dog line—by both sense and juxtaposition, in that stanza's strict double ranks. Within the not-so-tightly-binary second stanza, the middle two lines are linked by mention of blood, again rather unsubtly for the printed page: the men's bleeding hammers suggest both the bloody, black branch and the children's more efficient weapons.

The "highway of diamonds with nobody on it," unlike the first stanza's crooked and tiring highway, hints of an escape route toward a fantasy goal, like the yellow brick road to the emerald city of Oz. But, in striking contrast to the hordes of people elsewhere, this road is deserted. The "white ladder all covered with water," three lines further on, presents another image of thwarted hope. Its implications do not become clear until the third stanza, when a listener pictures the "wave that could drown the whole world" and realizes too late that an escape route is itself already immersed.

The ladder image stays in the background of a listener's response to that "roar of a wave," however. Images keep piling up; the tidal wave is closely linked to the thunder just before it, which likewise roars. Each third-stanza line begins, "I heard." But the scenes remain visual as well as aural. Stanza by stanza the song progresses from the narrator's continuous movement at first, to the set scenes he observes in the second stanza, to his both hearing and seeing each scene in the third—just as a responsive listener both hears and pictures each line. In midsong, thus, listener and narrator begin to merge. And then the listener too must stop moving long enough to meet each character in the fourth stanza; the listener too stands still in the depths of the deepest dark forest. And after the narrator sinks into seven-measure oblivion, the listener has experience enough to go on alone, to witness, understand, and speak out against atrocities. The listener has been Dante to the narrator's Virgil, but if there is a Paradiso, after the Cuban missile crisis, the listener will have to create it herself—by knowing her song well before she starts singing. If, that is, she has time to come to know it or anything else. Indeed, if this narrator had started singing sooner, without worrying quite so much about exact facts and a perfect performance, perhaps he would have reached with his message more of those forgotten souls. Perhaps he would still be speaking out from atop the ocean, even, just like Jesus.

This closing hint of Christian imagery reverberates with the other obviously biblical symbol, the rainbow of hope for after the impending flood. A young girl, not a demanding god, holds out the rainbow. Unfortunately for the printed lyrics' sporadic clutchings toward optimism, she is firmly paired with the young woman whose body is burning—whether with lust, scabies, or suicidal gasoline, a disconcerting image.

The last couplet of this fourth stanza creates polarized emotional auras, clearly oppositional. "Wounded in love" suggests Cupids, Romeos, Frankie and Johnny—an overdramatic, timeworn romanticism. "Wounded in hatred" comes as a shock, then: because outside the song, too, love and hate are both in binary opposition and, as they say, very close; because unlike the cliché "wounded in love," this phrase is fresh and literal; because war wounds should happen painlessly among abstractions like patriotism and courage, not in a face-to-face confrontation with hatred. And death by nuclear fallout, unlike death by eels, comes to an individual not because of love or hate or anything human: wounding and death simply, unavoidably, come.

But the listener, even during repeated playings of the album cut, experiences only the opposition and oddness of the phrase "wounded in hatred." She cannot stop to analyze, for the refrain follows without instrumental break, as usual, and the scenes march on. The parent asks, "And what'll you do now?" (note that the younger generation has all the answers in this song), and the son tells his plans, picturing the future as he has the past. In the fourth stanza and latter half of the third, each scene had shown one person—one of the forgotten, hungry, empty-handed multitudes who now reassemble in this final vision. The landforms among which they once built homes are now poisoned, perverted, destroyed. And the face of the executioner, whether the gleefully evil figure staved off by ballad heroes or the nameless button pusher in Washington, is now and has been and will remain hidden.

And so death comes to Dylan's narrator. It comes not because of the rainfall he has warned of so often but because of the ocean that has been there all along and now rises to treachery, in cahoots with the executioner and the oppressive guitar. Bryan Ferry's narrator instead mocks the executioner and the ocean: Ferry's closing "it's a ha-ha-ha-ha-ha-ha-ha hard" acts as culmination of the vocal tricks that throughout his 1973 performance suggest triumphant laughter.

The 1973 version accentuates the line-by-line shifts in emotional response that Dylan's version represses. To do so, Ferry uses sound effects, along with backup vocalists, instrumental effects, and his own vocal inflections. Ferry's version does not end with hard rain still threatening, for example; the listener need not feel impelled to rush out and tell, speak, and sing before the downpour. Instead, tension is resolved by a closing sound effect of pouring rain—one that would remind many listeners of early-sixties sentimental songs, like "Rhythm of the Rain" by the Cascades, and would further soothe away politically motivated discomfort.

Imitative sound effects also appear after every line of lyrics in the third stanza. After its first line a listener hears, as does the narrator, the sound of thunder. After the second line she hears surf; after the third, a drumroll; next, the female backup group whispering. Then, in the single most irreverent moment of the performance, these backup singers go "ha ha ha ha" after "many people laughing." They next mark the death of the poet with a mock-sympathetic falling "a-a-aw," but do not imitate the clown's crying because, as in Dylan's version, no break precedes the refrain. In this and each refrain, the vocalists echo "hard!" on a high note each time Ferry sings "it's a hard," and they harmonize with him on "hard rain's gonna fall."

In each refrain somewhat differently, Ferry and the backup vocalists bring out the harsh consonance in the phrase "hard rain" by giving each word equal force. (Dylan, in contrast, makes each "hard" a brief stairstep into a louder "rain," howled for four beats.) In this third stanza, Ferry cuts short the final word "fall," but the backup singers hold and stretch the word, their voices descending in four long steps to merge there with the organ's repeated chords, ready to lead into the next stanza.

Their voices fall on the word "fall," in oral onomatopoeia that, like the sound effects, helps interpret the lyrics for the listener. Other instrumental and vocal effects also illustrate the text. A glockenspiel (probably) gives an effect of crinkling gold foil after "gave me a rainbow," "What did you see?" and "What did you hear?" A distinctive guitar riff follows the second line of each stanza except the first, separating question from answer, like quotation marks. A drumroll behind each "darling" further marks the shift in speaker. A bass guitar (probably) goes "boing" after "hammers a-bleeding" and "body was burning." The backup vocalists follow the white man/black dog line with an "o-o-o-ooo" that suggests both wariness and a howling dog. And they come in to lead the last stanza toward a triumphant climax by backing up each line with "a-a-ah," rising in pitch as if to challenge the rain soon to fall.

This "ah" is an incomplete aural mirror image to the "hard!" with which the vocalists reply to most of Ferry's renderings of the phrase "it's a hard." With this and with the hollow "ha ha ha ha" after "many people laughing," the backup singers turn against it one of the song's most important syllables, using what is already there in the lyrics as a banner of mockery. Ferry does the same. The variety of ways he renders the second half of each stanza's penultimate line ("it's a hard, it's a hard") can demonstrate his vocal expressiveness. In stanza one he adds two "and"s to the published text: "and it's a hard, and it's a hard." In stanza two he sings, "and it's a hard... ha-hard... hard," his vocal pitch highest on the last syllable. In the next he sings, "and it's a hard... hard... hard... hard" on a level pitch, increasing in loudness. In the fourth stanza he pauses after "and it's a" and then stretches "ha-ha hard" across nearly three measures. The last stanza echoes the "many people laughing," as "and it's a ha-ha-ha-ha-ha-ha hard." To end the song he twice repeats the refrain: first he renders this half-line with a less emphatic laughing effect, as "and it's... ha-ha hard"; then, finally, as "and it's so-oh-oh-oh ha-ha hard."

Ferry's voice plays with other lines as well. To set apart the vow that ends the song, for instance, he increases the alliteration of "none is the number" by stretching the initial *n*s and swallowing the *uh*s; then he sings the last two verse lines staccato. Vocal manipulation continues in a swallowed "well," the bouncing consonance of "singing," and the thrice-repeated laughing refrain. Ferry thus closes with the narrator's self-confident control over language, not his drowning.

The two opening lines of the song are likewise set apart by Ferry's voice and also by instrumentation. The 1973 version opens with only the organ, getting louder and louder on a repeated chord four times per measure, until Ferry starts singing. He sings the question almost in a whisper, with distinctly articulated syllables and an aristocratic "been," with long *e*. The drum comes in on "darling young one"; then the rest of the band enters.

Throughout the performance the drum and organ carry a strong backup beat, seeming to battle one another for prominence. Between them they mark a fast tempo as steady as is the guitar-strummed beat of Dylan's version. Ferry actually sings the words at about the same speed as Dylan does. But Ferry's version sounds a third again faster because the instrumentation is marking four beats per measure instead of three, as in Dylan's. Dylan's version in metronome measurement (M.M.) allows a dotted half note approximately 76 units; in Ferry's version, a whole note has that same value. That is: Dylan, M.M. $\:\dotted{d}.\:$=76; Ferry, M.M. $\:\circ\:$=76.

In addition, Ferry's version has no instrumental breaks between any of the verse lines, where Dylan had allowed three strums of thinking time. Ferry squeezes the lyrics into exactly four measures in each line; even his breath break is usually crammed full of sound effects, and sometimes he phrases a breath break midline, with not even a pause at the end. His performance allows the listener much less time than does Dylan's to grasp at relationships between poetic images. And it allows no time at all to contemplate them. The listener can relax and let herself be whisked effortlessly from scene to scene, emotion to emotion, with no call to interpret anything for herself or to struggle toward dialectical understanding.

The fast-moving instrumentation joins forces with vocals and sound effects to increase the lyrics' contrasts, the ups and downs in emotion that a listener to Dylan's version is forced to repress. Dylan's performance can create in a listener the feeling of helplessness with which one had to repress fear and anger in October 1962. Ferry's version, instead, takes the variety of emotions expressed in the lyrics and uses performance techniques to increase the variety—to add the complexity, even, of laughing while people starve and hard rain threatens. Ferry's version does the responding for the listener and leaves her entertained, amused, or perhaps annoyed at the sacrilege. Dylan's version shows audience members that their own responses have been flattened, repressed. Thus, as a "protest song," it may incite individual action that will use those aroused emotions of terror, anger, hope, and indignation.

The Cuban missile crisis had come and gone, with no help from Dylan's audience, before this song was released in May 1963. At that time, Richard Nixon had announced his retirement from politics, John F. Kennedy was alive, and massive escalation of the war in Vietnam was just a twinkle in the eye of the military-industrial complex. By the time antiwar protests had become possible and, finally, effective, Dylan had long since moved on to "Some Other Kinds of Songs..." (cover notes to *Another Side of Bob Dylan,* 1964). Ten years later fell the hard reign of Richard Nixon. Fifteen years later, after the near disaster at Three Mile Island, this song was still being invoked, by college students who were busy being born when those missiles went to Cuba.

The characteristics that I have pointed out in Dylan's protest songs continue through the years in his other kinds of songs. Dylan allows no easy-listening bystanders: he draws a listener into a song, often by means of pronouns and other bland-looking words that acquire meaning in performance. His songs often feature unresolved oppositions in the lyrics, and can produce other kinds of tensions that do not appear on the page. Many of his songs are proven flexible in performance across the two decades covered in this book, a manageable unit of time for observing how the same artistic work can shift its meaning in shifting social conditions. What *did* Chaucer do so well, anyhow, that lets a nineteenth-century critic condemn

Alysoun for her amorous adventures and an eighteenth- or twentieth-century reader thoroughly enjoy them? Texts of the longest-lived literature intended for oral performance writhe with unresolved ambiguities, tensions, conflicts, oppositions. And most literature, after all, ought to be read aloud.

However, a justly obscure album called *Sebastian Cabot, actor—a dramatic reading with music—Bob Dylan, poet* (MGM E/SE4431) will prove to any doubter that Dylan's lyrics ought not to be read aloud. They are not poems; they are songs. They represent a developing art form, one made available to a mass audience because of advances in sound recording technology in the late fifties, one in which performed words and music are mutually dependent and mutually effective.

> *If dogs run free, why not me*
> *Across the swamp of time?*
> *My mind weaves a symphony*
> *And tapestry of rhyme*
>   *—"If Dogs Run Free," 1970*

I I

Developments

I still listen to the same old black-and-blue blues. Tommy McClennan, Lightnin' Hopkins, the Carter Family, the early Carlyles.... Big Maceo, Robert Johnson. Once in a while, I listen to Woody Guthrie again. Among the more recent people, Fred McDowell, Gary Stewart.... Memphis Minnie.... Blind Willie McTell.... bluegrass music....foreign music, too. I like Middle Eastern music a whole lot.[1]

The title of *Bringing It All Back Home*, Dylan's fifth album, features one of the more enigmatic pronouns in the history of rock. Speculation penetrated college classrooms in the sixties: a philosophy of education professor at Madison, for one, devoted an entire class session to discussion of "It." The class suggested bringing back home truth, love, self-realization, the Vietnam War; the more cynical spoke of Dylan's money. No one mentioned the blues.

This, Dylan's first album to employ electric as well as acoustic guitar, was recorded in January and released in March of 1965. In May of 1964, during his first concert tour of England, Dylan had encountered the Beatles, Rolling Stones, Animals, and other musicians whose transformations of black American gospel and blues, as the "British Invasion," had already reached back to the white American audience that itself would probably never have bought "race records."

Very briefly and oversimply, rock merges two streams of American folk music: black traditional music, formerly distributed on race records, and white rural music, called "hillbilly" and then "country western" on records. Elvis Presley's 1954 fusion of the two styles has had the most lasting impact, although there have been other crossovers—white men who could sing the blues, like Jimmie Rodgers or Hank Williams. Within black tradition are maintained separate categories, by intention if not always in practice: secular vs. religious music, or blues vs. gospel. Blues style usually involves interaction of a single (or lead) voice and instrument, sharing responsibility for expressiveness; gospel style tends toward groups of singers, weaving elaborate vocal harmonies to a strong beat.

Not until after World War II were American race records available at all in England, to kids in London and in ports like Liverpool. The Beatles put secular lyrics to gospel style; their vocal harmonies set into motion other Merseybeat groups and then American groups like the Beach Boys. Dylan did not adopt gospel sound for another fifteen years, though, until *Street-Legal* and *Slow Train Coming*. Instead, inspired by the Animals' "House of the Rising Sun" and by the Rolling Stones' early albums (traditional blues set to a rock beat),[2] Dylan in 1964 brought back home the electric-guitar-led music that black American musicians had themselves developed in the forties, when defense-industry jobs in cities like Chicago had enabled them to leave behind their southern shacks that had no electricity nor much of anything else.

Dylan's music from the mid-sixties has solid roots in the blues, then. But he brought it all back home to an audience quite unlike urban blacks, and he adapted the style—not at all by forethought or plan, of course—to lead his listeners gradually away from their culture's fixation on words and to introduce them to the possibilities of nonverbal communication.

The transition was gradual, in the sixties, to appreciation of words and music together. Listeners to each newly released Dylan album would first try to figure out exact words, especially if mumbled or garbled. Much discussion, speculation, and interpretation—plus a few pirated transcriptions, such as the mimeographed *Approximately Complete Works* (Holland, ca. 1969)—fed this audience craving for words until the 1973 publication of *Writing and Drawings*. Controversies have continued, however. An exchange of letters in the *New York Times* debated the exact wording of a Dylan line that Jimmy Carter paraphrased while accepting the 1976 presidential nomination.[3]

In retrospect, though, the lyrics shrink in importance. "What used to be called protest music," says Robert Christgau, "accomplished less with words than rock and roll did with nothing but sound—inflections that shook teenagers out of their white-skin gentility, rhythms that aroused their sexuality and aggressiveness."[4] Fifties rock and roll had begun to bring to whites, including the teenage Bob Zimmerman, the excitement of black music—but combined with simple lyrics, most often composed by grown-ups for the rebellious children they pictured as the record-buying audience ("Yakety-yak, don't talk back").

But Bob Dylan spoke directly to his peers, first in articulate words of protest accompanied by a few strummed guitar chords, then in songs that combine increasingly elaborate instrumentation with increasingly evocative lyrics—or simple instrumentation with straightforward lyrics, as he chose. Sociologists might well describe Dylan's style as "the unique combining of precedents by an individual," which results in innovation, the basis of cultural change.[5] Especially in the sixties, Dylan intertwined words and music from any traditions he fancied into an innovative form in which words and music create meaning together, inextricably.

Although Dylan's songwriting and performing style have developed over the decades, the subject of most of his songs—like most all songs ever—is love.[6] Like most all male singers ever, he sings to or about women. Like most all men, like Freud, like the knight in the "Wife of Bath's Tale," he doesn't know what women want. However, neither do we women know what women want.

Let me pause to make an emphatic point. The narrator in the lyrics of a Dylan song may show some attitude toward women, toward war, toward authorities, toward whatever. But the "I" in a song is *not* Bob Dylan. Like poems, songs can sometimes rework into artistic patterns the songwriter's own experiences. But a song is absolutely not biographical evidence. Much of the discussion about exact lyrics in the sixties spilled over into speculation about Dylan's private life. Is "Visions of Johanna" about Joan Baez? Is "Mr. Tambourine Man" about his dope dealer? Is "It's All Over Now, Baby Blue" about us, his audience? "I *do* know what my songs are about," Dylan told an interviewer in 1966. "Some are about four minutes; some are about five, and some, believe it or not, are about eleven or twelve."[7]

I will discuss four songs, spread over a decade of Dylan's career, that are "about" goddesses: that is, words and music combine to create atmospheres of reverence toward females in "She Belongs to Me" (1965), "Sad-Eyed Lady of the Lowlands" (1966), "Shelter from the Storm" (1974), and "Isis" (1975).[8] In each song, a male narrator stands in uncomprehending awe of the Female, which can be understood as whatever is irrational, unorganizable, uncontrollable in the human mind and human experience.

Keeping in mind that the theme linking lyrics of these songs does not necessarily occur in other songs Dylan wrote at those times and that each of the four male narrators speaks of himself, not of Bob Dylan's personal life, these four songs might still seem to show a linear development through Dylan's career. At first glance, the male narrators appear to be expanding their understanding of allegedly mysterious womanhood. In "She Belongs to Me" the female is unapproachable; the narrator remains aloof and orders the listener to worship her. In "Sad-Eyed Lady," the narrator dares to approach her and in so doing comes to understand that her gentleness as well as harshness makes men want to worship her. In "Shelter from the Storm," the female has rejected the narrator; looking back, he sees that he had expected to stay soft forever in her womb. Although he doesn't understand why he had to be born, he accepts that he now is on his own. And in "Isis," the narrator leaves on a quest to prove himself worthy, finds male heroism dead, and returns not to the goddess he idealized but to a woman with a life and ideas of her own... for a moment. But in the last stanza, Isis is still a "mystical child," as the woman in the 1965 song is "nobody's child." And still what drives him to her is what drives him insane.

I would warn against overrating the Western-European worldview, which demands that all parts of anything—even art, even creativity, even an individual's life—be forced into a developmental schema such that linear evolution through time takes precedence over close examination of possible complexities.[9] Academicians as respectable as musicologist Wilfrid Mellers and literary critic Frank Kermode have divided Dylan's career that far into three developing periods, although Kermode takes a grain of salt with the division: "Shakespeare and Beethoven are traditionally allowed four periods, so how is Dylan using his up so fast?"[10] Yet such premature schematization, and any conclusion based on it, may well be knocked askew by the next album or the next decade.

Judging from Dylan's previous few albums, for example, hardly anyone would have predicted the gospel lyrics, as well as sound, of *Slow Train Coming* (1979) and *Saved* (1980). Yet such intense Christian imagery does make sense in relation to the religious imagery of these earlier four songs. *Slow Train* narrators address women as "You" in "I Believe in You," for example, or as "Baby" in "Do Right to Me, Baby (Do Unto Others)." Before, human women were goddesses. In late-seventies albums, the Judeo-Christian God has become female—and in several images, she's black.

A brief overview of the instrumental effects of the four songs that share goddess imagery can illustrate the point that artistic changes need not imply linear development throughout the artist's career. The most recent song, "Isis," has the most complex instrumentation. Dylan plays piano and harmonica, the latter intertwining with Scarlet Rivera's violin, while bells and other unfamiliar sounds add to the music's eerie, unsettling effect. The arrangement of "Shelter from the Storm" is soothing, not unsettling, using only two instruments that seem male and female in performance—a melodic bass and a scampering lead guitar.

But "Sad-Eyed Lady," eight years earlier, employs instrumentation just as complex as in "Isis." The terse cover notes to *Blonde on Blonde* list ten musicians besides Dylan. However many are playing on "Sad-Eyed Lady," they coordinate into a sort of featherbed of soothing instrumentation, into the "fluid yet structured sound" that, as Jon Landau says, gives Dylan "a point of reference against which he can create a genuine artistic tension."[11] And the earliest song I discuss, "She Belongs to Me," creates an unsettling effect, as does "Isis," but with comparatively simple instrumentation: a steady drum and acoustic guitar carry the rhythm, while the electric guitar and harmonica persistently and irregularly intrude.

Thus, the four songs create different musical effects on two axes: soothing vs. unsettling, simple vs. complex. The instrumentation shows no more linear an historical development than do the lyrics. As words on paper, the two earlier songs have clustered images, like lyric poetry, but with fewer syntactic links than written poetry would require. The later two songs tend toward narrative instead, each telling a story of a male/female relationship. But Dylan's songwriting career certainly did not develop from lyric to narrative, as early narrative songs like "Talking New York" (1962) and later lyric ones like "Buckets of Rain" (1974) go to show.

Other apparent developments over the decades could also be disproven with evidence outside these four songs. For instance, "She Belongs to Me" takes the structural form of the twelve-bar blues, which Dylan used frequently in the mid-sixties. But then so does "New Pony," from 1978: in each, as in twelve-bar blues, a stanza consists of three lines of words, each filling about half of its four-measure musical line. The second line of lyrics repeats the first, often incrementally, while the second musical line repeats the first; then the third line rhymes and completes both thought and musical segment.

In "She Belongs to Me," structure and instrumentation from the blues combine with words that idealize a woman. Blues frequently use religious imagery about women: "Well, a long, tall woman will make a preacher lay his Bible down," for instance, or "She's got ways like an angel, and she's sweet like heaven above."[12]

"Bow down to her on Sunday," says the narrator of "She Belongs to Me." How does Dylan's "artist" differ from an idealized woman in the blues? A blues performer creates poetic images that can be understood aurally, without efforts toward figuring them out. And he usually embeds such an image in a literal, explanatory context. Washboard Sam sings, for example: "I've got a woman stream-lined from her feet to her head/.... She's a river hip mama and [men] all wanna be baptized."[13] Here one can spot the wordplay on "hip" and on "stream" and "river," and perhaps even glimpse a shade of James Joyce's Anna Livia Plurabella. But these two lines occur within a more literal description of a woman who wears patent leather shoes and makes men whine and cry. Sometimes a poetic image continues for an entire song, as in Robert Johnson's "Terraplane Blues" or "Milkcow's Calf Blues,"[14] but extended metaphors like these can be translated most often into literal sexual descriptions.

"She Belongs to Me" cannot be so translated. Only "her keyhole" suggests, obliquely, sexuality; one bows to and steals for the artist because of some irresistible and undefined attraction. She has power over the narrator, over the listener "you," over darkness and light, and over the law. The song does not directly celebrate her sex appeal, as the blues most often do. Nor does it resemble the sentimental religious idealization in white American songs, such as "You're the nearest thing to heaven that I know," in country-western tradition, or Tin Pan Alley's "Nature fashioned you and when she was done/You were all the sweet things rolled up in one/.... The angels must have sent you."[15]

Dylan's song, instead, is deliberately evocative, indirect. If a keyhole here seems sexual, it equally suggests the woman's mysterious unattainability and furthermore suggests the meaning of the song itself—a meaning glimpsed by its overeducated audience, peeking through the closed door of black American culture and wanting words to interpret it all. Dylan's love songs, like his protest songs, force listeners to ask their own questions. But love, unlike political oppression, yields not at all to dialectical analysis.

This performance, the second cut on the first side of *Bringing It All Back Home*, follows "Subterranean Homesick Blues," which has opened the album with an electric-guitar shriek. "She Belongs to Me" begins with acoustic-guitar strumming, alone only briefly. The drum joins and then the electric guitar, which continues throughout, playing high, plucked notes and occasional runs during every sung line except the first, and during every instrumental break that completes each four-bar segment. Sometimes, as at the start of the second stanza, the electric run overlaps such that the break ends with a few beats of rhythm instruments alone. But inevitably the electric guitar returns to demand its share of the attention.

The unpredictable demands of the electric guitar create tension with the calm, structural insistence of the rhythm instruments—drum and acoustic guitar defining four-measure musical lines. Together, irregular and regular instrumentation expresses the inevitability with which the listener must follow commands to bow down and worship the artist in the lyrics, who becomes increasingly divine through the five sung stanzas. (See text in Appendix A.) Her first-stanza attributes could apply to a human woman, the final line neatly combining human artistic powers with a hint of the cosmic. "Don't look back," which D. A. Pennebaker used as the title for his documentary film of Dylan's 1965 British tour, may have come to Dylan from the oft-quoted list of advice that black baseball star Satchel Paige composed in the fifties: his last admonition is, "And don't look back. Something may be gaining on you."[16]

The song's narrator acts as priest, never naming himself, gradually drawing the listener into the service of "she," the artist. The pronoun "she" dominates the first, third, and fourth stanzas, occurring twenty-one times; nearly a fifth of the words in the song, in fact, are "she" and "her." This repeated "she" keeps in the foreground the long-*e* sound that governs the second- and fourth-stanza rhymes, and winds throughout the song—"needs," "steal," "peeking," "keyhole," "Egyptian," "Halloween." Other vowel-consonant patterns also recur, such as the third-stanza *um/n* in "stumbles," which anticipates the last stanza's end rhymes as well as its "Sunday" and "trumpet." But the long-*e* sound is widest spread, and is notable too as the vowel sound most resembling the sound of an electric guitar. Dylan was not the first to make artistic use of this vocal/instrumental interface: Elvis Presley, for one, often flips into falsetto on syllables containing long-*e* sounds in his early electric-blues-derived rock and roll.[17]

The other major pronoun in "She Belongs to Me" stands more isolated in sound: "you" rhymes only with "through," sandwiched firmly between the "peeking" and "keyhole" that evoke "she." "You," however, indirectly echoes the *ow* sound pattern: in the second stanza "out" and "proud" and "down" describe "you," and then "bow down" commands the listener "you" in the last stanza. In meaning, though, this pronoun starts out as the impersonal. The second-stanza "you," who stands and steals proudly but then kneels in humiliation before her still-closed door, refers to a worshipper—but not yet necessarily to the listener to this song.

The tangled negatives of the third stanza, again describing "she," leave the artist even less subject to human limitations. "She got no place to fall" remains particularly enigmatic, seeming visual until one tries to picture it:

even perched solidly on that pedestal, a woman would have a place to fall to. The image upsets earthbound notions of space, like the point in Dante's *Inferno* where down becomes up. "She's nobody's child" evokes the prophecy that Macbeth will be slain by man not born of woman, as well as the virgin births of Jesus and other deities. Finally, her freedom from "the law" suggests the Old Testament and, more forcibly for most of Dylan's audience, America's military draft and parking meters and compulsory education, which one could no more avoid than enter life as nobody's child.

In the fourth stanza, the artist wears a ring with the exotic aura of ancient Egypt and, like the keyhole, with oblique sexual symbolism. In this line she seems an oracle; her ring signals her every utterance as she hypnotizes with sight and speech. And the last line of this stanza proves her irresistible, not just exotic and therefore fascinating: she wants, and she will get, "you" for her collection of walking antiques. As the fourth stanza ends, "you" has become the listener, no longer an impersonal pronoun. The fifth sung stanza shifts to the imperative, with "you" understood. But there is a stanza not there on paper: between the third and fourth stanzas, both about "she," Dylan plays an entire stanza on harmonica. Because of the alternation of "she" and "you" stanzas, this instrumental stanza seems directed at "you." Thus the voicelike harmonica, seeming to articulate what words cannot, helps the listener make the difficult transition from observation to commitment. In the second stanza a listener can remain impersonally detached from rituals in honor of the artist; by the last stanza, she must participate.

So, "you" begin observing her rites, no longer paying homage to other deities on their holy days. Halloween suggests the spirits of the dead, neglected for her sake; Christmas, of course, she preempts from Christ. The artist prefers musical offerings: a trumpet, to announce the apocalypse or the royal presence, and the drum, which has kept a steady up-tempo beat behind and around all the lyrics of this song.

The narrator of "Sad-Eyed Lady of the Lowlands" likewise makes an offering of drums. But that narrator remains unsure whether the goddess he addresses will deign to accept his gifts: the sad-eyed lady does not care whether she is worshipped. This earlier artist, however, demands subservience, commitment, awe, worship. "She Belongs to Me"? An ironic title, a love-song cliché disproven—for in this song, you belong to her. And insofar as "she" evokes religious frenzy and other extreme emotions that get repressed in white American musical tradition, you belong to the electric blues.

"Sad-Eyed Lady of the Lowlands" instead evokes the unfrenzied emotions of Western-European religious traditions. The lyrics portray the sad-eyed lady herself as a cathedral before whom the narrator stands and wonders. (See text in Appendix A.) The instruments, particularly the organ, help create an atmosphere that is respectful, quiet, predictable, culturally familiar even to a listener who does not actually attend white American church. Throughout the song the drum stays calm and as dependable as a heartbeat. The drum's part—which includes the snare and cymbal struck softly and together on the fourth beat of every 6/8 measure, four times during each musical line—varies only slightly, during twelve of the thirteen lines in each stanza.

For every refrain the drum changes drastically, however, and thereby sets apart the line "My warehouse eyes, my Arabian drums." After each "no man comes," other instruments fade while the drummer strikes firm, separate beats that lead into, accompany, and then lead away from "My warehouse eyes, my Arabian drums." Then the drum reverts instantly, every time, to back up the question "Should I leave [put] them...?" with its usual riff. Throughout the song, the drum's steadiness provides security. Its one repeated variation sets apart the sung line that tells what the narrator can offer to the lady.

Dylan's harmonica also spotlights the "warehouse" line—not during every refrain, but rather at the end of the song. The harmonica plays for four measures at the song's opening, after the four-measure instrumental introduction and before the words; then it does not reappear until after all five sung stanzas. There, while the rest of the band plays through eleven more musical lines and fades during what would be the "warehouse" line (if this instrumental stanza were sung), Dylan plays an unusually mellow harmonica. He seldom plays the sung melody, though. For example, in the fifth instrumental line, his harmonica notes blur into a harsher sound than elsewhere; in the ninth line he plays a series of high, then low, pitches. Most noticeably, in the third and seventh lines, he replaces what would have been the sung melody with a harmonica reproduction of "My warehouse eyes, my Arabian drums."

This melody can easily be identified, even though the five renderings of the "warehouse" line differ. In the first three stanzas, Dylan sings each syllable of "My warehouse eyes, my Arabian drums" on a separate, descending pitch. In the other two stanzas, instead, it becomes:

<pre>
        My
           y
             warehouse eyes, my A
                                rab
                                 ian
                                  dru
                                    u
                                     ms
</pre>

So, during the final instrumental stanza, the narrator holds out his offerings even more frequently and insistently than he does during the lyrics.

Divisions and transitions in this song, other than the setting out of his offerings, are marked by full, rich organ chords. Only occasionally—as after each "Sad-eyed lady of the lowlands" line—does a guitar emerge from the plush instrumentation to add, softly, a decorative riff. Otherwise, the organ shapes the song. Its chords mark the four measures behind each sung line as regularly as do the snare and cymbals. In addition, the organ divides each stanza into four distinct segments: a four-line unit, then another four lines, then two lines, then three, all precisely correlated with the syntax and rhyme scheme of the lyrics. After every four-line unit—after every question ending "… you?" that is—the organ plays a little-varying sequence of three descending chords and a fourth ascending one. A louder organ arpeggio coordinates with the drum lead-in to each "warehouse" line. Also following every stanza, the organ plays a brief melody sandwiched between two longer-held chords.

While the organ-led instruments mark off the song's recurring structural patterns and create a calm, churchlike aura, the lyrics too are as vital as are the exact words to the Lord's Prayer or the four questions at Passover. Dylan articulates carefully, never slurring words as he does in other songs on *Blonde on Blonde*. (For "Rainy Day Women #12 & 35," for example, his slurring helps convey the song's idea that "everybody must get stoned.") For instance, he clearly separates the two *k* sounds in each phrase "think could."

But apparently the words are not so sacred that Dylan hesitates to deviate from them in performance: this, probably his only public performance of the song,[18] differs from the text as later published (bracketed in Appendix A). Some of these variant lyrics seem poetic improvements: in the fourth stanza, for instance, the "dead angels" line as performed creates a picture of men pointing toward the sky or an empty tomb—not at corpses of angels, as the published text suggests.

However, Dylan presumably would not make changes in performance with planned-out artistic intentions. Furthermore, and more to the point, we cannot know whether text or performance came first. In the studio in 1966, Dylan would have sung from his own notes or typescript. The text published in 1973 was prepared by employees of the music-publishing house, working from the sound track itself and perhaps from other sources, probably not recoverable. Maybe Dylan checked through and okayed the lyrics published in *Writings and Drawings*—or maybe not. For consistency, when the two clearly differ, I in all cases regard the performed text as primary. But, as for other chicken-or-the-egg issues, the relationship between published and performed texts is nowhere very certain.

What is certain is that the sad-eyed lady is just as awesome and holy at the end as at the beginning of the song. There is no linear narrative; instead, scenes steadily alternate from her past and her present, flipping back and forth like flipping a single card. In the two central stanzas, the narrator dwells longer on her past, on the side that made her what she now is. And in every refrain, he stops flipping the card to reassess his attitude toward her. But he never does decide what he ought to do... except to play that harmonica, and with it to keep offering her his warehouse eyes and Arabian drums, over and over.

Each stanza's poetic structure resembles the Petrarchan sonnet. For eight lines the narrator wonders about her present and about "them" in her past; in an abrupt shift of thought, as for the sestet, the narrator then wonders for five sung lines and one instrumental line about himself in her future. The tight syntax and the rhyme scheme, alliteration, and other vowel/consonant patterns all help the instruments frame a listener's response to the poetic imagery. Each of the five stanzas is rhymed *AAABCCCBDEEFF*. Most *A* and *C* lines, with narrative exceptions, fit into long prepositional phrases beginning "With your..." and listing the lady's attributes, most often as two nouns whose combination forms a not-quite-visual image—"match-book songs," for example, or "magazine husband." Each *B* line, asking about "they," ends with a verb and "... you?" rhyming one or both syllables of the verb.

The opening line introduces three of the major vowel/consonant patterns that continue throughout: "With your mercury mouth in the missionary times." The soft, suckling sound of *m* occurs frequently among the lady's attributes, softening even her "sheet-metal memory." Sounds of *s* and *sh* also continue through the song, from the sad-eyed lady's "eyes like smoke" to her "ghostlike soul." And the long-*i* sounds throughout, as in "sympathize with their side," keep in the listener's semiconscious aural awareness what is only periodically articulated but is always present in the song: the lady's eyes and the "I" of the narrator.

Although the song tells how this "I" feels toward the sad-eyed lady, speculation about what "they" have said or done to her fills the narrator's musings. But this potentially threatening "they" is overpowered, for it must share its long-*a* sound with her "saintlike face" and, more often, with her "gate" and the narrator's "wait" for the "lady" herself. The third and fourth stanzas hint that "they" include kings of Tyrus, farmers, and businessmen, whereas the active verb of each *B* line tells what they have tried to do to her. The narrator, instead, regards her passively. The two alternatives he sees are not mutually exclusive ones: he can leave his gifts, and/or he can wait.

His warehouse eyes and Arabian drums, representing all he has to give, seem momentous. The drumbeats make them seem so, as does the poetic meter. These words would move slowly even if spoken, for nearly every syllable requires a strong stress. The assonance of the open vowel pattern also slows down the line, especially the careful articulation of "eyes, my."

The "warehouse" line contains the *m*, long-*i*, *s*, and long-*a* sounds that also permeate the lady's attributes, thus suggesting her influence over what the narrator has to offer. His two gifts reverberate with the poetic imagery as well as the vowel/consonant sounds of the rest of the lyrics. "Warehouse eyes," to begin with, combines two strands of imagery: the lady's eyes variously described, along with other parts of her face, and the harsh, metallic quality of her past experiences, always overcome by softness and gentleness.

The lady's repeatedly sad eyes appear also smokelike and swimming with moonlight. Metallic images, more varied throughout, culminate in her "sheet-metal memory of Cannery Row" (in which Dylan pronounces -*ory* and -*ery* identically). The metallic images begin gently, in religious metaphors: a silver cross and a voice like chimes. Her mouth of mercury— an elongated *mer-kree*—seems elusive, a metal/human oxymoron but not clearly, yet, a harsh/gentle one. Mercury itself is a mediating substance in the Lévi-Straussian sense, a substance neither metal nor nonmetal; its appearance as opening image sets the tone for the woman's combining of other apparent binary oppositions. "Missionary times," also ambiguous, suggests the olden days, when religion could provide meaningful goals, and equally suggests religion blared from a newspaper headline.

"Streetcar visions" is the first image to use metal in a harsh/gentle oxymoron. She places these visions on the grass, taking action to cushion with a natural substance the jangling feel of city traffic. In the second stanza, "sheets like metal" suggests that she can calmly accept, as well as take action to change, harshness, can even fall asleep in metal bedsheets… until "sheet-metal memory" twists the concept. Her "belt like lace" forms another harsh/gentle oxymoron: what for others is leather and metal buckle, for her is soft and delicate. The fifth stanza labels her "gentleness now," which, in all cases, can engulf what is coldly metallic in the world.

The narrator's own "warehouse eyes" combine harsh and gentle, metallic and human images. The lady's sad eyes have so influenced the narrator's way of seeing that his own eyes share her oxymoronic, nonrational power. The metaphor also carries the sense of a warehouse as a vast storage area, filled with myriads of images of her.

The narrator also stands ready to offer the sad-eyed lady his Arabian drums: he will voluntarily give up both the eyes he needs to see the world and the drums he needs to communicate with it. "Arabian" here, like "Egyptian" in "She Belongs to Me," makes its noun seem exotic and thereby valuable. The narrator knows she doesn't need his warehouse eyes, for she already has her sad ones; he knows too that among all her attributes she has the female counterpart of his drums, her "gypsy hymns." But still, knowing she can well do without them, he is willing to give up all he has—his music, which lets him speak publicly, and his private visions of her gentleness, her harsh past, her cathedrallike beauty, her mystery, her pride, and her innocence.

Her innocence, throughout the song, has overtones of sexual wholesomeness. More thoroughly, she remains innocent of crime, even when associating with criminals. She can protect her own pockets and stack the deck to win. (In addition, her "deck of cards missing the jack and the ace" lacks the extra male—the threatening oedipal son?—and the superpower. The high cards are king and queen, an ideal couple.) In the third stanza the sad-eyed lady confronts and conquers the kings with their convict list. They judge whether she and her kiss are properly "geranium," meekly domestic, peeking coyly from behind gingham curtains and picket fence. But they also stand ready to rape her, in line like a bike gang at a turnout.

The farmers and businessmen, in the fourth stanza, seem less formidable. Rather than threatening conviction or force, they try to persuade her to be like their "dead angels," their lifeless romantic ideals. But the sad-eyed lady is too proud and too certain of her innocence before the valid laws of nature—the sea, as distinguished from the arbitrary laws of male society—to be convinced she should take any blame for the farm or for other social problems, petty false alarms. To show how easily she ignores social conventions, she stands on the beach hugging the child of the hoodlum.

That baby shows the futility of those who would try to accuse her of corruption by association. Although she is both sexually and criminally guilty because of the baby, in the fifth stanza she inspires the same religious devotion as she did in the first. The transition to the final devotional phrases comes neatly in the word "thief," which ties backward to the criminal imagery and forward to the intensifying religious metaphors, suggesting the thieves crucified alongside Jesus.

These two major patterns of imagery—harsh/gentle mostly in her attributes, innocent/guilty mostly in the narrative flashbacks—add to the song's overall feeling of religious devotion: it is unresolvable oppositions like these that religious rituals and myths can mediate for a believer.[19] Both themes appear in "She Belongs to Me," but briefly—"The law can't touch her at all" proves the artist innocent, and she is mysteriously invulnerable, behind closed doors, though not as certainly gentle inside.

Oxymorons and other mutually contradictory images occur evenly throughout "Sad-Eyed Lady." Images do not pair off to imitate dialectical thought processes, as in "Hard Rain," nor do they remain as frustratingly unresolvable as "she got no place to fall." As a Christian accepts Mary as both virgin and mother, and Christ as both god and man, so too this song's narrator accepts that the sad-eyed lady encompasses what the rational mind would term mutually exclusive attributes.

The sad-eyed lady is portrayed most frequently in Judeo-Christian terms, both in words like "holy medallion" and in sounds like the stately organ. But the song also hints at ancient mother-goddess religions (at the popular idea of them, that is). In a strand of light/dark poetic imagery in the second and third stanzas, the sad-eyed lady has the darkness of basement and moonlight and midnight, with her "silhouette when the sunlight dims." A few images of fire, "curfew" and "matchbook songs" and "childhood flames," also suggest surrounding darkness. Such associations with the goddess of moon and twilight, birth and death, in whom oppositions like light and dark can be irrationally contained, appear more fully in "Shelter from the Storm" and "Isis."

As poetry, the C-line images in the third stanza may seem isolated from the rest. "Spanish manners" could be gentle ones, brought from afar like his drums. "Mother's drugs," if those drugs are sleep-inducing downers, gives to the dream state appropriate to a mother goddess a rather ugly modern twist, as in the Rolling Stones' "Mother's Little Helper." "Curfew plugs" has ugly overtones, too, perhaps of a teenage tease. A "cowboy mouth" sounds rugged, quite unlike a "mercury mouth." These unlinked attributes, however, widen the range of emotions that the song evokes about the woman. A listener to a song does not need the rational, narrative, or even imagistic links that a reader would. A listener, experiencing each emotion while the phrase evokes it, understands what these third-stanza lines have to do with the rest of the song: they share its vowel/consonant patterns, its syntax, its rhymes; they are delivered in the same soothing voice and the same velvety instrumentation. Sound creates connections, also, within each phrase: the *an* of "Spanish manners," the *uh* of "mother's drugs" and "curfew plugs," the *ow* of "cowboy mouth." Thus, a listener who relaxes into music and aurally experienced words has understood the song without straining to interpret such phrases precisely.

Most listeners, though, do think about these lyrics that Dylan so carefully articulates. Not-quite-visual imagery raises questions in a listener's mind—especially when, as here, the imagery is framed in interrogative syntax. And such questioning has gotten deflected into biographical speculation in the past. Dylan has uncharacteristically revealed—in the 1975 song "Sara"—that he wrote "Sad-Eyed Lady of the Lowlands" one night in the Chelsea Hotel about his (now ex-) wife. My discussion of the song has demonstrated, I hope, just how limited such biographical interpretation would be in analyzing the artistry of Bob Dylan's work. (I may be a little jealous, too.)

For decades, Dylan's reticence about his private life was matched by his reluctance to talk about the artistic processes by which he fuses words and music. But his 1978 articulation offers more precise information than we have for most artists in any medium:

> That's the sound I'm trying to get across. I'm not just up there re-creating old blues tunes or trying to invent some surrealistic rhapsody.... it's the sound and the words. Words don't interfere with it. They—they—punctuate it. You know, they give it purpose. [*pause*] And all the ideas for my songs, all the influences, all [the feelings] come out of that.... I'm not doing it to see how good I can sound, or how perfect the melody can be, or how intricate the details can be woven or how perfectly written something can be.... I symbolically hear that sound wherever I am.... the sound of the street with the sunrays.

He also singles out *Blonde on Blonde* as his best album:

> The closest I ever got to the sound I hear in my mind was on individual bands in the *Blonde on Blonde* album. It's that thin, that wild mercury sound. It's metallic and bright gold.... I haven't been able to succeed in

getting it all the time. Mostly, I've been driving at a combination of guitar, harmonica and organ, but now I find myself going into territory that has more percussion in it and [*pause*] rhythms of the soul.[20]

Dylan's characterization of his ideal musical sound shows yet again how inextricable are music and poetic imagery in "Sad-Eyed Lady"—even to her "mercury mouth." The musical territory that Dylan was then entering, which includes "Isis," has more percussion in the instrumentation and in the imagery as well. That is, although the "Sad-Eyed Lady" narrator ends the song still wondering what to do, the soothing instrumentation joins the stable structure and the list of female attributes in oppositional pairs to teach him something soothing about the appeal of what is Female. The narrator of "Isis," accompanied by bells and other jangling percussion, tries hard to please the Female but ends the song even more baffled than at the start.

In "Shelter from the Storm" the relationship of words to music (more precisely, of discursive sense of lyrics to instrumentation) is more complex. Instead of reinforcing each other, the simple instrumentation quite negates what the words say. The despondent narrator of "Shelter" has been rejected by the woman forever. But the acoustic guitar and bass, as a mutually contented couple, deny the narrative situation, and the nonlinear narrative structure combines with the dependably strophic musical structure to suggest that time is more controllable than we assume, that forever may someday end.

"Shelter from the Storm" is on *Blood on the Tracks,* an album outstanding for its aesthetic unity and thematic balance. Each cut tells of a male/female relationship from the male point of view. The power to begin or end a relationship is symbolized most often as the Road—as the power of male or female to take to the road or to let the searching partner find him or her.

"Shelter from the Storm" describes the male quest for the female in an aspect unique on the album. (See text in Appendix A.) The narrator knows just where she is. But since it was she who forced him out onto the road, into the "foreign country" (no exotic place name here), he may not return to her. And the road holds no challenge or adventures for him: it is "full of mud," and he is "burned out from exhaustion" and "blown out on the trail." The "world of steel-eyed death and men who are fighting to be warm" is one of male-heroic behavior, daring and finally fruitless, shown in contrast to the "place where it's always safe and warm" that the woman has denied to him.

The narrator's exile stems from his attempt to continue male-heroic behavior from within her womblike security. Heroism, throughout the song, appears in related images of gore and battle, of the road, of authority figures, and of Jesus Christ. None of these types of hero gets the glory or satisfaction that a believer in each would expect. Toward the end of the song, predominant imagery shifts from the wandering, fighting, knight-errant hero, who suffers *in spite of* our expectations for his glory, to the Christian hero, who ought to attain glory *by means of* suffering on the cross—but who, instead of attaining salvation, is forced into exile by the female.

Another exiled narrator, one who is stuck inside of Mobile with the Memphis blues again, makes explicit a connection between exile in space and disruption in time: in Mobile, "people just get uglier, and I have no sense of time" (1966). The "Shelter" narrator is likewise suspended in time. The song's imagery does not develop neatly from hero who suffers to suffering hero, and the narrative too is intricately nonsequential. Each stanza tells a bit of what would be a narrative sequence, as the narrator meets and falls in love with and gets rejected by the woman. But all these scenes are disrupted, the linearity of time disarranged. In a song, as distinguished from a poem, linear development of imagery is not needed for artistic coherence. While the music keeps time, somehow, the listener need not. "Shelter from the Storm" pointedly demonstrates its freedom from linear time in both nonsequential development of imagery and nonsequential story line.

The song tells of four points in time, around a male/female relationship: (1) the narrator on the road before he met her, (2) the moment of meeting, (3) the moment of parting, and (4) the narrator on the road after they part. The repeated refrain "Come in, she said, I'll give you shelter from the storm" continually evokes (2), the moment of meeting. In the other three lines of each four-line stanza, a scene appears from one of these four points in time.

The first stanza shows (1), the narrator on the road before they met. The second stanza leaps to (4), him on the road after they part, in exile. The third stanza describes (2), the moment of meeting; the fourth returns to (1), before they met. The fifth stanza expands on (2), the moment of meeting. The sixth and seventh are not as clear but are certainly out of sequence: the sixth combines (3) and (4), the moment of parting and the road afterwards; the seventh could describe both (1), before, and (4), after their sheltered interlude. The eighth stanza seems more probably (4), afterwards; the ninth describes (3), the moment of parting; and the last, misleadingly in order like the first, comes during (4), the narrator's time in exile after her sheltering.

In "Sad-Eyed Lady," the narrator's musings shift from the lady's past to her present to his future, but these points in time are merged, not disarranged. In "Shelter," time is deliberately askew. The entangled narrative reproduces the narrator's entangled emotions as he looks back on love, and it also disrupts Western-European assumptions of time as a neatly controllable linear force.

 · The opening and closing lines of the song articulate this skewed sense of time. "'Twas in another lifetime," it begins—but Western notions do not allow for reincarnation, as cyclical conceptions of time do. The song's closing line is powerful, and not only within this song's suggested contrast of patriarchal and matriarchal religions: "If I could only turn back the clock to when God and her were born." In that tenth stanza, the narrator begins to muse about a possible future, but he ends the song realizing he has no more power over her beauty than he has over time or God.

Although other gods were born as humans (avatars), this song's imagery is predominantly Christian. The eternal Christian god was born, paradoxically, on Christmas Day of the year one. The woman in "Shelter" is both born and eternal likewise, always safe and warm. The narrator tries to imitate Christ, wearing a crown of thorns and dying while "they" gamble for his clothes. But only the female can offer or withhold salvation. The ninth-stanza ideas that he bargained for salvation and prepared his own offering suggest that he tried to take back the active hero's role, which he should have abandoned when he passively let her remove his crown of thorns.

Images besides those of Christ also portray the heroic world, both before and after the sheltered respite. Images of battle and hunting—"toil and blood," "steeleyed death and men who are fighting," "Hunted like a crocodile, ravished in the corn"—overlap with images of the wanderer on the road in the wilderness. The seventh stanza features lone male authority figures proving themselves by making life more difficult than it need be. A Wild West deputy need not test himself like a Far East fakir; a preacher could choose an easier life than that of a circuit rider. The "one-eyed undertaker" tries to usurp the role of the goddess of birth and death. His horn, suggesting Gabriel's at the Last Judgment, is "futile" (and equally, in performance, "feudal"). It is futile because the wombed female, not some patriarchal angel showing off his trumpet, holds the power over life and death, power to decide who gets a lethal dose of what might otherwise heal. In the second line of this seventh stanza, "nothing" becomes a positive concept, equal to "doom"; reciprocally, "doom" (or "do 'em") becomes empty and melodramatic, like so much else in the male-heroic world.

The eighth stanza specifies that the male-heroic world lacks love. A newborn baby will presumably stop wailing after mama picks him up. The old men are worse off, for they are at the far end of the birth-to-death spectrum of the mother goddess; lovelessness there is not as easily remedied. Their broken teeth, as in much folklore, seem an image of impotence.[21]

Besides its metaphorical and mythological dimensions, this song also, vitally, describes a "real-world" relationship in ordinary, even clichéd language: "Everything up to that point had been left unresolved"; "I took too much for granted, I got my signals crossed"; "I'll always do my best for her, on that I give my word." The song tells, on one level, of a relationship that breaks up just as a listener's might; on other levels, the woman is an earth-mother goddess, and the narrator has failed at every sort of male heroism.

The second sung line, "When blackness was a virtue," ties backward to Dylan's early protest and love songs, forward to "Isis," and all around to the mythological dimension of "Shelter from the Storm." To paraphrase a popular "comparative mythologist," matriarchal religions had combined in the mother goddess attributes like light and dark (as in moonlight), birth and death, good and evil, right and wrong. But patriarchal systems set concepts like these into opposition so that "all that is good and noble was attributed to the new, heroic master gods, leaving to the native nature powers the character only of darkness—to which, also, a negative moral judgment was now added."[22] If blackness was once a virtue, then the moral oppositions of Western thinking are no more absolute than its linear time.

Dylan had been articulating the shortcomings of dichotomization at least since "My Back Pages" (1964):

> Lies that life is black and white
> Spoke from my skull....
> Good and bad, I defined these terms
> Quite clear, no doubt, somehow
> Ah, but I was so much older then
> I'm younger than that now

In other early songs besides "Sad-Eyed Lady" and "She Belongs to Me," the combining of binary oppositions characterizes the ideal female. The idealized object of "Love Minus Zero/No Limit" (1965), among many examples, is "true, like ice, like fire.... She knows there's no success like failure, and that failure's no success at all."

The lyrics of "Shelter from the Storm" tell of a terminated relationship that can be renewed only at the disinterested female's bidding. How, then, does the song sound so soothing? For one thing, the disrupted time sequence suggests that past is not unalterably past. For another, Dylan's voice and the gentle instrumentation counterbalance the harshness of the narrator's exile— counterbalance, but in no way cancel out, what the words say. The loose melody and lack of pulsation in the vocal line give precedence to the words. Nevertheless, the rhythm guitar keeps an undercurrent of steadiness such that the lyrics move at a driving pace, a faster tempo than would seem appropriate to the despondent narrator's situation. The lyrics and the musical performance of them—each contributes contradictory emotions to the experience of a listener.

The soothing quality of this performance can be perceived easily in comparison to another released version of "Shelter," that on *Hard Rain,* the 1976 concert-tour album. In this rowdy up-tempo version, Dylan's often sarcastic voice combines with complex and self-involved instrumentation to tell the woman in the lyrics that the narrator can get along just fine without her, that he couldn't care less.

In the *Blood on the Tracks* version, instead, Dylan's voice expresses regret and sadness. Also, his careful phrasing of each sung line into two separate images expresses the narrator's thorough but unsuccessful attempt to figure out what all happened. Dylan sometimes shifts the volume of his voice to more clearly bisect lines, as in the loud command "Try imagining a place," followed by a gentle "where it's always safe and warm." He articulates carefully, consistent even in pronouncing "you" as *yuh* in every refrain.

The studio version opens with four measures strummed on acoustic guitar. Tony Brown's bass joins it for four measures, then continues throughout the vocals. Behind each sung line the bass marks the first beat of each measure and fills in the fourth measure, usually with ♩ ♩ ♫♩ , while the acoustic guitar cheerfully carries higher-pitched chords. Their warm and satisfying relationship is quite unlike the one the lyrics describe.

In almost every line, the voice accents the same beats as does the instrumentation, adding to the effect of calm cooperation. Between stanzas, the instrumental break varies from four to eight measures at first; with increasing predictability, then, the vocal of each of the last five stanzas begins during the final upbeat of the eighth instrumental measure. After the last sung stanza, bass and guitar continue alone for two measures. Then Dylan's harmonica joins them for an entire stanza—not playing the vocal melody, and toying a bit with the regular beat. But the harmonica fades midway through what would be the refrain if sung, and the guitar and bass finish the musical line and then the song. They slow down as they fade; the last sounds are a rising arpeggio plucked on the guitar and a final, high-pitched strum.

This finality, this musical ending that could not pass for a middle or a beginning, contradicts the lyrics' implication that, because time is not linear, endings need not be final. Any potential upset a listener might sense because of a disrupted narrative sequence gets calmed because the whole song is solidly framed in white American musical tradition. Time is both there and not there; neither words nor music overpowers the other, and the contradictory complex of emotions remains not tense, not resolved, but somehow balanced.

The innovative Eastern music of "Isis" has quite a different effect on the listener and quite a different relationship to the words, in both the song and the glimpse we get of Dylan composing this and other songs on *Desire*. In the liner notes, Allen Ginsberg says that "Half-month was spent solitary on Long Island with theatrist Jacques Levy working on song facts phrases & rhymes, sharing information seriousness." Dylan alone wrote the music to all songs on *Desire*. But for every song save two, for the first time in his career, he shares the credit for the original words. Since separating Levy's contribution to "Isis" from Dylan's would be a task as formidable as seeking the communal origins of a Child ballad, I must refer to the song as if Dylan wrote it.

Throughout *Desire*, Dylan experiments with musical sounds unfamiliar within what has jelled into the white rock tradition. Besides the usual bass, other guitars, drums, and piano, musicians play violin, mandolin, bells, congas, and a bellzouki (presumably invented by Vincent Bell, who plays it). Dylan shares vocals on *Desire* with two men and two women well known from solo careers, Ronee Blakley and Emmylou Harris; except for a duet with Johnny Cash on *Nashville Skyline*, one scat singer on "If Dogs Run Free" (1970), and the ill-fated *Self Portrait* album, sharing his vocals on a studio album is another innovation. Dylan plays harmonica and rhythm guitar and, the jacket specifies, piano on "Isis."

"Isis" opens as Dylan's piano, repeating low-pitched chords, plays for two measures alone and then is joined by a metallic instrument struck once in each of four measures. Three sharp drumbeats lead into the first sung word, as Dylan comes down hard on "I married Isis."

Throughout his vocals, Dylan continues to come down hard on four syllables in each line, often coinciding with the four accented beats in each musical line and always waiting for the first accented beat of each line to come around. The four-measure musical line quite overwhelms any objection that poetic meter or narrative continuity might wish to raise. But a glance through the printed text shows why this musical insistence detracts little from the articulateness with which words tell the man's story. (See Appendix A.)

The vast majority of sung lines contain four evenly spaced syllables that convey most of the verbal meaning. In a line like "So I *cut* off my *hair* and I *rode* straight a*way*" in the first stanza, Dylan's voice and the musical beats (marked here as =) pick out the four main ideas; the same goes for the last stanza's "What *drives* me to *you* is what *drives* me in*sane,*" the entire twelfth-stanza dialogue, and more. Dylan may purposely play with the musical beat, though: in the eleventh stanza's "*Blind*ed by *sleep* and in *need* of a bed =," he sings the last phrase fast so that the accented musical beat falls well after the word "bed." And Isis, in fact, needs no bed, except in the narrator's continued misunderstanding of her.

This regular beat is carried by nearly all instruments involved—bass, piano, drums, and (loudest and least familiar) bells. The shaken bells go 123 123 123 123 during every musical line, including the lengthy breaks between stanzas. The drums, which one would expect to carry the beat, do so unobtrusively, noticeable only in brief, decorative riffs. The piano (which Dylan has occasionally played on albums since *John Wesley Harding*) repeats its low-pitched chords, 123 123 123 123, loudest behind the first two sung lines but steadily throughout. After two lines the piano passes beat-marking honors on to Rob Stoner's bass; it is plucked at each 1 of the piano's 123, and plays four chords that descend in even steps behind each sung line. Thus the bass gives to the song an overall feeling of inevitable sinking— this in spite of scattered efforts from the harmonica and violin to raise or at least shake up the listener's spirits.

While all these instruments (none of them the familiar rhythm guitar) mark rhythm, Scarlet Rivera's violin and Dylan's harmonica playfully trade off licks that make each instrumental break between stanzas sound as different as possible from its eleven corresponding breaks. These breaks vary in length from four to twenty measures. The longest one follows the ninth stanza: it imitates the narrator's confused state of mind when he finally breaks into the tomb to find "no jewels, no nothing" and before he comes to realize that this tomb will no longer be empty once it holds the dead body of the male-heroic stranger. As the narrator reenters Isis's presence, in the last three stanzas, each instrumental break becomes sixteen measures of harmonica and violin together, balanced. (See Appendix C for sketch.) Then the song fades abruptly into a splash of shaken bells, a drumroll, and a piano run upward. The last sounds to fade are a highpitched chord on the same piano that has played low chords throughout, and the not-quite-stilled bells.

The uneasiness created by unaccustomed and unpredictable instrumentation affects the listener's understanding of the narrative. The music throughout anticipates the unsettling last stanza, in which the narrator finally addresses Isis directly and finds that he still does not understand what the Female wants or needs from him... if anything. On paper this narrative—until the last stanza—seems a straightforward story of a man who sets out on a male-heroic quest to prove himself to the woman he has deified, and who returns, wiser, to a satisfying dialogue with a human companion. The narrative proceeds in chronological order, with few of the gaps that characterize the traditional ballad or Dylan's balladlike songs, such as "Lily, Rosemary and the Jack of Hearts" (1974).

His voice recounts the story mostly in a tone of drily humorous self-deprecation. Some phrases he sings more gently and seriously, such as the eager "I love her" that ends the tenth stanza. His voice creates special effects on certain words, as well: in the ninth stanza, for instance, "empty" sounds hollow and "mad" quietly desperate. Allen Ginsberg, in the liner notes, describes this quality in Dylan's performance of "Isis":

> Dylan's spontaneous ritards & talk-like mouthings for clarity, "It's only *natchural*." So you can *hear* it! ... Steady rhythm behind the elastic language, poet alone at microphone reciting-singing surreal-history love text ending in giant "YEAH!" ... So he now lets loose his long-vowel yowls & yawps over smalltowns' antennaed rooftops. To Isis Moon Lady Language Creator Birth Goddess, Mother of Ra, Saraswati & Kali-Matoo. Hècate, Ea, Astarte, Sophia & Aphrodite. Divine Mother.

If there is a development to be labeled, from the narrator's baffled worship of the artist in "She Belongs to Me" to this narrator's quest for and return to the eternal earth goddess, it is a realization that cultures other than Judeo-Christian America also cannot explain the Female. None can explain what is emotional and chaotic and dark and appealing and, by nature, precisely what cannot be encompassed by psychological drives toward dialectical organization and rational analysis.

This male narrator does not try to analyze Isis, though. He sets out on a quest that borrows elements principally from two mythologies, one Male-centered and the other more balanced. The first, the tough-guy mystique of

James Bond or Philip Marlowe, tries to ignore the power of the Female by treating human women as decorations and by killing whatever it can't understand. The second, more complex mythology, having developed over thousands of years of ancient Egyptian history, does deal with the Female. In most stories about Isis, she is both sister and wife to Osiris. Their son, Seth, slays his father and scatters him in fourteen pieces up and down the Nile. Isis, a protective and sheltering goddess, weeps and wails and searches until she has found thirteen of the pieces: her rebuilt husband then lacks only a penis. In Egyptian mythology, thus, Female seeks Male. In Dylan's thirteen stanzas, Isis's husband seems to be seeking some missing piece of himself. The narrator leaves the Female behind, to go off on a harebrained quest with a male stranger, seeking some unnamed prize.

Images throughout the lyrics suggest patriarchal religions in general besides these two clusters in particular. The action begins as the man, after Isis marries and then leaves him, strikes out into a wilderness where he can tell wrong from right and dark from light. "I cut off my hair," he begins. Hairstyle indicates social status in almost every society. Usually, uncut or unkempt hair symbolizes a status outside the norm—children, shamans, visionaries, freaks—whereas short, carefully styled hair symbolizes full participation in structured adult society. First, then, this narrator attempts to conform with male-oriented, goal-directed, moralizing society.

In the next stanzas, he takes the same kind of action as did supposed patriarchal conquerors:

> I rode straight away
> For the wild unknown country where I could not go wrong
> I came to a high place of darkness and light
> The dividing line ran through the center of town
> I hitched up my pony to a post on the right

By choosing the right, the opposite of both left and wrong, he chooses what the dichotomizing Male world has defined as virtue, or heroism.

His adventures begin as he sits incongruously in a men-only wilderness, a cowboy or knight-errant stopped off at a laundromat. A stranger asks for a match—an opener familiar from Humphrey Bogart films—and starts bragging about an apparent get-rich-quick scheme. As they set out for the north, the hapless narrator gives away his blanket. This stranger begins to come across like a parasite hitchhiker who will next ask about spare change, food, dope, cigarettes, and a place to crash. The narrator becomes wary but is relieved to learn that they'll be back by the fourth, which date evokes both the Fourth of July and his wedding to Isis on the fifth of May—contradictory associations with Male and Female worlds, so that the narrator can announce his relief publicly while privately feeling happy for another reason. As they ride, then, his thoughts drift to his past and future life with Isis and to the material wealth he will bring her.

They reach the ice-embedded pyramid and begin to dig. The stranger reveals finally that they are seeking not treasure but a body. The body might be a valuable mummy—even though up north, so far from Mother. But the image suggests also the castrated body of Osiris, who, in this song, is... the digging narrator himself. The stranger and the narrator engage in a male-heroic contest of physical prowess, resembling the oedipal contest wherein the son slays the father and takes the kingdom—as Seth was trying to do by chopping up Osiris. This contest, though, the Osiris/narrator wins by default. The stranger, the male-heroic adventurer, the rival, the usurper, the other man in Isis's song—he dies of exhaustion.

"I was hoping that it wasn't contagious," says the narrator, rhyming "contagious" and "outrageous" with the wryness that was an early trademark of Dylan's (as in "Bob Dylan's 115th Dream," 1965), and he keeps on digging. He breaks into the vault finally, to find no body, "no jewels, no nothing," and to realize without malice that the stranger had seduced him along on a male-fantasy quest for what never existed. But, he further realizes, he has indeed found a body there—not a mummy's, not Osiris's, but the stranger's. He buries it there, at the far end of the quest, at the point farthest from Isis and all that the Female represents. The Osiris/narrator buries whatever led him off into male-heroic social conformity and power seeking, and he rides back empty-handed "to find Isis just to tell her I love her." But they do not live happily ever after, back where Isis sleeps by her stream. The narrator has eliminated the chauvinism that had made him want to hold onto Isis in the first stanza, to declare perhaps that "She Belongs to Me." He returns to her now—not castrated like Osiris or dead like the stranger but alive and ready for "the next time we wed." What more could she want? What more could he do? Yet, he returns not to kiss awake his fair damsel but to curse her.

Or does he? The published text here says, "I cursed her one time then I rode on ahead." But in performance, Dylan pronounces the second word as much like "kissed" as "cursed." Linguistic philosopher Roland Barthes claims that although there is an intermediate sound between, for example, the initial phonemes of *bière* and *pierre,* this sound "cannot in any way refer to an intermediate substance between *beer* and *stone*... the opposition is still in the *all-or-nothing* category."[23] Such a generalization is given the lie by Dylan's performance here: by creating a sound midway between short *i* and *ur*, he calls up an emotional state intermediate between kissing and cursing. This one pronunciation, as oral onomatopoeia, imitates the emotional tug-of-war within Isis's husband.

· Seldom, elsewhere, does Dylan's slurred pronunciation merge two words that would create unresolvable conflicts in sense if heard as one or the other. When each of two separate words can be understood, they often combine their meanings within the song's imagery toward an effect more complex than either alone. Another example here, besides kissed/cursed, is "I was thinking about Isis, how she thought I was so reckless/wretched/rugged." Greil Marcus suggests for "Sad-Eyed Lady" the alternative understandings "My warehouse eyes/hides my Arabian drums/drugs."[24]

The futile/feudal horn in "Shelter from the Storm" is yet another example. "Futile" enriches that song's mythological dimensions; "feudal" would add another image of pointless male-heroic behavior. A feudal horn suggests the trumpet blasts during jousting and tournaments, and in particular the horn with which Roland summons aid with his dying breath. In that same stanza of "Shelter," the second line sounds equally like "it's doom alone that counts" and "it's do 'em alone that counts." Again, both images of male-heroic behavior merge, for it's more macho to do it all alone, to ride off alone toward a romantic doom.

Two more examples of words merged in performance occur in the line of "Isis" that is published as "Blinded by sleep and in need of a bed." Before a songbook came out, I transcribed this line as "Lightly asleep…" and Greil Marcus hears it clearly as "…in need of a bath."[25] The printed line condenses already established patterns of imagery, but so would these possible alternate understandings. "Lightly," like "right" in the second stanza, puns: a lightly sleeping Isis combines the light and dark the narrator sought to separate. And "in need of a bath" suggests, as does much else, Isis's freedom from socially defined propriety. She can bathe without plumbing, soap, protein conditioner for those annoying split ends, or even effort: she can keep on sleeping there in her meadow until the creek again rises to meet her. This line and the next, in the eleventh stanza, use densely packed imagery to suggest what is still askew in the narrator's attitude toward Isis:

> [She was] Blinded by sleep and in need of a bed
> I came in from the east with the sun in my eyes

In spite of his quest and his epiphany, still, all the narrator shares with his wife is "I"—his entire name, the sound of which only just begins hers. For her, sleep allows darkness and dreams and a respite from action. But the narrator still cannot accept what is Female. He thinks sleep blinds her; furthermore, she ought to sleep only on socially acceptable furniture. Even more confusing, though, he finds himself just as blinded as she is—blinded not by darkness but by too much light, by the glare of sun as it sets in the west. The narrator did ride east as well as north, then, to explore ideas other than Western rational/heroic ones about the mystery of the Female.

But the narrator has returned from his quest. Isis awakes by herself, needing no prince's kiss, and asks questions as a human lover might—an ideal lover, concerned but not demanding. But then again... not even all that concerned. She does not bother to arrange her remarks sequentially, and she ignores his strained attempt to justify his actions as "natural." She feigns no interest in the details of how or why he has gone off on this quest for her sake. She will let him stay, though, while she goes right on sleeping and dreaming in the meadow by her Anna Livia Plurabella creek.

The last stanza makes the narrative cyclical, referring again to the day of their marriage. The "drizzling rain," a muffled and misty *driz-uh-lin ruh-AYN*, might have made a romantically ideal bride frown. But Isis smiles equally on sunshine and rain, on darkness and light, on sleep and waking, on sane and insane, on child and woman, on bed and meadow, on bath and creek, on any dichotomy by which what is Male in the psyche tries to figure her out. She is still a "mystical child," still "nobody's child," as a decade before. And what drives him to her is what drives him insane—a line whose poetic meter helps convey its meaning if ever there was one. Like the narrator who absurdly claimed that "She Belongs to Me," all the Osiris/narrator can do is to move helplessly, inevitably, into her hypnotized collection of fruitlessly analytic male-heroic minds.

In none of these four songs are the artistic effects exclusively or even primarily verbal. In "She Belongs to Me," words and different aspects of instrumentation combine to command the listener's awe. In "Sad-Eyed Lady," the narrator's uneasy verbal questions are answered not by other words but by soothing music. The metallic/nonmetallic poetic imagery and the metallic/nonmetallic musical sound allow a listener to realize that one need not set up dichotomized choices for future action: why not *both* leave gifts by her gate *and* wait? In "Shelter from the Storm," the comforting music contradicts the words, insofar as they tell of a narrator not just uneasy but downright miserable, but also reinforces the words, insofar as the lyrics' nonsequential time implies future hope. And throughout the potentially optimistic narrative of "Isis," the eerie Eastern music anticipates the conclusion, in which Female remains impenetrably, oxymoronicly Female.

The last great development in analytically describing the effect of music on the human mind was made by Pythagoras. Musicologists and philosophers from all angles agree that no technical vocabulary can substitute for hearing a piece of music and that no set of techniques can predict how an individual will respond to it.[26] In these four songs, Dylan uses the unanalyzable force of music to help convey what words fall short of—the nonlinear, nonrational nature of the Female, of darkness, mystery, awe, and passion.

> *For there's no use in trying to deal with the dying*
> *Though I cannot explain that in lines*
> —*"To Ramona," 1964*

III

Performances

*[Jann Wenner:] Are there any albums or tracks from the albums that you
think now were particularly good?*
*[Bob Dylan:] On any of my old albums? Uhh... As songs or as
performances?*[1]

"Don't criticize what you can't understand," Dylan told all our parents
for us in "The Times They Are A-Changin'" (1963). Yet, in some of
his most influential and artistically complex songs, narrators do just that.
They fight the Female, attack what can't be controlled, scorn the woman in
the lyrics. These songs—including "It Ain't Me, Babe" (1964), "It's All
Over Now, Baby Blue" and "Like a Rolling Stone" (1965), "Most Likely
You'll Go Your Way (And I'll Go Mine)" and "Just Like a Woman" (1966),
and less-known ones like "If You Gotta Go, Go Now [or else you gotta stay
all night]" (1965)—share their theme of rejection with a handful of Rolling
Stones songs but with few other songs by anyone before or since the mid-
sixties.

In religious imagery or otherwise, nearly all songs ever have urged a
woman to stand by her man and a man to offer her the world's biggest
necklace plus drums, trumpets, fifteen jugglers, five believers, and—if
necessary—"to die for you and more." An occasional blues or country-
western song rejects a woman who has been untrue or otherwise has failed
to fulfill male romantic expectations. There is almost no precedent for
Dylan's nonlove songs,[2] for songs that reject women *because* they are
accepting sex-role stereotypes.

The postwar baby boom probably produced no more tomboys than any generation before, but an unusually high proportion continued to believe in tomboyism and to articulate, as they became adolescents and then adults, just what is wrong with the female roles that the male romantic imagination emits. The women's movement was underway five years after the release of "Just Like a Woman." Yet that same year of *Blonde on Blonde,* 1966, I was drawn into my first antiwar protest in Madison by the call "Chicks inside! We need more chicks inside!" Without the slightest shudder at such a term, I helped block the building and got my head bashed by cops, right along with the guys.

My point is that in spite of vicious attitudes toward women in the printed lyrics of Dylan's nonlove songs, those songs were helping me subconsciously articulate what kind of a woman I did not want to be. Listening over and over, it never occurred to me to identify or even sympathize with the beribboned and curly-headed Baby being rejected by such a song's narrator. Even before the lyrics were published in 1973, I could probably have said that in "Just Like a Woman" or "Sad-Eyed Lady" or "All I Really Want to Do" (1964), for instance, the "I" is a man addressing a woman. But while listening to these songs, slipping into their respective moods of rejection or tenderness or bemusement, I never had to imagine myself as a male. Pronouns can remain neuter in performance, as they seldom can on paper.

A narrative situation, likewise, can remain both neuter and unified in aural understanding. On paper, "Just Like a Woman" appears a random narrative indeed. (See Appendix A.) A traditional ballad leaps, stanza by stanza, from scene to scene of intense drama. In "Just Like a Woman" the scenes are briefer—couplets, usually. Transitions are lacking; furthermore, less neatly than in "Shelter," the time sequence is deliberately scrambled. And instead of balladlike moments of dramatic action—for the ribbons and bows have already fallen, the introduction already has been made—each scene focuses on a moment of extreme emotional intensity. A listener, rather than visualizing external action or overhearing dialogue, shares in one after another violent internal state—the feeling of saying what one knows will hurt, for instance, or of meeting a former lover in public.

Imagery throughout the song incorporates sets of binary oppositions, many mediated by a third term—"Baby" and "woman" with "little girl" between, for example. Love does not encompass Female contradictions here; instead, nonlove wrenches apart such pairs, exposing those mediating terms like barbs. As in "Hard Rain," however, elements of performance can push such textual irresolution toward one pole or the other.

Dylan has released two very different performances of "Just Like a Woman": a 1966 performance with electric backup band at a Nashville studio, on *Blonde on Blonde,* and his 1974 solo performance with acoustic guitar, in concert at the Los Angeles Forum, released on *Before the Flood.* Although the same performer sings nearly the same words, and although each performance's narrator rejects Baby, the lover/mother/little girl/woman, the two narrators' personalities differ. In the 1966 version, the narrator sounds gentle and regretful as he sends Baby off to fend for herself. A listener, far from feeling rejected herself, can feel encouraged to reject Babylike attributes in her own life. In the 1974 version, the narrator rejects Baby venomously, maliciously, gleefully. And so does the responsive listener.

"But she breaks just like a little girl." Dylan's vocal inflections on this line, more specifically on the key word "girl," can exemplify this major difference in effect between his two performances of "Just Like a Woman." In 1966, Dylan pauses before each "girl," takes in enough breath to stretch the word across several musical beats—then instead cuts off his voice to let the musical space fill mostly with that version's familiar piano arpeggio. In 1974, Dylan makes a four- and then a three-syllable descent on "girl." In the last refrain he plays with the word even more, like a cat with a mouse: his voice swoops to a higher pitch so that the three downward steps are particularly distinct. As characterized by vocal inflections, the 1974 narrator gives over none of his control to the harshly strummed guitar: he manipulates the word "girl" and with it the narrative situation.

Comparing the 1966 "girl" to the 1966 "woman" can demonstrate further how Dylan's voice there interacts with the velvety instrumentation of *Blonde on Blonde* to express the narrator's regret and to comfort a responsive listener. Dylan's voice drips scorn on "just like a woman," sung three times per refrain, creating tension between harsh voice and soothing instrumentation. But for every "just like a little girl," his voice defects to the instruments' side to express pity and sympathy for a broken child.

The relationship differs between these two incrementally repeated lines, backed by harsh guitar in 1974. The extended falling pitches on each 1974 "girl" let burst the bitter venom that Dylan's voice, during each "just like a woman" phrase, has just barely held in check. Each 1974 "girl" twists like a knife into the listener's gut, giving the lie to the song's opening line, "Nobody feels any pain."

In the lyrics, this first-line "Nobody" gradually becomes a positive being—becomes the same "Nobody" who, in the second stanza, has to guess that Baby can't be blessed. The pain that "Nobody" feels (pretends not to feel, that is, at first) merges with the "ache" he inflicts on Baby, refrain after refrain, thus expressing the hurt not just of lovers' parting but also of himself being born from her womb, midsong, amid

> this pain in here
> I can't stay in here
> Ain't it clear that
> I just can't fit

Even the elsewhere-scornful 1974 narrator softens his tone slightly, then, at the last stanza's "I was hungry and it was your world," as he recalls his newborn dependency on Baby. But, he asks, "Please don't let on that you knew me" then. This last-stanza word "knew" ties back to the first stanza, linked as verb with "Everybody knows" and as homonym with the "new clothes" they all know about. Yet only "Nobody," the narrator, can see past Baby's clothes and curls, can go see another woman, and can thereby force Baby to come to see that she's like all the rest—just like "Everybody."

"Just Like a Woman," in whatever performance, would not yield to neat line-by-line analysis of its densely packed poetic imagery. A glance at verbs and adverbs shows the extent to which Dylan, writing for oral performance, has disallowed the words any linear progression in time. The narrative situation jerks from "Tonight" to "lately" to "finally" to "the first" to "When we meet again" and then back to when it was her world. Verb tenses wander between present and present perfect in the first stanza, present and future in the second, past and present in the third (bridge) stanza, and in the last stanza—when "it's time"—present and future and past. Any attempt to figure out exactly who said and did what, in what order, is inappropriate—for this is a song, not a poem.

Within about four minutes, these 252 words writhe with unresolved oppositions that arouse ideas of seeing and knowing, appearance and reality, selfhood and nonentity—not to mention cursing, blessing, death, birth, hunger, thirst, rain, fog, clearness, pain, ache, hurt, woman, Baby, girl, queens, friends, everybody, and nobody. Furthermore, seeing is not believing. All these are simple words, everyday language. Dylan has a particular skill at reviving the dead metaphors in the clichés of ordinary speech—with his singing voice, to some extent, but more notably in imagery even as it appears on the page. Time after time, Dylan makes a worn-out metaphor suddenly literal or otherwise foregrounded. This characteristic has remained constant throughout his career—from "Good car to drive, after a war," through "You can have your cake and eat it too," to "Later on as the crowd thinned out/I's just about to do the same" and "Like a cork screwed up my heart."[3]

The title "Just Like a Woman," incrementally repeated throughout the song, begins as cliché but acquires tangles of meaning in performance, helping to characterize the gentle 1966 narrator and the scornful 1974 one. "Dying... of thirst," another foregrounded commonplace, interacts with "hungry" and with undrinkable "rain" and "fog," as well as with the unnamed act of birth. And in the final stanza, the mustily nostalgic "I knew him when" is paraphrased to introduce the infant's viewpoint, which everybody has experienced but nobody quite remembers.

Dylan's 1966 voice puts quotation marks around the "when" of "you knew me when" and around its rhyme word, "friends." There his vocal inflection makes "when" more clearly part of a converted cliché and "friends" more clearly a term for what they precisely are not. But society has no better label than "friends" for former lovers, nor for the kind of casual sexual relationship implied in the second stanza's "Queen Mary, she's my friend"—"Queen Mary" suggesting, in no particular order, the mother of Christ, the luxury ship, the killer of "Mary Hamilton" in Child ballad no. 173, and the "Queen Jane" who comes to "see me" on this same album.

"I believe I'll go see her again" uses a modern slang sense of the multidimensional word "see": "Are you still seeing Mary?" would refer most likely to a continuing sexual relationship without long-term commitment. In the last sung stanza, similarly, Baby's "knowing" the narrator during their now-elapsed relationship involves sexuality, with implications enriched for listeners who realize that the King James Bible uses "know" for "have sexual intercourse."

Thus, referring to Queen Mary, the sexual overtones of "see" help the word "friend" mean just friends, as distinguished from committed lovers. In the last stanza, referring to Baby, the sexual overtones of "knew" combine with the word "friends" to intensify the contrast between the lovers they once were and the so-called friends they will be labelled in social situations. The word "lover," to which "friend" is opposed from these two angles, never occurs in the song. And "love" itself—a word bogged down in the very ribbons and bows that the narrator denies to Baby—appears only in the euphemism that is no euphemism, "makes love."

As the two instances of "friends" interact with the absent "lover," so too the related ideas of seeing, knowing, and believing cluster into two not-quite-oppositional terms and a mediator. Another such threesome involves "Baby" and "woman," mediated by "little girl"; another—with precedents aplenty in literatures and mythologies—links birth, death, and sexual intercourse. And mediating between the "hurt" that her curse inflicts on him and the "ache" he keeps inflicting on her is the "pain" that he at first denies and then shares from within her womb.

"Baby can't be blessed," and her longtime curse hurts him. In between blessing and cursing occurs the most unresolvable opposition with mediator in the song: "With her fog, her amphetamine and her pearls." Syntax offers no help. Does the phrase refer to what she ought to acquire or to what she ought to get rid of? Do they represent what she will discard, after she sees that she's like all the rest, or what she will find within herself underneath those ribbons and bows?

Furthermore, who are "all the rest"? The phrase as cliché seems negative; especially in conjunction with "just like a woman," it would toss her into a heap of nonessential, disregarded females. The narrator wants her to see that she's like all the rest, though. And because he, in the first stanza, sees what's left beneath her bows, this second stanza implies that she should see the same—see that she's just like everybody, that is, and just like nobody. Fog, amphetamine, and pearls thus suggest artificial social trappings and, equally, what humans have in common underneath such trappings. What people share could be either a common human bond or else emptiness. Because "Nobody feels any pain," and because the woman aches in every refrain, the narrator holds over her the threat that she too is "Nobody" under it all. But in the bridge stanza, he himself feels pain just like "Nobody," and in labor pains her female power of procreation appears.

Her world-encompassing strength, which the narrator admits in the last verse line of the last sung stanza, stands in contrast to her helplessness in the last verse line of the first stanza, where the force of gravity alone can destroy her superficial glory. Thus the last verse line of the second stanza—the fog/amphetamine/pearls image—acts as a transition from her weakest social role, as curly-headed bow wearer, to her strongest natural role, as mother.

The three attributes themselves form an unresolved opposition plus a mediating term. "Fog" and "amphetamine" each contain an emphatic *f* yet are otherwise in contrast. A short word for a natural phenomenon is linked with a polysyllabic, manmade substance. Fog comes upon a person from without, whereas amphetamine sharpens internal sight—at least as an illusory clarity that will dissipate as the drug wears away. Mental fog is not dissipated as easily. So, external fog blocks external seeing, then leaves of its own accord; internal fog must be eliminated by individual effort; internal amphetamine clarifies internal vision, then leaves of its own accord. The terms do not balance: they keep tugging back and forth such dichotomies as seeing vs. not seeing, individual vs. environment, nature vs. culture.

And what of pearls? Like no other gem, pearls grow into their culturally defined worth from a grain of sand, within an animal, in the sea. A pearl is neither animal nor mineral, neither land nor water. It differs from other jewels too in being cloudy (suggesting fog, itself a mediator between rain and not-rain and between seeing and not-seeing) and in being excretory in nature but valuable within society. Because pearls just don't fit into the category of precious stones, they appropriately make up the biblical gates that separate heaven from earth... as well as the third term of this blessed/ unblessed Baby/woman's three transitional attributes.

The other two terms interact with imagery elsewhere in the song. "Fog" has poetic links with seeing and rain and thirst. "Amphetamine" has reversed associations: its internalized seeing temporarily suggests knowing, and its opposite, numbing downer drugs, are what Baby needs for continuing aches. But pearls stand isolated in the imagery, excluded even from the category of female decorations by the closed-off chumminess of ribbons and bows and their mediator "curls," which neatly converts a ribbon to a bow and also provides a tousled head for their nestling. "Curls" goes on to form a rhyme set with "girl," for whom curls are appropriate, and with "pearls," a woman's decoration, and with "world," a woman's natural strength. This structure and positioning more precisely show why the described shift in Dylan's vocal inflection on the word "girl" can so shift the meaning of the song: as pearl mediates between natural and cultural values, between crystal and oyster, between excrement and jewel, so also "little girl" mediates between infant and adult, Baby and mother, birth and the maturation that leads to death.

The word "girl" also contains one of the song's two principal sound patterns, the growled *uh/ur* that, throughout the song, characterizes the female—from her "curls" at the start through "I was hungry and it was your world." The other major vowel/consonant pattern, likewise far more apparent to ear than to eye, is the long-*a* sound that blends toward the narrator's "I" (as in Cockney dialect). Using this male long-*ay* as weapon, each refrain pounds at the woman with takes/makes/aches/[wakes] /[fake]/breaks. Dylan's voice forces long-*ay* rhymes out of words as diverse in print as "pain" and "blessed," and the narrator bursts from Baby's womb proclaiming his male selfhood with a howled "*Ai-yai* just don't fit" that is particularly forceful in the 1974 version.

The words alone provide no linear sequence for understanding the song. And the melody is strophic, repeating in three of the stanzas plus the closing harmonica stanza. But a linear progression does occur each time the song is heard: the female *uh/ur* sounds come to quite engulf the increasingly desperate male long-*ay* sounds. "I was hungry and it was your world," for me, climaxes the song. In the last sung refrain, the long-*ay* verbs brandished at "you" sound automatic, rather flimsy.

But in neither version is that final refrain much quieter, faster in tempo, or in another objectively measurable way less emphatic than are the two earlier refrains. Thus, mine may well not be the only possible interpretation of the sounds. But there are valid critical advantages to analyzing thoroughly one's own responses rather than pretending—as (mostly male) scholars so often have—that absolute objectivity is a valid goal or even a possible one in literary criticism.[4]

Literary criticism? No, this is performance criticism, and still lacks a schema for descriptive analysis of aural meaning. So far I have merely hinted at the relationships among aspects of performance: in "She Belongs to Me," for example, the repeated long-*e* sound creates a vocal effect like the shriek of an electric guitar, and the harmonica resembles a human voice. Let me now propose a spectrum for analysis with terms that will vary somewhat for every performance of any song.

First, consider what music does that words cannot, what words do that music cannot, and where other elements of performance would fall on a spectrum stretched from purely musical effects to purely verbal ones. Music keeps time: that is, a regular beat can somehow free a listener from awareness of clock time's passing. But unlike words, a given passage of music cannot be labeled with a predictable discursive meaning. For "Just Like a Woman," such a spectrum would stretch from the discursive sense of the lyrics, at the far "words" end, to the instruments that mark rhythm—one guitar in 1974, and the band with regular drums, piano, and guitars in 1966:

> (nonsequential) sense of lyrics
> sound of lyrics, as on the page (rhyme, assonance, meter)
> vocal effects (i.e., sound of lyrics, as performed)
> (voicelike) harmonica
> rhythm instrument(s)

All five elements in this spectrum interact to create a listener's understanding of the song. In a poem read silently, the sense of the words is primary, reinforced secondarily by imagined sounds of meter and rhyme and assonance/consonance. In a performance, sound is primary. The sense of the words is at least partly controlled by their sound, by their meter and vowel/consonant patterns. Furthermore, in both performances of this song, such word sounds are themselves controlled by Dylan's voice, for he forces assonating words to rhyme and otherwise creates connections not there in print. Next on the spectrum, Dylan's harmonica mediates between what a voice can do and what an instrument can do—differently in each of the two performances, as I will show. And by keeping time, the rhythm instruments allow the nonsequential lyrics to make aural sense. As in a game of scissors/paper/rock, no performance element finally wins: each both overcomes and is subject to another.

For each performance of "Just Like a Woman," the whole spectrum tips toward the right, weighted toward the "music" end. In other of his songs—"Like a Rolling Stone," for example, discussed in my next chapter—Dylan sets up tension between the poetic meter in the words and a musical beat that differs. In "Just Like a Woman," though, the would-be dactylic meter capitulates quite totally to the 4/4 musical rhythm, to its right on the spectrum.

As to rhyme, in "Just Like a Woman" an end-rhyme scheme does appear on the page. Using A' to indicate a slant rhyme with A (e.g., pain/again), it goes:

$$AABBBCDDDC \,/\, A'A'A'A'A'CDDDC \,/\, C'C'EC'C'EEE \,/$$
$$FFA'A'A'CDDDC$$

On paper, also, other assonance and consonance appear. The A-line long-*ay* rhymes, pain/rain, reverberate with the strong long-*ay* verbs midline in every refrain, for example; and the "it" of "Ain't it clear that" shifts to become a clear end rhyme in the last sung stanza.

But no text could show what Dylan's voice does with such phonetic resemblances in performance. Describing the bridge (third) stanza of the 1966 version, in the first book-length analysis of Dylan's art, Michael Gray says,

> Dylan somehow moulds and holds out to us a hand-made object, a sort of clever toy with a lot of tactile appeal.... [Notice] the indescribably plaintive resonance the voice yields up on those simple little words like "rainin'", "first", "came" and even "aint";... [and how] "but what's worse" becomes three equal fur-mouthed jerks and that "what's" rhymes gleefully with "hurts". You really have to hear Dylan doing it,

he concludes, here as elsewhere straining against his unfortunate resolve to treat Dylan's work as poetry.[5]

Gray hears, as I do, how thoroughly assonance or slant rhyme on the page can become voice-forced rhyme in performance. In that bridge stanza, during the narrator's final painfully fetal moments, the female *uh/ur* sounds squeeze so tight that for two lines every single word rhymes—"your [longtime] curse hurts/But what's worse"—save only "longtime," which thereby stands out and seems to take longer to sing, as oral onomatopoeia.

In both the 1966 and 1974 versions, a listener is carried through "Just Like a Woman" not by words primarily or by music primarily but by the middle term in my proposed spectrum: vocal effects. Dylan is a musicians' songwriter, creating songs that others can perform in their own styles. But in addition, his own remarkable trait as a performer—whether of his own songs or of someone else's—is his voice "of an outraged bear," "like a dog with his leg caught in barbed wire."[6] Primarily with that voice he creates the two narrators of such different characters, from the unresolved and bursting oppositions that stud the text.

The song opens with each narrator, in 1966 and in 1974, declaring his control over the sounds and sense of language. The pure rhyme pain/rain first declares his soldierlike bravado, then twists the commonplace "in the rain" to "inside the rain." The manipulative narrator tricks nature's rain into itself becoming a shelter for him, where he stands well protected by the long-*i* sounds of "Tonight" before and his newly created "inside" after "I."

The first portrayal of Baby likewise uses a pure rhyme, the *ohz* of knows/ clothes/bows. This long-*o* sound, echoing "Nobody," appears only twice elsewhere in the song: as a transitional "so" in the bridge stanza and in "Please don't" in the last. The *z* of this *ohz* rhyme reappears in that same "Please," in "curls" and "pearls," and in the auxiliary verbs "does" and "was." Neither of these latter words is inessential to the song's meaning. "Does," as part of the "yes she does" in the first two 1966 refrains, makes that narrator seem to crave more self-assurance than does the 1974 narrator, when the "yes she does" is replaced by forceful guitar strokes. The word "was," carrying on the *z* sound, combines with the *uh* that is part of the woman's "just"—twice in anticipation ("It was" and "I was" in the bridge stanza) and then twice in fulfillment, during "I was hungry and it was your world."

In both versions, Dylan expresses the narrator's control over the opening situation by rendering the already strong rhyme knows/clothes/bows with vowels that move toward two-syllable end rhyme, as *oh-wohz*. The slightly different inflections help characterize the two narrators. In the gentler 1966 version, the vowel of "knows" is moving slightly toward diphthongization, with only a hint of a *w* sound. "Clothes" eases a bit further toward *ow*, along a rising vocal pitch, and "bows" is an almost fully reduplicated *boh-wohz*.

The more self-confident 1974 narrator instead starts right in manipulating those three rhymes. The first two vowels are clearly and similarly reduplicated. Yet "bows," in contrast, is one syllable, with no *w* in its *oh* sound. "Bows" is held on a loud, level note and stretched out like a diving board over the following line's oral onomatopoeia, "Have fallen... from her curls."

Here, in 1974, Dylan sings "fallen" ahead of its musical beat and fills the resulting gap with guitar strums that are unusually soft, so that Baby and all those ribbons and bows perch, teeter, and then fall into a hole in the performance. Vocal phrasing imitates "fallen"; a vocal flourish, in addition, makes the two-syllable "curls" sound curly, as Dylan's voice loops up and around before descending to the pitch of the second syllable. This rendering can be compared to its rhyme word "pearls," which descends two steps without the loop. And the last-stanza "world," ending the only line that causes the 1974 narrator to hesitate from gleeful rejection of all aspects of Baby, makes three, instead of two, descending steps. Dylan's voice wavers on each pitch, sounding particularly tentative on the middle one. But this narrator is still in control. He knows that he is hesitating, in 1974, and he knows why.

In the 1966 version, a guitar arpeggio after "curls" somewhat imitates curliness. But it simply echoes the familiar piano arpeggios that back up most sung lines and instrumental transitions throughout. The 1966 narrator thus culminates his tentative moves toward diphthongization of *ohz* by giving up vocal control in the face of insistently familiar, comforting instrumentation.

He comes back on strong, as strong as the 1974 narrator, by relishing the pure midline rhymes of the battering-ram refrain—takes/makes/aches/breaks. In the first 1966 refrain, Dylan's vocal phrasing creates a harsher and a milder effect in the four lines. An intake of breath follows "takes" and also "aches" so that each term has an extra moment of impact on a listener. But the "makes love" line flows evenly, without breath breaks. And the last line is phrased "But she breaks just... like a little... girl": the "just" cushions the male "breaks" and with its female *uh* vowel anticipates the first occurrence of the word that is the 1966 narrator's undoing, the sympathy-dripping and isolated "girl."

In 1974, instead, Dylan phrases each of the first three refrain lines evenly; then, after "breaks," he breaks the line sharply. As in the "fallen" line, his onomatopoetic phrasing helps express the narrator's strength and control over language—in this case, his gleefully sadistic breaking of a little *guh-hu-hu-hurl*.

In the second stanza, both end-rhyme sets—friend/again and guess/blessed/rest—rhyme with the male long *ay*, and in both performances Dylan increases the rhyme by tending to reduplicate all vowels concerned. He toys the most with the triplet in 1974. One would expect a two-syllable "guess" to become *gay-yess*; instead, Dylan drops in pitch from one to the next syllable, swallowing the transition to leave a gap instead of a *y* sound. "Blessed" is a more usual reduplication, *blay-yest*, and "rest" resembles the first-stanza "bows" by remaining one syllable. But instead of being stretched outward on a level note, as was "bows," "rest" slides upward at the end—melts upward into the fog that follows.

These voice-forced, not-so-pure rhymes in the second stanza give an effect of each narrator's losing control of his long *ay*. And in the lyrics, sure enough, the narrator is turning to outside help: with studied cruelty he goes to see Queen Mary, and with "can't be blessed" he invokes divine support for his own vision. To the relief of the flagging 1966 narrator, the refrain comes round again with his solidly long-*ay* words. This time, Dylan leaves a pause that increases the impact after "takes" and "aches" and even "breaks" in the 1966 version. But "girl" remains isolated and tenderly sung, as before. The 1974 narrator is still unconcerned with the woman's aches, for a carefree guitar run follows that line, and still he hates that little girl.

The bridge stanza, recreating a painful memory, is hard on the respective states of mind of both the hesitant 1966 narrator and the brash 1974 one, for there male and female sounds get crammed together. The bridge's midline rhymes echo the refrains and the opening couplet, with rain/came/pain/can't/stay/ain't. The female set of sounds, heretofore represented principally by curls, pearls, and two girls, now explodes with first/thirst/your/curse/hurts/but/what's/worse. Its *r* sound reverberates with "in here," repeated at closer intervals which increase the urgency. "Here" also rhymes with the final, tortured howl of "clear" and stands in opposition to the "there" where he was dying of thirst. The long *i* of the thrice-named "I" links the narrator to the foreboding terms "dying" and "longtime." The two "was" verbs anticipate "I was hungry and it was your world." The "So," just before "I came in here," is the last gasp of the *ohz* with which the narrator had described her in scorn, when he was fully in control. Of forty words in this bridge stanza, only eleven fail to fit snugly into an already established vowel/consonant pattern.

The imagery and the respective instrumentations join with the vowel/consonant sounds in the bridge stanza to force each narrator's acceptance of her world "in here," then his birth trauma and newborn howl of "I." The bridge's opening "rain" recalls the "tonight" when the narrator controlled both sound and sense of the word. But as he here remembers "the first," rain is a natural phenomenon from which he, just like all the rest, must seek shelter. Then the "I"—which, in the first stanza, smugly tells what "I see" that "Everybody" doesn't—gets linked tightly to dying; he cannot even take advantage of natural rain to prevent his "dying there of thirst." So the narrator too is trapped by social conventions, not the least of which is the absurd, male-world pretense that nobody feels any pain.

With false bravado, still, he pretends he made the choice to enter her womb, declaring so with the long *ay* of "came." But all around him the *ur* sounds are welling up louder and louder, more and more overwhelming—until at last he admits that his opening claim was wrong, admits that pain hurts him just as aches must hurt her. After "pain" come "can't stay" and "Ain't," the shorter intervals between long-*ay* sounds adding to the sense of urgency, as in the three "in here"s. Then he bursts free from all those *ur*s into a clear statement expressed with the help of the woman's word "just": "I... just can't fit" in 1966, "*Ai-yai...* just don't fit" in 1974. The shift in inflection and in one word helps differentiate the narrators. The 1974 narrator denies that he ever wanted or tried to fit, all that much; four lines later he includes his momentary admission of weakness in a command: "Please don't let on."

The instrumentation in each version joins the gathering thundercloud of vowel/consonant sounds to thrust the narrator out of his womb-shelter. Up to this point the 1966 piano has predominated, its mellow arpeggios falling to the background only after *ur* end rhymes: because of a guitar arpeggio echoing the piano, after "curls"; because of a guitar figure after "pearls" that instead descends and thereby seems foreboding; because of a likewise negative downward progression of organ chords, after the "girl" that ends each refrain. In the 1966 bridge, apparently emboldened by the swelling *ur* sounds, the organ and guitar then replace the piano at center stage. They back up vocal lines but at first aren't sure what to do in the spotlight: the mingled guitar and organ after the first "in here" imitate the narrator's confused state of mind. Then the drum joins them and gives them direction. It becomes louder and louder after the two "in here"s, and drives the narrator out in a bursting drumroll that ends abruptly just before his "I... just can't fit."

One acoustic guitar, in 1974, performs this entire same task of ejection. For the first two stanzas the guitar has strummed a solid backup to lines of lyrics, with potential instrumental breaks mostly buried beneath Dylan's vocalization of bi- to quintasyllabic rhyme words. In the bridge stanza, however, at the point where the 1966 instrumentation writhes in momentary confusion, Dylan's guitar creates a three-beat musical space after "in here" such that "here" is filled with foreboding strums. Musical spaces after the other two "in here"s become shorter.

Meanwhile, threat is expressed also in the pounding coordination of the 1974 guitar's musical beat with the voice's volume and phrasing. Dylan forcefully bisects each line of lyrics except the anticipatory, rising "But what's worse." His voice comes down loud and hard, exactly synchronous with the guitar strum, on "rain," "first," "dy-," "thirst," "here," and— progressively louder now—on "pain," "stay," "ain't," and *cle-heyear!"* He also imitates orally the events in the lyrics. The narrator's hesitation before he first comes "in here" is indicated by a break after "I"; the length of her curse is suggested by stretching "long... time... curse-hurts." "Hurts" gets tucked into the back end of "curse"'s beat. Thus the 1974 narrator keeps his upper lip stiff during "hurts," then lets loose with a no-holds-barred, feel-it-and-get-it-over-with "pain."

The first couplet in the last sung stanza links back to four of those eleven words in the bridge stanza that did not fit into earlier vowel/consonant patterns. The last-stanza fit/it's/quit echoes the two instances of "it" in the bridge, one referring to rain and the other to clearness, and also to the phrase "Is this," which acts as the narrator's final verbal barrier before he admits pain. With "I believe it's time for us to quit"—the 1974 "quit" becoming *quee-it*, echoing the long-*e* sounds that surround it—each narrator siezes the "time" that was part of Baby's longtime curse, and combines time with the rainy/clear "it" to state what "I" do not merely "see," as in the first stanza, but now "believe."

Yet another cliché flops belly up. A whole song has interposed to show that seeing may well not be believing. In the second stanza, "I believe" combines with a nonvisual use of "see" as the narrator cruelly declares his intentions regarding Queen Mary. This last stanza "I believe" expresses his conviction rooted not just in seeing past appearances but also in feeling pain. But it is used in the same ironically casual sense as in the second stanza, "I believe" meaning "I suppose" or—like "Nobody"—"I guess."

The long *e* of "believe" otherwise appears in the opening "feels," in the shifting senses of "see," and in Baby's other name, "she." In the last stanza, by incorporating his newly gained knowledge of feeling, seeing, believing, and birth, the narrator can predict the future and ask that she then keep up external appearances, with the long *es* of "we meet," "Please," and "me." The 1974 narrator sarcastically stretches "Please"; he goes on to clip "let on" to *leddon*, to sneer the "you" (in both versions a transition from the bridge-stanza "your" to the final refrain's decisive pronoun shift) as a disrespectful *yuh*, and to make two syllables of "when." The 1966 narrator actually pleads.

Each narrator uses the same again/friend rhyme with which, in the second stanza, he had intentionally hurt Baby. In the last stanza, instead, he speaks of an event that will be thrust upon them in the future, one that both would prefer to avoid because they will be forced to assume fake social roles, as evoked in empty phrases like "when we meet again" and "you knew me when"—phrases that, despite their well-worn melodramatic overtones, mark the passage of time within human society. And if time did not pass, if babies did not become girls and girls become women (who give birth) and lovers become "friends" and "she" become "you," then the narrator could have remained where he once was, torn from Baby's womb but still hungry and still inside her world.

A whole stanza remains after the lyrics cease. In each version the harmonica goes on to say, in different styles appropriate to each, what the words stop short of saying. Deriving his harmonica style from those of blues musicians and Woody Guthrie, Dylan slurs notes by sliding off and onto pitches and by blowing into several holes at once. Richard Middleton says that as distinguished from most white popular music—wherein the singer is clearly human and the background clearly instrumental—in the blues characteristically "the instrument [is] not separate from the player... not a machine with respected rules and demands, but an added part of the body, which amplifies human expression and is spoken through, not played."[7] Dylan brings to this tradition an awareness of his particular audience, so well educated that it needs almost to be taught that instruments also have voices, that music can communicate feelings even better than words can. His harmonica, more noticeably than in the blues, can make a choice either to break into word-length clusters that sound like English-language inflections or else to go its own instrumental way.

The harmonica stanza that closes the 1966 "Just Like a Woman" tends toward the former effect, and Dylan's 1974 playing toward the latter. The entire 1966 version opens with a drumroll. The drum then begins to mark two measures behind each vocal line, while Dylan plays harmonica with the precise phrasing, melody, and inflections that his voice will produce for "Nobody feels any pain/Tonight as I stand inside the rain." After all of the 1966 lyrics the closing harmonica again sings like a voice, over the still velvety instrumentation. This harmonica, calmly articulating as much as it can nonverbally, reassures the listener after the rather cruel shift from "she takes" to "you fake" and the panted, publicly orgasmic "You make... love..." aimed at her in the last sung refrain. Moreover, it gives to the 1966 narrator's babyhood the timelessness denied in the discursive sense of the lyrics: the not-quite-verbal harmonica suggests a baby just learning to talk, when only its mother can understand its babbling. The instrumental background, during what would be the refrain if sung, expands to envelope and quiet the harmonica. Band and harmonica together fade, at last, into the simple arpeggio that has carried the song.

Dylan's 1966 harmonica sounds gentle, almost didactic, especially as compared to the harmonica gymnastics he performs for the 1974 concert audience, which is more accustomed to the mingling of black and white musical traditions in rock music. His 1966 version, of course, does not lose its comforting effect for a more musically sophisticated listener in a later decade. The carefulness with which the 1966 harmonica eases the traumas of breaking relationships, umbilical cords, and social roles echoes the gentleness and regret elsewhere on the spectrum of performance—most importantly, in the interaction of Dylan's voice with the soothing instrumentation.

Dylan's 1974 harmonica likewise fits that performance's unified effect, that of a devil-may-care narrator who breaks free of Baby with much less backward glancing. The 1974 harmonica creates its own cheery barrelhouse world, quite oblivious to any limitations on the human voice. It ignores any opportunity for wordlike phrasing or melody; it jumps an octave midline; it dances in and out of the beat, teasing the guitar. The 1974 harmonica carries right through to the end of the song, ceasing only when stomped out in the last few fast strums of guitar. The effect is of the harmonica declaring its independence and then of even trying to tell the guitar what to do—just like a little girl who grows up, who needs no more help or comfort from the musical beat. And the 1974 narrator's viciousness becomes, as it has been becoming throughout the song, each individual listener's triumph over what Baby may mean to her.

The audience reaction during this live-album cut of "Just Like a Woman" shows a conscious appreciation that music, as well as words, conveys a song's meaning. The audience cheers in recognition of the opening "Nobody" after Dylan has been toying with expectations by playing riffs that might open "Mr. Tambourine Man" (1964). Yells come after the first "just like a woman," in fulfilled recognition, and after each "just like a little girl," as a sadomasochistic wallowing in the varying venomous depths of Dylan's voice. Then just as wildly, the 1974 audience cheers not at words but at a place during the harmonica stanza where Dylan exhales one long piercing note across what would be two or three sung lines.

If our coming to understand the power of nonverbal communication means growing up, such an audience reaction declares, we have grown up. We don't need Baby and her social roles anymore. Never did, so there. Or... well, anyway, we can go home in 1974 and put *Blonde on Blonde* on the turntable and be reassured yet again, by a different performance of the same song, that we were right to throw it all away.

"The blues had a baby and they called it rock and roll," sings master bluesman Muddy Waters. The rock-and-roll baby kept on growing during the eight years between these two performances of "Just Like a Woman." Dylan, like Elvis Presley, was a white boy who could sing the blues—not just sing them, though, but transform them into new ways of combining music and words and voicelike instrumentation and instrumental vocalization for a mass audience coming of age in a world of hypocrisy and plastic and twenty years of schooling and the Vietnam War... and just starting to find new ways to deal with that most unresolvable of binary oppositions, male vs. female.

> *For he not busy being born*
> *Is busy dying*
> —*"It's Alright Ma," 1965*

I V

Causes

My recording sessions have tended to be last-minute affairs. I don't really use all the technical studio stuff. My songs are done live in the studio; they always have been and they always will be done that way.[1]

Literary critics have long mapped the pitfalls of a search for "author's intention." At best, it leads one toward social history rather than literary appreciation; at worst, it deadends at a dreary document like Poe's explanation of how he wrote "The Raven." Now-elderly New Criticism began as a reaction to such biographical/circumstantial interpretation. New Critics ask what a text means to a reader, not what the ever-elusive author intended to put into the text.

My approach to Dylan's work has so far been New Critical: I have analyzed what occurs in between a revolving plastic disk and the eardrum-connected cells of my own brain. Only tangentially have I mentioned how those sounds got onto the disk or what they might mean to somebody else. Such limits are needed for precision in close analysis.

But close analysis, in the end, cannot be separated from subjective aesthetic judgment. In processing those sounds, my brain cells of necessity apply what Michael Owen Jones terms the "ohhh-ahhh/ugh-yuck complex."[2] I analyze not all that I hear, that is, but rather what I like and don't like hearing. Furthermore, although "performer's intention" is even more elusive—fleeting and inarticulable—than is "author's intention," still, performers do sound better and worse on different occasions on account of discernible causes, one of the most immediate of which is audience response.

I have suggested the extent to which folklorists and others are now examining the kinetics of performance and of audience reaction, and the aesthetic standards upheld by performer and audience.[3] I have bemoaned the scarcity of videotapes of Dylan performances—albeit halfheartedly, I admit, since I've plenty to say about sound alone. Still, among the mass of recorded data available for Dylan—more than for anyone else, perhaps, except for the Grateful Dead, some of whose fans would tape the whole of every concert—is plenty of material that can contribute toward these more recent issues in performance analysis. Some idea of audience response at a Dylan concert can be gleaned from bootleg tapes and released records, as well as from comments by people who were there. Such comments have been fairly extensive, especially for those Dylan concerts that have come to be regarded as historic moments for the folk group self-defined as sixties counterculture.

"Like a Rolling Stone" has been called the anthem of my generation too often to credit. Dylan considers it his best song.[4] Many performances survive on tape; I will discuss four that take place under historically significant circumstances. The 1965 studio version, released on *Highway 61 Revisited*, demonstrates Dylan's precedent-setting recording style, live in the studio: on this cut, Al Kooper is playing organ for the first time in his career. The Newport '65 version comes from the much-discussed concert on The Day Dylan Went Electric, 25 July 1965. On the Manchester '66 concert tape, Dylan performs for an audience of hecklers who sound openly hostile to his "new" electric style. And in the 1974 concert recorded in Los Angeles and released on *Before the Flood*, he and those same musicians—called the Hawks in 1966, the Band in 1974—play before an openly ecstatic audience.

Interaction with the audience may be one of the many "why"s behind a live performance's particular effect. The Newport '65 musicians sound flustered, and audience reaction could be why—but Al Kooper has a simpler explanation, as I will show, and other eyewitness accounts vary wildly. The Manchester '66 performers seem to insult their audience. And the L. A. '74 group sounds unopposably triumphant, interacting with audience expectations that this performance of this song will mark some kind of high point in the decade.

Without extensive interviewing, far beyond my own authorial intentions, I cannot finally prove what was going on in even the 1974 audience. I can assume only that audience reaction at the L. A. Forum on 13 February 1974 resembled that of 11 February 1974 in the Oakland Coliseum, where I was.

But I can describe and substantiate a different aspect of audience response. When I replay the *Highway 61* version now, I find myself surprised at its mildness. I have been hearing this performance of this song in my head for fifteen years now, hearing it somehow with more sneerings and howlings in Dylan's voice, more intensified rhymes and backup instrumentation, more dramatic pauses and vocal tricks. In fact, the performance inside my head sounds remarkably like the one on *Before the Flood*: the excitement expressed during the 1974 concert seems somehow latent, set like a spring in the studio version. A listener not only responds to a recording while hearing it, then. She may also interact with a particular performance over a period of time, not changing it out loud as a folk performer would but remembering the song such that it sounds the way she wants it to sound, to express what she wants it to express.[5]

The 1974 "Like a Rolling Stone" is performed one day after the 1974 "Just Like a Woman," whose mood is venomously triumphant. The former is just plain triumphant, as is the "Like a Rolling Stone" that plays inside my head. It is not entirely coincidental that my personal experiences, during the eight years between the two released versions, had included learning how to live out in the streets with nothing to lose nor that sociohistorical events included Watergate and the end of the Vietnam War.

Any member of the 1974 concert audience, asked whether she felt triumphant about leftist politics, would probably have mumbled something about multinational corporations and continuing oppression of prisoners, women, old people. But still, in 1974, the need to celebrate was there. And if you had asked Bob Dylan why he then went on his first tour since before his 1966 motorcycle accident, he would almost certainly have mentioned money to produce his film. But still... he and the Band were participating in a mass community celebration. "Even the president of the United States sometimes must have to stand naked"—the audience went wild at this line in every 1974 concert (from "It's Alright, Ma," 1965). Victory, waiting in the wings, seized center stage during Dylan's return to public performances—and for the finale of every concert he chose "Like a Rolling Stone."[6]

Since 1965 also, the mass audience had come to better understand the musical question that the song's Miss Lonely still does not—the unfinished-sounding chord change that follows each line of the refrain. Such a chord change (tonic-subdominant-dominant) occurs in all four performances, but surrounded by different instrumentation. The riff is speeded up to be gotten over with in Newport '65, it is slowed to scornful simplicity in Manchester '66, and it is enlivened with drumrolls and dramatic organ runs, getting louder and louder as the 1974 performance progresses. In the 1965 studio version, the musicians vary the C-F-G chord change just enough, refrain by refrain, that "How does it feel?" gets reasked by what is both the same riff and a different riff. It seems an ideal teaching technique. But Dylan, totally lacking didactic intentions, was himself just learning to coordinate black and white musical traditions, as were other rock musicians at the time.

A dramatic example is that of Al Kooper, who had played guitar at other Columbia studio sessions and who, by his account, sneaked into the session at which this "Like a Rolling Stone" was recorded:

> The band.... weren't too far into this long song Dylan had written before it was decided that the organ part would be better suited to piano. The sight of an empty seat stirred my ambitions.... If the other guy hadn't left the damn thing turned on, my career as an organ player would have ended right there. I figured out as best I could how to bluff my way through while the rest of the band rehearsed one little section of the song. Then.... Check this out: There is no music to read. The song is over five minutes long. The band is so loud that I can't even *hear* the organ, and I'm not familiar with the instrument to begin with. But the tape is going, and that is *Bob fucking Dylan* over there singing, so this had better be me sitting here playing *something*. The best I could manage was to play kind of hesitantly by sight, feeling my way through the changes like a little kid fumbling in the dark for a light switch. After six minutes they'd gotten the first complete take of the day down, and all adjourned to the booth to hear it played back.
>
> Thirty seconds into the second verse, Dylan motions towards [producer] Tom Wilson. "Turn the organ up," he orders.
>
> "Hey, man," Tom says, "that cat's not an organ player...."
>
> But Dylan isn't buying it. "Hey, now don't tell me who's an organ player and who's not. Just turn the organ up...."
>
> At the conclusion of the playback, the entire booth applauded the soon-to-be-a-classic "Like a Rolling Stone," and Dylan acknowledged the tribute by turning his back and wandering into the studio for a go at another tune. [7]

In the studio version, the organ tends to stir up whatever emotions the piano simultaneously calms down. This two-way pull, between Paul Griffin's professionally melodic piano playing and Kooper's instinctive and isolated organ chords, creates one tension that keeps the album cut emotionally unresolved, ready to become what each listener wants or needs. The 1974 concert version has less leeway: a listener not swept into the overwhelming beat of its music would join Miss Lonely in the out group, among those who do not know how it feels.

At a live performance, though, it would take a stolid listener indeed to ignore the sense of community in the crowd around her. That sense is so strong that, in the Newport '65 and Manchester '66 concerts perhaps and in other concerts certainly,[8] the audience united *against* Dylan and acted out an oedipal slaying of this figure they had followed and loved and respected. The booing incidents were a sort of rite of passage, releasing hostility and declaring independence for each participant. Only a few months earlier, though, Dylan's "Subterranean Homesick Blues" had begun to tell this audience, "Don't follow leaders/Watch the parking meters." By booing they were simply obeying—were refusing to follow leaders, even him.

Lines from rock songs, such as "Don't follow leaders," have functioned like proverbs among the subculture that, at the time of these booing incidents, was just beginning to define itself with recorded rock music as communication. One line from "Like a Rolling Stone" has passed into this kind of proverbial usage: "When you ain't got nothing, you got nothing to lose" may be spoken to express sympathy at another's loss or else bravado before a coming challenge.

Folklorists and others have often noted the wisely advisory tone of proverbs—epecially that almost any proverb advising a course of action can be matched with one advising the opposite course for the same situation. (A Victorian parlor game consisted of pairing, for example, "Haste makes waste" with "He who hesitates is lost"; more modern examples would include "You can't fight City Hall" and "The harder they come, the harder they fall.") This characteristic also applies to lines from rock songs, which convey advice without usually being spoken aloud. But I have heard one person, comforting another, use the Rolling Stones' line "You can't always get what you want [but sometimes you find you get what you need]" and the other reply, from Dylan, "Yeah, but your debutante just knows what you need [I know what you want]."

Whole conversations, not just advisory exchanges, can be carried on in Dylan lines—in half-lines, actually, since everyone knows the rest. As I negotiated permission to quote lyrics for this book, for example, I had the following exchange with an executive at Special Rider Music:

> him: "Look, I'm not saying it's all over now...."
> me: "Yeah, it's just that—oh, you know, to live outside the law...."
> him: "I know, but some of us are prisoners...."
> me: "OK, well, if you don't underestimate me...."

Among the hard core, occasionally, sessions even start up of "wisdom questions"—"Which Dylan song mentions a cat?" for example. Like biblical riddles, these questions call for thorough, esoteric knowledge of one's subject.[9]

"Like a Rolling Stone," the only Dylan song that mentions a cat, has an obvious link to the traditional proverb "A rolling stone gathers no moss." The image "rolling stone" figures in both white and black American oral tradition. In white culture the image is frozen into formulaic words of wisdom, although interpretations vary: either the rolling stone gathers no wealth and is a bad thing to be (mostly in Scottish tradition), or the rolling stone stays free from ties and responsibilities and is a good thing to be. This one proverb, then, wisely and knowingly advises two opposite solutions to the same problem.

In black tradition, "rolling stone" is a popular floating image in the blues, implying both responsibility-free traveling and male sexuality. As an important example, Muddy Waters's first hit record was "Rolling Stone." As recorded in February 1950 and rereleased on the album *Muddy Waters* (Chess 2ACMB-203), the song goes:

> Well, I wish I was a catfish swimming on the deep blue sea
> I would have all you good-looking women fishing
> Fishing after me... sho nuff after me...
> Sho nuff after me...
> Oh lord... oh lord... sho nuff...
> I went to my baby's house and I sit down on her step
> She said come on in now Muddy, you know
> My good man's just now left...
> Sho nuff he's just now left...
> Sho nuff just now left...
> Oh lord... oh well... oh well...
> Well, my mother told my father just before I was born
> I got a boy child's coming, gonna be
> He's gonna be a rolling stone...
> Sho nuff he's a rolling stone...
> Sho nuff he's a rolling stone...
> Oh well he's a... oh well he's a...
> Oh well he's a...

Each ellipsis in the lyrics is filled by a dramatic chord change on guitar. In the third stanza, thus, the chord change actually replaces the phrase "rolling stone." The Rolling Stones chose their name from Muddy Waters's song, according to the cover notes of this album. Dylan's "Like a Rolling Stone" came out a couple of years later, 1965; by 1967 the first major counterculture publication, *Rolling Stone*, began reaching a nationwide community united by rock music.

"Rock" is shortened from "rock and roll," a term also borrowed from the blues. "Rock and roll" originally referred to sexual intercourse but as early as 1948 "was being used in a number of songs to suggest both lovemaking and dancing."[10] The sixties counterculture developed this metaphor complex of rocks, stones, and rolling—generally dropping the blues' sexual food imagery ("jelly roll," "biscuit roller") but expanding in its stead the use of "stoned" as high on drugs. And—as in Dylan's "Rainy Day Women #12 & 35" (1966), with its punning verse lines and refrain, "Everybody must get stoned"—the metaphors never lost their solid grounding in geological stones. In "Like a Rolling Stone," the oft-repeated "rolling stone" image has as its unsuccessful counterpart the mineral symbol of sexuality proper to Miss Lonely's romantic world of wealth and promises, the "diamond ring."

The phrase "rolling stone" focuses not only imagery but also vowel/consonant patterns in this, probably Dylan's most popular song and certainly one of his most complex. (See Appendix A.) Stretching American English to its limits, Dylan interweaves sound patterns such that in the entire song hardly a syllable fails to fit into one of the major patterns of interlocked sound and meaning. Each rhyme set in the song is governed by a different strong vowel: long *a*, *e*, *i*, and *o*; diphthongs *ow* and *yew*; and the short *a* of "at" and *i* of the loaded word "it."

Although Dylan's voice makes these rhymes particularly distinct, he seldom forces barely assonating words to rhyme. His performance of this nonlove song differs otherwise from that of "Just Like a Woman" as well. A spectrum for analysis of the 1965 studio version of "Like a Rolling Stone" would go:

> sense of lyrics
> sound of lyrics, as on the page
> vocal effects
> instrumentation

Although still not as sequential as a poem would be, these lyrics do suggest a linear shift in the relationship between narrator and Miss Lonely, a progression marked by the interplay of her elegant Latinate diction and his blunt Anglo-Saxon-based language. But the progression that most directly leads a listener through this song is not the sense but the sound of the lyrics, in rhyme and assonance/consonance that appear even in print. Poetic meter holds its own against musical beat, as well, and the harmonica is no more voicelike than are the guitar and other instruments that ask how it feels. All in all, the effects created by this song—recorded about half a year before the 1966 "Just Like a Woman"—lean more toward the "words" than the "music" end of such a performance spectrum.

Considering vowel/consonant sound patterns as primary in effect, then, we see that the phrase "rolling stone" contains two of the vowels and two of the consonant sounds most often repeated throughout the song: long *o*, short *i*, *l*, and terminal *m/n/ng*. The *l* and *ohm/n* elsewhere occur in the end rhymes of each refrain: first "feel," with an extended *l*, and then [own]/home/ unknown/stone. Throughout the song, key phrases like "all right Miss Lonely" and "live on the street" also echo "rolling stone." These and other vowel/consonant patterns interact with musical riffs and poetic images in four stanzas, each with two long (eight-bar) couplets rhymed *ABCB*, two short (four-bar) couplets rhymed *DDDD*, a final verse line *E*, and the refrain rhymed *EE(F)FFF*.

The 1965 performance on *Highway 61 Revisited* opens with a drum crash, then four bars of the steady piano/guitar riff that backs up sung lines throughout, then sharp drumbeats at the start of the words. The first long couplet introduces the song's two main characters and its two major patterns of poetic imagery: the finely clothed princess of "Once upon a time," addressed as Miss Lonely, and, in contrast, the "bums." The narrator identifies himself with these bums and with the "mystery tramp" and "Napoleon in rags" later: although the recurring tramp figure is always in the third person, the overwhelming presence of "you" makes one expect "I" throughout the song. The tramp therefore is understood as the narrator, using third-person reference to distance himself from Miss Lonely's unfeeling world. Furthermore, the absence of any first-person pronouns in the song creates a vacuum: the listener herself becomes the unstated "I" who repeatedly attacks "you."

Besides evoking the fairytale princess, the phrase "Once upon a time" also sets up the time contrast between then and now, between the romance and riches she had then and the street-world reality of now. In addition, the phrase from Western-European storytelling tradition signals the moment to suspend rationality and disbelief until the formula "they lived happily ever after" ends the period of fantasy. In "Like a Rolling Stone" the narrator destroys the evoked fantasy world over and over, not by such a formula but instead by battering her "Once upon a time." He begins in this first couplet with monosyllabic, blunt street language and the immediate intrusion of bums.

The first couplet sets up vowel and consonant patterns that recur throughout the song. The hissed *st* in "dressed" anticipates the "stone" of every refrain, the "street" she can't live out on and the "stare" that does her no good and the "steeple" she used to inhabit, the "Siamese cat" and "where it's at" and "steal" that tell of her diplomat, the "used to" in varying senses, and the "secrets to conceal" that the narrator emphatically denies her in the end.

The thrice-repeated word "so" extends this *s* sound; "so" reverses the "Once" that begins the song and echoes the "stone" that ends each refrain. Here "so" accumulates meaning by repetition—so fine, so loud, so proud—becoming an attribute of Miss Lonely. It does not recur until the last stanza, when the narrator's sneer "You used to be so amused," paraphrasing the first stanza's "You used to laugh about," gives him control over her kind of diction, including her defense word "so."

Each rhyme word of this opening couplet, time/fine/dime/prime, combines a long *i* with a final nasal consonant, *m/n,* as also in the refrain rhymes [own]/home/unknown/stone. The long *i,* as in each refrain's "Like," appears further in the second stanza, where the narrator paraphrases Miss Lonely's Latinate diction with compromise/realize/alibis/eyes. Long *i* thus links the fairytale "time" to Miss Lonely's intellectual pretensions; the narrator shows both façades, romance and education, to be insufficient. And although he never says "I," we know by sound that an "I" is watching all along.

In addition to the rhymes in time/fine/dime/prime, each word's initial consonant anticipates sound patterns through the song. The *t* of "time" occurs in "tricks" and "tramp" and the loaded uses of "it." The *f* of "fine" recurs in "fall," "find out," "finest," and most often "feel." These *f*-alliterated words tend to characterize what is internal. Words with initial *d,* as in "dime," more often refer to some outside phenomenon that impinges on Miss Lonely: "doll," the streetwise address she ignores; the "deal" of the second stanza and the soon-to-depart "diplomat" of the third and the soon-to-be-pawned "diamond" of the fourth; and the "direction" that each refrain tells her she cannot find within herself. The *d* alliterates also with the "does" in "How does it feel?" demanding repeatedly that feeling be defined at a point in time. Finally, the *pr* of "prime" recurs in words that try to substantiate the romantic world being shattered: in the "proud" of the first stanza and in the last-gasp cluster in the fourth of "Princess" and "pretty" and "precious."

Dylan pauses after "prime," then raises his voice in pitch for the first time on "didn't you?" or, more accurately, *din yooo?* (His voice seems to descend on each line before, but is staying on one pitch while organ chords ascend.) As in conversation, the raised pitch asks a question; here it also seems challenging or threatening. This phrase sets up the "you" that the narrator will attack throughout the song; its diphthong *yew* will be repeated in the "used to" phrases, in the "vacuum" she faces when she finally asks for help, and in the last-stanza rhyme amused/used/refuse. After instrumental break with piano and drum prominent, Dylan returns to his original vocal pitch until "kidding you," again a third raised. Because "kidding you" is not a question, its raised pitch seems more threatening than did "didn't you?"

Because of midline rhyme and the four-beat poetic meter, both of which coordinate with the four four-beat measures behind "Once upon a time you dressed so fine/You threw the bums a dime in your prime," the opening lines of the song much resemble the "overwhelming majority of English nursery rhymes [which] have sixteen beats divided into four lines of four beats each," a characteristic of children's rhymes in non-European cultures as well.[11] As children turn adolescent, in many cultures also, rhymed words become a weapon in verbal duelling.[12] A rhymed insult can both give extra power to the insulter, by demonstrating control over language, and ritualize the insult to absolve the attacker from personal responsibility for hurt caused by the words. The narrator of the intricately rhymed and alliterated "Like a Rolling Stone," likewise, can simultaneously insult "you" with his controlled language and also imply that social ritual itself is to blame for her downfall.

Although in the opening *AB* couplet the narrator starts out combining rhymed insults with nursery-rhyme meter, in the *CB* couplet he immediately deviates from it. The musical four beats go on, but the poetic meter forces together five strong stresses: "call, say beware doll." Four words precisely rhyme—call/doll/fall/all. But they coincide with neither the middle and end of the metrical lines nor with the second and fourth isochronic beats. The shift away from nursery-rhyme meter in the *CB* couplet coordinates with that couplet's clear narrative warning that her fairytale world cannot last.

The "beware" that conveys this warning alliterates with "bums" just before and "bound" just after; all three convey threats to her romantic world. A warning is conveyed also in the fourth stanza, in the later words that begin with the letter *b*: "you better pawn it, babe." And like every sound so far except the stubbornly fairytale *pr*, *b* also occurs in the refrains. In "To be on your own [without a home]," "be" holds center position in each refrain; with a long *e* it extends the earlier sound of "feel" toward the rhyme set that climaxes in "stone." Paralleling this phonetic effect, "be" also extends the sense of "feel," by starting to name the street-world situations that give rise to feelings. The refrain warns Miss Lonely that she will have to do what she never did in fairytales—to "be," not seem. Once upon a time she could hide behind fine clothes and seeming pride; in each refrain the "be" puts her in her street-world place, with three clichéd literal descriptions and a resounding final simile.

The second-couplet word "bound" alliterates with these words of warning. With its diphthong, it also anticipates the sequence about/out/loud/ proud that end-rhymes in the short couplets that follow. The musical bridge after "kidding you" is louder than after "didn't you," with percussion more prominent. During this passage Kooper's organ swells, to then back up the four-bar short couplets. Behind each of the first two lines it marks every other measure with a high, then low chord; then, softer, it plays four descending chords, one each measure behind each of the lines that end "loud" and "proud." Thus the organ, not midline rhyme words as in the *ABCB* couplets, divides each line that tells how she used to act and used to seem to the narrator.

Dylan's vocal phrasing also bisects each *D* line—very distinctly in this first stanza, which has fewer words in the musical space than later. For the first two he pauses midway through each line, allowing instruments equal time with his voice; in the last two he stretches the midline "don't" that precedes "talk so loud" and "seem so proud." "Don't" anticipates the refrains' "stone" in its sound... and in its meaning as well, because the narrator's "don't" strips away from Miss Lonely the loud talk and seeming pride that, like the covering moss of the proverb, once kept her secure from rolling.

In each of these two lines, the loud and isolated "don't" of the narrator's world overcomes the "so" that is trying hard to defend her romantic attributes. The sound of "so" will get sucked into the resounding "stone," right along with "don't"; here, more immediately, it collapses into the sound and sense of "seem."

"Seem," next to the active verbs "laugh" and "talk," shows the emptiness of her superficial defenses. The long *e* and *m* of "seem" mirror the sounds in "meal," which in its turn leads to the refrain's repeated "feel." No one would eat a "meal" in her fairytale world—a banquet perhaps, or even a dinner, but "meal" is a solid, sensible Anglo-Saxon word. Dylan stretches the word, making its mouth-filling *l* slide over the instrumentation before the refrain.

The fullness of this *I* suggests that scrounging for a meal does work. "Scrounge" itself, like many well-established slang words, is onomatopoetic, a mouthful by itself: few English words have more than two consonants in a cluster, whereas "scrounge" begins with three consonants and—counting the *w* sound from the diphthong—ends with three. Its *ow* diphthong ties the word to the "proud" rhymes that precede it, highlighting the contrast between her defenses, which don't work, and the scrounging, which does.

The discursive meaning of this first verse is obvious. The monosyllabic street slang poses no poetic images. In diction as well as sound patterns and narrative situation, it pulls Miss Lonely down to street level. One phrase that contrasts sharply with her "Once upon a time" is "hanging out." One person might hang out but would do so at a "recognized rendezvous," expecting to be among others doing the same.[13] "Hanging out" evokes an entire community of the low-life types she would scorn—working-class or unemployed men, "bums," probably at a bar. The mystery-tramp narrator is never alone; he is among "Everybody."

Instead, it is Miss Lonely who is outside society. In the last three refrains of the *Highway 61* version her isolation is specified by the added line, "To be on your own." In this first refrain, however, the narrator makes no attempt to help her define her feelings: she is simply without a home, not—as afterward—on her own with no direction home, such that home must exist somewhere. Michael Gray feels that in the course of this song the man comes to regard Miss Lonely more sympathetically.[14] Gray's impression comes, in part, from this added line of refrain, which defines her situation more precisely to a listener and, by extension, to Miss Lonely.

In the two "How does it feel?" lines in the first refrain of the studio version, the two words "feel" differ in performance. On the first "feel" Dylan's voice rises; on the second it sinks. A contrast is formed: the rising pitch can imply questioning, threatening, possible continuation, and hope; the sinking pitch of the second "feel" implies dejection, finality, hopelessness. Dylan does not repeat this rendering in every refrain. In the second refrain both "feel"s rise, the third refrain is similar to the first, and in the last refrain the first "feel" rises and the second one maintains a level pitch. This level "feel" might imply her emotionless invisibility at the end. But more certainly, the variety of ways in which Dylan renders "feel" reproduces a listener's own internal experience of up-and-down feelings in any confusing situation, particularly in one all alone with no home.

The "it" in "how does it feel?" is Miss Lonely's loneliness, literally, but with sexual implications. Doing it, making it, getting it on, getting it off...

the word "it" functions as the bland, white, middle-class equivalent of the colorful metaphor "rolling stone." As "rolling stone" means most literally a homeless wanderer but has sexual overtones, so too this "it" refers to homelessness and implies sex. The street experience Miss Lonely lacks is not exclusively sexual, but it includes sex while excluding fairytale romance, ornate diction, and euphemisms like "it."

Each line of the refrain contains four strong isochronic beats, like nursery-rhyme meter. But only the first two musical beats occur during words; the second half of each line is carried by guitar. Predictable four-beat meter thus conveys to the audience the security that the narrator denies to Miss Lonely. Words stop; the beat goes on. The audience can share the narrator's scorn for Miss Lonely—for she exists only, after all, in the text that music transcends.

The power of the line "How does it feel?" comes not from its question as much as from the reasking of that question by instrumentation alone. In three and a half measures, guitar chords change from the secure-seeming tonic, behind each end-rhyme word, to a subdominant and then an unfinished-sounding dominant. This chord progression both repeats the sung question before it and anticipates a question to follow, even after the line that ends the textual refrain.

In the studio version, the instrumentation accompanying this chord change is similar after the first three lines of the first refrain (after the first four lines of the expanded refrains). Following the unknown/stone lines that end every refrain, however, the instrumentation becomes more level and calm, and the organ loses prominence to the piano. Gentler-sounding instruments assure a listener that being "a complete unknown" and "a rolling stone" need not be as bad as they are for Miss Lonely. A "complete unknown" would at least have privacy, untroubled by anyone's expectations. A "rolling stone" has conflicting implications, as well—potentially unpleasant homelessness but potentially pleasant sexuality.

While the organ and lead guitar and piano go from forceful to reassuring variations on the distinctive riff, the bass guitar and drum and tambourine keep up a steady beat that unifies the refrain from "scrounging" to "stone." As the words to the first refrain end, the riff is further elaborated by instruments, including Dylan's harmonica for a few notes. A burst of drumming leads into the "You" that opens the second stanza.

The word "you" occurs forty-four times in "Like a Rolling Stone." In comparison, there are four "they"s, ten occurrences of he/him/his, and no other personal pronouns. The narrator aims anger at "you," over and over;

the song makes it overwhelmingly clear that "you" must be attacked. The undefined resentments writhing within each listener, whether sociopolitical pressures or parental or sexual or, likeliest, all of the above and more hopelessly entangled—all these emotions get channeled onto the time-after-time-repeated "you."

In the long couplets that open the second stanza, "you" resounds with the two different senses of "used to." The first "used to," marking past tense, puts Miss Lonely's schooldays back into "Once upon a time." The long-*i* vowels of "finest" and "right" echo the first stanza, as do the words "fine" and "used to" themselves. The second "used to" in the second stanza, however, stands in extreme contrast to those auxiliary "used to"s. On the streets, she has to get "used to" whatever all "it" is; she used to be in control of her surroundings, but here and now she must adjust.

The blunt street language of the first stanza had shown no clear visual scene. There Miss Lonely, perhaps on a high white horse, scorns bums, callers, and hangers-out—vague, separate groups. In this second stanza, Miss Lonely becomes easier to picture: a prep-school type who would sneak whisky into her dorm and there giggle about Boys, waiting in hair rollers for a big weekend date. (The possibility that she gets juiced on that date and does something she regrets, let us leave for the next stanza.) The people she scorns also become more individual. There is the "mystery tramp," a precise Latinate term that nonetheless evokes the rough rock-and-roll fifties, Elvis Presley's "Mystery Train." And there is, besides, "Nobody."

Like "don't" in the first verse, the negative "Nobody" becomes an attribute of the street world, in opposition to Miss Lonely's world of fairytale and, now, school. The third stanza will flash weaponlike negatives as well, such as "wasn't," "shouldn't," and "ain't it hard." And this pattern of words that negate her romantic assumptions, as the narrator takes control, will burst at the end into the twisted negatives of "When you ain't got nothing, you got nothing to lose/You're invisible now, you got no secrets to conceal."

These *ABCB* couplets of the second verse lack the regular internal rhyme of the "Once upon a time" lines. And where those first-stanza couplets rhyme "you," these rhyme "it"—still with sexual overtones, even though the first "it" refers to her school and the second to living on the street. Use of the same loaded pronoun for both school and street life sharpens the contrast. Despite pretensions of the finest schools, drinking is drinking and fucking is "it."

The higher-pitched "used to it" that ends this *ABCB* segment is followed by a tambourine-led instrumental break. The organ had marked measures behind the *DDDD* lines of the first stanza; the tambourine goes on to mark measures here. It fades behind the second short couplet, then returns loud and fast behind "make a deal."

Appropriately for a school scene, these short couplets employ elegant diction. Long Latinate words paraphrase Miss Lonely's speech and thoughts: compromise, mystery, realize, alibis, vacuum. The end rhymes (compromise/realize/alibis/eyes) link the long *i* of the song's opening rhyme set to the *z* that will govern the closing rhyme set amused/used/refuse/lose, there combined with the song's omnipresent *yew*/"you." In this second stanza, the rhyme words get shorter, line by line, until the "eyes" that their rhymes suggest finally do appear. Miss Lonely tries to attract his attention with her elegant diction, but even when she can look deep into his eyes, she gets no response, no "I," just her own *yew*/"you" reflected back from his "vacuum."

To communicate with the mystery tramp, she instead has to use his street-world language. By asking him to "make a deal" rather than "compromise," in an expression as solidly Anglo-Saxon as the "meal" it echoes, Miss Lonely comes to realize that her fine clothes and finest schooling will do her no more good than will her diction when she needs help from the tramp. "Alibis," a Latinate term nonetheless appropriate to rough criminals and cowboys, implies that she has already committed some Kafkaesque crime—that she cannot simply declare innocence but must pay to cover up what she did. She asks the narrator's help, but he leaves her on her own in the added line of refrain.

The instrumentation in this second refrain differs from that in the first. Piano and guitars, rather than organ, predominate; the tambourine keeps time more noticeably than does the bass guitar. Also, this questioning riff remains fairly constant after each of the five lines: the organ does level off as before, but regular piano chords can be heard throughout. After the second refrain, Dylan's harmonica coordinates with the band for one measure, turning the basic backup riff into a variation on the riff that reasks "How does it feel?" The tambourine and drum then explode into the first word of the third stanza—yet another "You." Dylan isolates this "You" by leading into it with "aaaaah" and by pausing afterward.

Then, he disrupts another couplet's expected nursery-rhyme meter. The rhyme words—around/frown/clowns/[down]—want to fall at the middle and end of each poetic line, at corresponding musical beats. Dylan had messed up the poetic meter of the "beware, doll" couplet by cramming together five stressed syllables. Here he takes the opposite tack, by inserting so many unstressed syllables that the stresses become haphazard to the discursive meaning as well as in conflict with the four-beat musical pattern that the rhymes try to coordinate with. The word "jugglers," in particular, needs a stress to help convey the line's sense but is buried among six consecutive unstressed syllables.

In this third stanza's *AB* couplet, Miss Lonely can again be visualized: no longer in a dorm room but rather at a circus, her own private one with "all the clowns that you have commissioned" (as elsewhere on this album— "Queen Jane Approximately," 1965). From servants' quarters they descend her marble staircase, perhaps to juggle and clown while she—puttering at whatever ladies do in mansions—treats them like a TV set left on.

The *CB* couplet then gives direct advice from narrator to Miss Lonely, in precise nursery-rhyme meter with midline rhyme: "You never under*stood*... that it ain't no *good*/You *should*n't... let other *peo*ple get your... kicks for you." He combines her fairytale meter with his street-world diction; the Anglo-Saxon but also polysyllabic "understood" mediates between the two kinds of language. The narrator, who ignored her plea for alibis, now makes an effort to communicate. It also becomes clear that she, who had earlier ignored the people's "beware, doll, you're bound to fall," will be forced to follow such direct advice from the narrator. And in the last stanza, indeed, his advice will turn into commands, as "Go to him now, he calls you, you can't refuse." Here, the *oo* of understood/good/shouldn't is a more closed sound than is *oo* in the "you" that again end-rhymes in this third stanza. The narrator's advice stands apart from the accumulation and direction of hostility toward the forty-four "you"s. The regular meter and rhyme also make this segment less harsh, and all four long-couplet lines are backed by mellow piano chords.

The first short couplet of the third stanza again shows Miss Lonely in a scene from her former fairytale life. But these couplets are no longer as short in words. Each fills the same musical space as before, four measures, still marked by organ and tambourine. But where the first stanza, as aligned with the accented beat in each measure, says, "Y͞ou used to = laugh ab͞out =," this third stanza packs in the whole of "You used to ride on the chr͞ome horse with your = d͞iplomat.͞" The narrator's increased verbosity makes the scene more visual. He even employs a poetic image, "chrome horse," for a high-powered motorcycle. Both words suggest transportation (not, that is, wild horses or industrial chrome), but as *ro* of "chrome" reverses to *or* of "horse," so too the forms of transportation stand in contrast, old and new. The "horse" evokes her "Once upon a time" world; the "chrome" suggests bikers, hotrods, hanging out. But these street-world implications of "chrome horse" get momentarily deflected by the diplomat, so elegant, who takes her for a ride—in both senses.

The graceful Siamese cat, balanced on his shoulder in the wind, adds sinister overtones possibly half-remembered from two fifties films—*The King and I*, with Siamese diplomatic intrigues, and *Lady and the Tramp*. In this Disney production the villains are gleefully evil cats named Si and Am; and Lady and the Tramp, an upper-class female cocker spaniel and a lower-class male mongrel, parallel the social roles of Miss Lonely and the mystery tramp.

The long-*i* and *s* sounds in "Siamese" connect it to "once upon a time," "dressed so fine," "finest schools," and even "kicks"—to the romantic concepts the narrator has been destroying. And "Siamese cat," like "diplomat," sounds particularly elegant in contrast to the blunt words that then rhyme, "that" and "at."

The street-language phrase "ain't it hard," with Dylan's voice louder on "hard," makes an abrupt transition from the poetically evoked scene to the diplomat's treachery. The diplomat perhaps steals material possessions; this last line also suggests both outright rape and coldhearted seduction. The two uses of "it" in the couplet reinforce sexual overtones: "ain't it hard" refers to the theft but also suggests an erect penis, and "where it's at" suggests the glamour of movie stars and jetsetters.

By the end of the third stanza Miss Lonely has become a victim, albeit one who asked for it, instead of a haughty bitch. The feelings of the narrator edge toward sympathy. Thus, the third-refrain questions sound less threatening than in the first refrain, even though the performances are quite similar. Dylan's voice rises during the first "feel" and falls during the second, again suggesting feelings that shift. The organ and bass carry the riff that reasks each question, and the piano again backs up refrain lines. Dylan here stretches the long-*o* sounds, particularly in "home"; the long *e* of "feel," in comparison, seems not as sneering. The effect of this less-hostile third refrain continues into the instrumental break, where guitars—with less percussion than elsewhere—lead into the fourth stanza. Dylan plays harmonica for a few notes at the start and end of this break.

As if to make up for its relative timidity in midsong, Kooper's organ comes up behind the words throughout the fourth stanza. It plays four ascending chords behind the *AB* couplet, quickly descends in the break after "got it made," and then ascends more softly behind the *CB* couplet. It marks measures in the first short couplet, with a high, then low, chord; then it descends in four steps behind the narrator's crowed "Go to him now, he calls you, you can't refuse" and again behind "When you ain't got nothing, you got nothing to lose." Twice descending organ chords intensify this important couplet such that Dylan's voice seems to rise twice in pitch, in an atmosphere of imminent excitement.

These elements of performance reinforce the sense of the last stanza. The long couplets again describe Miss Lonely's fairytale life, but in a scene where she has more company than the one treacherous male who had appeared previously. The narrator edges closer to seeing Miss Lonely not just as snob but as victim of her high society, not only in, but also above, her world: Miss Lonely, the female in the song, is understood as "Princess on a steeple." A fairytale princess atop a white clapboard church: the image is hard to visualize because the worlds of romance and religion are so far apart. Or are they? From that incongruity emerges the latent sense of steeple as a phallic symbol for the dying-and-resurrected fertility god. Miss Lonely radiates something of sexuality and royalty and romance and religion above the bickering crowds. She is worth his trouble to save.

The *pr* consonant cluster describes her fairytale world with "prime" and "proud" in the first stanza, "Princess" and "pretty" and "precious" here. The consonant *p* by itself intrudes into "steeple" and "people," and thus prevents them from rhyming with the "feel" that rings through the song naming precisely what pretty people do not do. Pretty people drink and think, though, in this fourth verse as in the finest schools. The midline rhyme of the steeple/people line makes a listener expect that regular nursery-rhyme meter will follow, but Dylan shoves together the potential midline rhymes into a sort of rocking-chair effect with "drinking thinking." He further disrupts the meter by stressing three syllables, "drink" and "think" and "they," instead of the expected four.

Dylan's voice breaks this line after the stressed "they," as usual isolating and raising in pitch the tag-end phrase. The long *a* of "got it made" assonates with "they" and with its rhyme fellow "babe." The set of English vowels is now complete. Every orthographic vowel, in its most distinctive long form, has highlighted major concepts and governed rhyme and assonance patterns in this song. Other than "they" in the first and third stanzas, the only previous clear long-*a* sounds occur twice in "ain't," markers of the narrator's street language. Long *a* here comes also to characterize her high-class society. It makes her social context likewise a warning to her, a world without home or security.

In "got it made," "it" suggests wealth or success—a more businesslike type of success than the glamorous "where it's at." The indefinite "it" occurs fifteen times in the song, not nearly as often as does "you." But, like "you," "it" can focus a listener's emotions. Sex and success and whatever else one does not understand—the song's repetition of "it" in so many varying, clichéd contexts can reassure a listener that something is there, even if indefinite. The accumulated "it"s resemble in effect the adding of an extra line to the refrain. At first without a home, Miss Lonely attains the more defined situation of having a home, though not knowing where. Similarly for a listener, by repetition "it" becomes familiar, unthreatening, and certainly better defined (being a word) than is the entangled mass of emotions with which each listener wonders who she is and what she's doing here.

In performance, Dylan conveys the skewed nursery-rhyme meter of this "got it made" line. For the next couplet, the text published in *Writings and Drawings* (its relationship to this studio performance being, as usual, unclear) is "Exchanging all kinds of precious gifts and things/But you'd better lift your diamond ring, you'd better pawn it babe," with cross rhymes that would put "gifts" and "things" and then "lift" and "ring" at metrically unexpected places. The studio performance has two fewer rhyme words. Furthermore, increasing the confusion generated by closely packed, unstressed syllables, organ chords (as $\overline{\overline{=}}$) stress different words in each measure than does Dylan's voice (italicized): "ex*chang*ing all *precious gifts* but you *better* take your diamond *ring* and you better… " As organ chords and Dylan's voice fight both with each other and with the expected nursery-rhyme meter, the two lines imitate petty bickering among pretty people. The narrator gives Miss Lonely advice, as he did in the stanza before with the clarity of nursery-rhyme meter. Here, though, to introduce his street-world advice the narrator has to claw his verbal way out of the pretty people's metrical muddle to trumpet clearly "*pawn* it, *babe.*"

In this phrase "it" refers literally to her diamond ring, again with sexual overtones. A diamond ring reevokes the prep-school princess of the second stanza, who would try to trap a doctor or lawyer as husband, and the diplomat's broken promises of the third. In addition, the diamond ring stands in contrast to the rolling-stone image of every refrain. Even outside the context of this song, diamonds and stones are hard minerals with contrasting associations of wealth and dirt. A diamond ring symbolizes sexuality in its WASP manifestation—delayed gratification, men promising wealth while women promise to do it someday. A rolling stone evokes unrepressed sexuality and instability as portrayed in the blues, expressing black American culture. Within this song's lyrics, in addition, the diamond ring and rolling stone symbolize the fairytale past and street-world present of Miss Lonely.

And within this song's sound patterns, the long *i* of "diamond" connects it to "time," "prime," "finest," "compromise," and other elegant words that have tried in vain to overcome street language… until here, at last, the long *i* gets pawned along with "it." The *ing* of "ring" echoes the pretty people's drinking and thinking. Thus "diamond ring" represents the ultimate futile attempt of her and her high-class society to come up with a symbolic and phonetic equivalent for the *ing* that is smack dab in the middle of "rolling stone."

The two phrases "rolling stone" and "diamond ring" share the sounds of *r* and *ing* and *ohn*, similarities that heighten the contrast between vowel/consonant sounds that the two phrases do not share. Like the long *i*, the *d* in "diamond" recalls other words in Miss Lonely's fairytale defenses—"dressed" and "dime" and "doll," names for shallow concepts that helped her get her own way, and then the growing desperation of "deal" and the treacherous "diplomat." This unmatched long *i* and *d* of "diamond ring" echo words that stand in contrast to words recalled by the unmatched *l* and *st* of "rolling stone," both of which echo particularly unassailable concepts in the street world—"feel," "meal," "deal," "steal," and "street" itself.

In spite of the two phrases' being evenly matched in the *r*, *ing*, and *ohn* that imply both worlds, "diamond ring" loses this symbolic confrontation in performance as well as phonetics. In performance, the "diamond ring" gets buried in meter-muddled lines; a listener does not respond to it as to a strong poetic image like "chrome horse" or "Napoleon in rags" or, certainly, to the "rolling stone" that every refrain leads up to and nearly every sound pattern in the song echoes. The defeat of the "diamond ring" is ignominious, for it is gotten rid of with "pawn," whose initial letter had previously been permitted only to pretty people. "Pawn it, babe" stands in extreme contrast to the smug materialism of the triply rhymed phrase "got it made." And "babe" is street-world warning, reaching her now in the disrespectful tone she ignored when addressed as "doll" in the first stanza.

The first short couplet of the fourth stanza rephrases the first stanza's "You used to laugh about" with high-falutin' diction. Neither Dylan nor any listener needs to look up "laugh" (Anglo-Saxon *hliehhan*) and "amuse" (Old French *amuser*, from Latin *musus*) to sense the contrast between the two terms, in diction and implied social class. (The second suggests Queen Victoria's "We are not amused.") In the second verse, he had forced her to ask to "make a deal" rather than to "compromise"; now, at the end of the song, the narrator can use Miss Lonely's language to say just what he said in his own at the beginning. Furthermore, she used to laugh about a vague everybody hanging out; in this stanza, she used to be so amused at a concrete visual image provided by the narrator, "Napoleon in rags." "Napoleon" suggests both a heroic conquerer and a caricatured loony in a caricatured nuthouse. "Rags," inappropriate to either role, stands in contrast to the opening image of Miss Lonely's fine clothing.

In performance, Dylan breaks the line between "be" and "so." It is the first appearance of "so" since Miss Lonely was so fine, loud, and proud in the first stanza. And "be," at midpoint of every refrain, has called attention to her state of being on her own, forced to feel. This line not only uses her language but also evokes the two points in time—Miss Lonely's past defensiveness (with "so") and her present loneliness (with "be").

In print this couplet seems unsubtle: I conquered her world with my kind of language and my kind of clothes. But a song is not a poem. During the ten years I listened to this song without analyzing the words, it never occurred to me that "Napoleon in rags" might be a character who, during the song, has gone from resentment at the lady for scorning his diction to conquest of her by using her diction. To me, "Napoleon in rags" had much more to do with my always wearing jeans and that same black T-shirt to classes at Madison and staying stoned and still getting all *A*s.

The second short couplet of the fourth stanza contains the narrator's strongest advice so far to Miss Lonely—his command, in fact. Backed by descending organ chords, Dylan's voice aligns with musical beat and nursery-rhyme meter, all stressing the syllables that also carry the line's discursive meaning:

Go to him now, he *calls* you, you *can't* re*fuse*
When you *ain't* got *noth*ing, you got *noth*ing to *lose*

"You got nothing to lose" stands as a dare, a shrug at possible danger. Coupled with "When you ain't got nothing," it brings tough-guy glamour to the lack of possessions. But it is the listener, not Miss Lonely, who shares the narrator's devil-may-care attitude. The best she can hope for is that he will take care of her.

The narrator, with her language and his own at his command, is willing to protect her—not respect her. With dictionarylike precision, he now employs Latin-derived terms: "You're invisible now, you got no secrets to conceal." The two halves of the line undercut each other's discursive meanings; he is using her language not to communicate clearly but to keep himself in control. The patently nonvisual terms "invisible" and "conceal" culminate the pattern of negative terms with which the narrator has been undercutting Miss Lonely's defensive bulwarks throughout. The negatives in these lines strip Miss Lonely, starting with nothing and going on down from there. After the powerful double negative of the first clause, the narrator shifts the sense of the second, word by word. After "When you ain't got nothing, you got," Miss Lonely is about to get something positive in contrast to the "nothing" just named. "When you ain't got nothing, you got nothing" snatches away the possibility, leaving her with twice as much nothing. And after "When you ain't got nothing, you got nothing to lose," she has acquired all those maybe-positive overtones only to lose both nothings. In the last line, Miss Lonely is not only less than nothing but also invisible. If she were hiding secrets and then became invisible, those secrets would show. But no—none at all, not even under her fine clothes.

Dylan's drawn-out *l* on "conceal" and piano chords make the bridge to the last refrain. Through the refrain the organ continues with the prominence it has established in this stanza, particularly during the questioning riff. By "on your own" the guitars and tambourines become noticeably louder, and on the last line the other instruments and voice all swell in volume.

Dylan's vocal pitch rises during the first "feel" and remains level during the second. He emphatically rounds the long *o* of the penultimate rhyme, "unknown." His voice then drops in pitch, cutting off the "stone," and he uses his breath immediately for harmonica. The band continues for three backup riffs, then fades. Dylan's harmonica creates a new variation, adding shrill, fast, high notes to the third beat of the riff. And that is how it feels at the end of the studio version.

It all felt quite different in the Los Angeles Forum in 1974. The lyrics eliminate "To be on your own," each refrain in concert instead asking how it feels "To be without a home/With no direction home." The syntax makes less sense than before, but a listener experiences each line separately, not sequentially, so that the repetition of the powerful "home" image doubles its impact. Slight rewording does little to change the song, however. Other than the audience screaming in the background, loudest after each "How does it feel?" what details of this performance make it sound excited and exciting, a fulfillment of possibilities latent in the *Highway 61* version?

The immediately noticeable change is in rhythmic density. Although the tempo is nearly the same as in the studio, M.M. $\mathbf{d}$=120, the 1974 one sounds faster because the percussion comes to accent more than one beat per four-beat measure. A drumbeat marks beat 3 of each backup measure as the 1974 performance begins—as, throughout the studio version, one beat per measure was marked. But by the end of the second 1974 verse, the drummer is marking beats 3 and 4 and, later, beats 1 and 3. He fills in all four beats per measure of nearly every instrumental break, sometimes quickening further into a roll. By the last two refrains, though, he is teasing audience expectations that drumrolls will follow sung lines. Each first "How does it feel?" features a drumroll instead on "How"; each second one, a drumroll during "feel." In all refrains, the percussion makes the rhyme words more dramatic.

The piano starts off the 1974 concert version. The musicians tease the audience from the beginning: they pick at chords, coordinate with one another, even add in high organ notes for a slow, romantic song like "Lay, Lady, Lay" (1969). Then the drums come up, the piano plays four descending pairs of notes, and the audience is screaming in recognition of "Like a Rolling Stone" even before the organ has begun playing the ascending chords like those that back up *ABCB* lines on the studio version.

I would recognize anywhere that these four pairs of descending pitches mark the beginning of "Like a Rolling Stone." Similar tones, the guitar ascending and descending, open the Newport '65 version; similar piano tones, though closer together and mushed by other instrumentation, open the Manchester '66 version. But nothing like this musical pattern opens the *Highway 61* version. I will have to leave unexplained how these notes so clearly signal the opening of "Like a Rolling Stone." They do signal. And by descending they gather the audience's attention and focus it on the opening words, familiar from childhood and from a decade of hearing this song start, "*Once* upon a *time.*" Like the audience for a fairytale, this audience in the L. A. Forum will be covering familiar territory and reexperiencing familiar emotions, to emerge from the song victorious over "you" and not so confused about "it." In every concert reported on the 1974 tour, "Like a Rolling Stone" was carefully set up as climax (sexual innuendo intended). As the song began, house lights would come on and Bill Graham's ushers would step aside, allowing each audience to surge forward in anticipation of each adventure to come.

Throughout the studio version, the piano calms down what the organ stirs up. In 1974, both add to the excitement. The organ does most of the instrumental flourishes. It does chords behind the words, but during instrumental breaks it often plays instead fast separate notes and sometimes playful runs—including a tumbling act, with lead guitar as partner, to illustrate "the jugglers and the clowns when they all came down to do tricks for you."

The piano, after each rhyme line in *ABCB* couplets, plays high, fast chords. Stanza by stanza this interlude after *B* lines becomes louder and louder, until the piano reaches its loudest and most excited passage after the fourth-stanza "got it made." After the next couplet, though, the chords are softer and descending, for the first time in the song; thus the words "pawn it, babe" stand out extra clearly. This phrase, somewhat sympathetic advice in the studio version, here becomes a shout of pure victory. The feeling conveyed is that Miss Lonely has to obey, has to go pawn her ring—or that it makes no difference to anyone whether she obeys or not.

As another difference between this and the studio version, in concert the members of the Band sing the refrain along with Dylan, loudest on each "How does it feel?" So does much of the audience, reinforcing the feeling that each listener is not alone but rather part of a community all of whom know how it feels. The studio version hints at such a community, for there the listener stands apart from the textual Miss Lonely and participates in the music she does not hear. This possibility get fulfilled in the 1974 concert, as other voices join to ask "you" the questions Miss Lonely cannot answer, and other instruments—including the impossible-to-ignore drum—join to assure listeners that musical questions too should be asked over and over.

Dylan pronounces words, also, such that they fulfill the studio version's possibilities. The song's narrator seizes control of language, in part by making all the long vowels of English as distinct as possible from one another. In the 1974 version, Dylan reduplicates many of those vowels, especially those in rhyme position. The first line, for instance, becomes *Wu-unce upona ti-yime, yuh drest so fi-yine.* In the second stanza, each rhymed "it" becomes *ihit*; the *ize* rhymes also get reduplicated, especially *reali-yize.* Dylan pronounces other vowels as longer than they would be in normal speech. For example, in "You used to laugh about," he makes the first three words assonate as long *oo,* and the word "about" Dylan sings with a long *a* and reduplicated *ow,* as *ay-bowout.* The line that follows this one shows Dylan playing with consonant sounds as well, pronouncing the two *ng* sounds in distinctly separate syllables: *hang-ing.*

The last verse line of this first stanza demonstrates how a word added in performance, a word unimportant to the sense of the lyrics, can increase the song's sound-pattern cohesiveness. "Scrounging," as onomatopoeia, reproduces the long search and the eventually successful mouth-filling of the activity it names. In this 1974 concert the search becomes twice as long, more phonetically circular, and twice as successful—for the word expands to *scrounging uh-round.*

Dylan's voice becomes particularly expressive as he speeds up just before the final refrain. In the cocksure phrase "you can't refuse," he does not bring out potential assonance but rather imitates street-language accents with clipped words and a drawled last syllable: *yuh cain't ruh-fuyooz*. The effect is of one who will choose his own time and place to assonate, who can use all levels of language simultaneously, ignoring all restrictions and conventions. Then Dylan puts into the last word, "conceal," all the scorn he can. He does so by breaking the word sharply, taking a breath before the second syllable, and then both reduplicating the vowel and holding the *l* for even longer than he did on "meal" or "deal" or "steal." As the Band joins to sing this last refrain, then, neither they nor Dylan pronounce "feel" with such a reduplication of its vowel and extension of its final *l*. Thus, these two *eel* rhymes stand in contrast: "conceal" purges the most extreme anger at "you"; with "feel," then, the audience joins a community of mutual feeling.

One might compare these two words, "conceal" and "feel," as they affect a listener to the 1974 version and to the Manchester '66 version. In Manchester, Dylan reduplicates the vowel in "-ceal" and stretches the *l* somewhat, and he renders "feel" exactly the same way. The two words do not stand in contrast. The second does not include the audience in a community purged of pent-up anger at "you." And the Manchester band and audience do not sing along on "How does it feel?"

It is unlikely that reliable eyewitness accounts of audience behavior during this Manchester concert will surface because, for one thing, the bootleg tape is not certainly from that particular concert. My labeling of it as "Manchester" is based on Greil Marcus's recollection of his first receiving this tape, from Dylan's 1966 British tour. It could be Liverpool, Marcus says; he agrees with Sandy Gant and Roger Ford that it is not "The Royal Albert Hall Concert 1966," as this tape was called on a bootleg record. Presumably using press accounts, Scaduto describes audience hostility at the Royal Albert Hall concert 1966—which took place within a few weeks of what I am calling the Manchester concert.[15] But all that can be proven about audience reaction, audience hostility, is what the tape itself has preserved.

Throughout the concert (or concerts, if the tape is spliced from several), the audience applauds after each song—politely, fading before the musicians decide what to play next, seldom cheering. One possible source of misunderstanding is a British vs. American difference in signaling. At a U.S. rock concert, the audience's clapping in unison signals impatience, eagerness to hear more. For a British audience in 1966, clapping in unison probably signaled displeasure. (The American custom seems to have prevailed in England by the late seventies.) Before "Like a Rolling Stone" at Manchester '66, a portion of the audience is clapping in unison at the preceding song, "Ballad of a Thin Man" (1965). While the band is tuning up, suddenly the audience laughs at something shouted offstage. At least three more catcalls come; the loudest sounds like "Judas."

The performers are no longer in control. As the band starts up, Dylan tells the audience "I don't believe you"[16] and then, coordinating with musical lines, "You're a liar" and, more softly, "Whatcha talking about." The piano comes in with its distinctive four pairs of descending notes; then it ascends and descends again in a musical attempt to get the audience to focus on "Once upon a time."

In this version, Dylan does not do reduplications or other vocal tricks that keep language under the narrator's control. He slows down key phrases like "didn't you" and "kidding you," but makes no changes in the vowel/consonant sound of normal speech. The tempo is usually M.M. ♩ = 100, notably slower than the others' M.M. ♩ = 120. Each refrain, and each musical-question riff in particular, goes even slower. Also, this questioning chord change is rendered just the same after nearly every line of refrain—not accented by percussion or elaborated, as in 1974, nor passed from organ to piano, as often on *Highway 61*. Each verbal question is followed by a slow-tempo chord change, time after time. This tactic seems to insult the audience. The message of each refrain is, "You're stupid, and in fact you don't know how it feels. But maybe if we go over it slowly and often enough, you'll start to see what we can do that you can't."

The instrumentation throughout the song is loose. The musicians do not coordinate with each other or with Dylan's voice. Listening to this performance, one does not expect music to reinforce or otherwise interact with words. One only hopes that the Hawks will hit the same beat at the same time, with corresponding chord changes. The cymbals seem particularly intrusive, arbitrarily struck behind arbitrarily related phrases.[17] Dylan makes a couple of attempts to break the slow monotony with his harmonica and vocal phrasing. His harmonica plays a few notes after each refrain but never quite coordinates with anyone else. In his phrasing, Dylan divides the sung lines in places that the musical beat and poetic meter would not have predicted. For instance, the second-stanza *CB* couplet goes: "Nobody's ever taught you how… to live on the street/And you find out now… you're gonna have to get used to it." By moving "now," and by pausing after it and after "how," he creates a new midline rhyme. The *ow* sounds, thus isolated, echo the first stanza's "proud" rhymes that tell of her fairytale defenses. The contrast is highlighted between the past, when she was loud and proud, and the present, when she has to learn how. In order to create this new rhyme, however, Dylan has detracted from other words in this couplet that carry more discursive meaning and sound patterning than do "how" and "now"—notably "street" and "used to it."

In another instance, the music and Dylan's voice detract from the words. In the third refrain, the narrator could be feeling as sympathetic toward Miss Lonely as he ever would; to reinforce the mood the instrumentation would be relatively calm and mellow. But in the Manchester version, most of it is identical to the other refrains, except for one couplet. Behind "Like a complete unknown" the guitar ascends; in addition, Dylan sings each syllable of each word separately, each on the same high pitch, and loud. His voice drops in pitch, arclike, on the last syllable "known"; then he repeats this pitch drop for "stone." His vocal inflections make the lines hostile and aggressive. But the lines seem arbitrarily chosen out of the song—unless, perhaps, he has chosen this refrain to tell the audience just who among us is a complete unknown and who is not.

After the last refrain the band, accompanied by Dylan's harmonica, plays on slowly for the length of another stanza, with refrain. When it finally stops, some of the audience shout and whistle with approval as well as applaud. Dylan says "Thank *you*," in a sarcastic tone, to the Manchester '66 audience.

Audience reaction to the Newport '65 performance of "Like a Rolling Stone" is barely discernible on my third-generation bootleg tape. Dylan's set at Newport opens with "Maggie's Farm," a song first released four months earlier. Almost everyone in the audience would already have heard this song with electric guitar on *Bringing It All Back Home*. But Dylan and his band (including members of the Paul Butterfield Blues Band) perform it with little in common, except for most of the lyrics, with that studio "Maggie's Farm." The tempo is faster; shrieking electric-guitar runs follow each line and almost bury the words. After the song, someone shouts what might be "Mike! Mike!"—i.e., turn up the vocals.

The Newport '65 "Like a Rolling Stone" immediately follows this "Maggie's Farm." Al Kooper's account of the incident does not mention his and the other musicians' reaction to any hostile shouts from the audience—whether shouts of "Mike!" or (as some accounts have it) "Down in front!" or (as the romanticized oral history of the counterculture has it) "We want the real Dylan!" Instead, Kooper explains, "In the middle of

'Maggie's Farm,' somebody fucked up and Sam Lay turned the beat around, which thoroughly confused everyone until the song mercifully stumbled to its conclusion."[18] Kooper says that they were satisfied with the subsequent "Like a Rolling Stone." But on the tape they seem still uncertain.

A striking difference between this Newport '65 version and the studio one is, again, tempo. At Manchester '66, slow tempo seems to insult the audience's intelligence; at Newport '65, faster tempo suggests uncertainty, hurry to get the song over with. The tempo actually speeds up during the course of the song. Beginning at M.M. $\flat$ = 112, it increases to about 116 and then, during the first refrain, to 120 (the tempo of the studio version). The musicians tend to speed up during each refrain and stay there through the next verse. They stay at about 132 for a longer stretch, until the last refrain again quickens, to end the song at M.M. $\flat$ = 138.

This unsteady increase in tempo is reinforced in that the musicians, during the performance, gradually give up any attempt to elaborate musical patterns. Every line of every refrain is followed by the same C-F-G chord change on guitar, with organ accompanying. The instrumental question varies only once: after the first "How does it feel?" in the fourth refrain, instead of its usual riff there, the organ plays descending chords that echo what it does during most of the *DDDD* lines. (Note that Al Kooper had about a month's experience as a professional keyboard player between the studio recording session and his simpler Newport '65 part.)

As the other musicians take no chances with variant riffs, so also Dylan takes no chances with harmonica, guitar, or voice. Throughout the song he does nothing out of the ordinary for spoken language—no unusual vowels, inflections, pitch changes, phrasing. For example, Dylan sings the last four lines of the last refrain identically, his raised vocal pitch on each rhyme word coinciding with the musical beat. The unadventurous vocalizing that ends the song is a fulfillment, perhaps, of the uncertainty with which it begins. In the other two concert versions, the distinctive opening instrumentation gathers audience attention with each descending set of pitches, until "Once upon a time" begins at a low point in the music. In Newport '65, the guitar introduction goes up in four steps and then down, then up, then down, then up... until Dylan begins to sing at neither a valley nor a peak, out of phase. Dylan plays only a few notes on harmonica, after each refrain. He also forgets the lyrics to the fourth stanza, which becomes:

> Ah you've gone to the steeple and all the pretty people
> Drinking thinking that they got it made

You better take your diamond ring and things, babe
You better take it down and you're gonna pawn it, babe

All that can be heard clearly are "got it made" and "pawn it, babe." Dylan's raised pitch gives some narrative clarity, but his voice mostly conveys relief at seizing a bit of familiar lyric.

The musicians make no such mistakes: they simply do the changes as fast as they gracefully can. In this version, as on *Highway 61*, the organ marks the musical structures. The bass guitar differs a great deal: for Newport '65 it not only keeps up a steady backup beat but also adds decorative riffs. After every refrain, for example, where on *Highway 61* the guitars and drum together do fast, sharp beats leading into the next stanza, in concert the bass almost alone carries lead-in beats. A bass guitar is not an exciting instrument by nature—a drumroll is exciting by nature—and yet in these breaks and elsewhere the bass is supposed to whip up excitement. Behind "chrome horse" and "shoulder" and "steal," for example, bass chords also swell.

As the song ends—with a quick instrumental wrap-up—the tape records some cheering and applause but then shouts, possibly jeers, predominating within seconds. The musicians take a long time tuning up for the next song, as they did for "Like a Rolling Stone." Then, as Dylan says "OK, let's try that one," they launch into a version of "It Takes a Lot to Laugh, It Takes a Train to Cry" (1965) that is louder and faster and screechier, with longer instrumental breaks and less possibility of understanding the words, than is the version that may already have been recorded for release in August on *Highway 61 Revisited.* As the final jam ends, without waiting for any more audience response, Dylan says clearly, "Let's go, man, that's all."

Dylan stalked or strolled off stage after this third electric song at Newport '65. Some eyewitnesses claim tears in his eyes. Most accounts, including those by Dylan and Kooper, deny the tears. When Dylan comes back on the tape, he is singing alone with acoustic guitar "It's All Over Now, Baby Blue" (1965). And then—a performer in action—he charms his audience: "Has anybody got an E harmonica? E harmonica? Anybody? Pass 'em on up here." And with the borrowed harmonica and his acoustic guitar he launches into a rendering of "Mr. Tambourine Man" (1964) that is note for note, pause for pause, inflection for inflection, eerily identical to that released on *Bringing It All Back Home*—except that in concert no electric guitar skips around on high, plucked pitches behind the acoustic one, dancing like the tambourine man. The audience goes wild.

In discussing "Just Like a Woman," I suggested that the two versions portray two narrators with different attitudes—regretful in 1966, gleefully sadistic in 1974. Can the same be said for effects of these four performances of "Like a Rolling Stone," whatever their causes? I think not. Even in 1974, the effect of a narrator more triumphant than on *Highway 61* is less clear than is a listener's own direct interaction with the band, the merger of musicians and mass audience into a community whose members all do know how it feels. Individual involvement, individual identification with the unnamed "I" who lashes out at forty-four "you"s, is essential to the song's meaning, essential to the anthem of a generation. Similarly, a listener to Newport '65 hears a tentative band, not a tentative narrator confronting a thereby-more-powerful Miss Lonely. A listener to Manchester '66 is herself insulted, not drawn into a narrator's berating Miss Lonely for stupidity along with all her other shortcomings.

In my mind the distinction between the two, "Just Like a Woman" as malleable artifact and "Like a Rolling Stone" as malleable part of my consciousness, is quite clear. I know and like both, but "Like a Rolling Stone" draws me into it in a way that "Just Like a Woman" does not. Why? I have already suggested that the absence of any first-person pronouns sucks the listener into the song, in a effect that could be termed "the vacuum of his 'I's." I have suggested, too, that the song's "you" gets thoroughly conquered in both sense and sound. A listener is not left squirming among variously unresolved binary oppositions, as in "Just Like a Woman," forced to apply the barbs to herself or to someone else. Instead, she eases out of the song contented that good guys have beaten bad guys, cowboys have beaten Indians, we have beaten the grown-ups who forced us into fine dresses and schools—but still she has the hope, as words and music cooperate to ask the same question, that we'll all live happily ever after besides, Lady and the Tramp, with half the puppies mongrel but the rest still somehow pure cocker spaniel.

The song's resolution presents, after all, a nice white middle-class attitude toward class conflict. Give them a little education and a little watermelon, and then take what you need but leave the rest of their culture. Borrow a few guitar licks, just enough to sass the authorities we know we'll someday become. It's quite an anthem.

After Newport '65, in large part because of Dylan's move to electric guitar, the "folksong revival" broke ranks.[19] The old guard held out for white rural traditional music as the only "pure" folk music. Others left *Sing Out!* to start *Rolling Stone*, the articulate advocate of young white musicians making lots of money by adapting black urban folk music for an educated audience privileged to pick and choose their level of diction and to feel self-righteous through it all. But Dylan again had already moved on.

Hey! Mr. Tambourine Man, play a song for me
In the jingle jangle morning I'll come following you
                    —"Mr. Tambourine Man," 1964

V

Effects

How many singers feel the same way ten years later that they felt when they wrote the song? Wait till it gets to be 20 years, you know?... And a lot of my songs.... don't work so good as the years go on. A lot of them do work. With those, there's some truth about every one of them.[1]

Until the fifties, when recording studios began setting up elsewhere than New York City, most singers always interacted with live audiences, for little or no money. Before that, metropolitan record companies and academic folklorists played approximately equal roles in preserving performances by folk singers.

Record companies had the edge: they trucked the latest sound recording equipment along bad mountain roads to set up sessions in hotel rooms or storefront offices—as in Bristol, Tennessee, August 1927, when the Victor Talking Machine Company cut records for both the Carter Family and Jimmie Rodgers, the "Singing Brakeman." Record companies, furthermore, paid the singers. Folklorists more often listened in kitchens and porches, recording words and melody only on paper—or, if electricity was available, on probably outmoded recording equipment. The American Archive of Folk Song at the Library of Congress, for example, first got congressional funds to buy recording apparatus in 1937, after nine years of borrowing equipment from the Rockefeller and other foundations.

At first, radio stations and record companies went their separate ways, competing for an audience—until TV was invented. Radio usually broadcast live music, news, sports, and drama until a rather abrupt changeover in the early fifties to using most air time to play records. And just as abruptly came payola, culminating in the infamous disk jockey convention in Miami in 1959, as record companies bribed DJs to convince radio audiences that particular records were popular and therefore worth buying. The resulting congressional investigations led radio stations to adopt the Top Forty format—that is, to play records that sales charts had proven already popular.

Into this technological ferment, in the early sixties, leapt the Beatles, whose albums and singles sold in unprecedented numbers. During the entire first six months of 1964, Beatles songs held as many as five of the Top Ten slots—a feat unapproached by recording artists before or since in the ever-changing industry dynamics of live concerts, album sales, singles sales, radio air play, cassette tape recorders, and whatever technologies next appear.

During the months of extreme Beatlemania, Dylan composed "It Ain't Me, Babe," the first of his major nonlove songs. He recorded its album *Another Side of Bob Dylan* in June 1964, at which time his producer, Tom Wilson, told an interviewer that "it's all to be stuff he's written in the last couple of months."[2] The Beatles had until then sung simple love-song lyrics in adapted gospel style; Dylan, adapting blues style, exactly reversed the sentiments. "She loves you, yeah, yeah, yeah," they sang, and he sang, "No, no, no, it ain't me, Babe."

This is one of Dylan's songs that *does* work, ten and even more years later. Its title alone functions as a slogan or proverb, even in situations quite unlike that in the song's lyrics, wherein male rejects female. For example, in the mid-seventies, San Francisco feminists put out a newspaper called *It Ain't Me Babe*. The song itself has been recorded ("covered") by other artists very frequently and is still popular among street singers (especially in London).[3] In a survey of four performances by Dylan and two cover versions, spread over the decade 1964-1975, I will be suggesting what about the song allows it to survive, to be interpreted with different artistic effects in shifting social contexts.

In words on paper, the male narrator of "It Ain't Me, Babe" thoroughly rejects the romantic expectations of a woman who stands, at night, outside his bedroom window. His address to her is rich in personal pronouns (plus the indefinite "it" and "someone") and rich also in negative terms, assonance and consonance, long vowels, and phrases in binary opposition. The text varies only slightly throughout the six performances, as shown in Appendix A.

As Dylan's 1964 performance, live in the studio, the song can encourage each listener to take the chances needed to reject what must be rejected in her own life. In a 1964 duet by Dylan and Joan Baez, the same set of lyrics produced a happy love song. In 1965, a Los Angeles group called the Turtles performed an upbeat, simplified version that does the rejecting for the listener, letting her enjoy the sensation without feeling compelled to change her own life. By 1974, then, according to Bryan Ferry's performance, to end a relationship by declaring "It ain't me, Babe" had become a formularized social ritual. But that same year, on concert tour, Dylan and the Band shouted out the song as community celebration. And a year later, in Boston, Dylan and the Rolling Thunder Review clowned around as they turned the same set of lyrics into a lackadaisical denial of responsibility for anybody's hurt.

Even during one decade, this song has expressed very different artistic impulses and intentions. Many Child ballads (until recently the only oral literature deemed worthy of study by the paper-bound literary establishment) have lasted two or three centuries, usually with extensive textual variations. Now folklorist Tristram P. Coffin was being pretty radical, in the 1950s, when he proposed that traditional ballads be regarded aesthetically as songs, not poems, and that a ballad's "emotional core" is what matters to singers and audiences: "melody, setting, character, and plot are used only as means by which to get [this emotional core] across."[4] Advancing technology now helps demonstrate just how shifting such an emotional core can be; it seems that the performance that a silent reader of a text hears inside her head is only one among its many possible variants. Instead of assuming that the text as read silently somehow has primacy, we should analyze it to see what on the page might allow flexibility in performance. Texts, whether intended for recitation or dramatic action or song, are all we've got left of any performances of anything before Edison invented the talking machine. Analyzing texts for potential flexibility will lead to aesthetic considerations—to understanding why some authors' works survive the centuries whereas others' don't.

Dylan composed "It Ain't Me, Babe" under particular sociohistorical conditions, at a time when he and his listeners had a lot of rejecting to do. In his earlier songs, from 1963, male narrators had rejected women (but somewhat regretfully, as in "Don't Think Twice, It's All Right"), and women had rejected men (but lightheartedly, as in "Gypsy Lou"). In subject matter, the closest precedent to Dylan's first major nonlove song is his unreleased "Hero Blues":

> Yes the gal I got
> I swear she's the screaming end
> She wants me to be a hero

So she can tell all her friends
Well, she begged, she cried
She pleaded with me all last night
Well, she begged, she cried
She pleaded with me all last night
She wants me to go out and find somebody to fight
She reads too many books
She got new movies inside her head
She reads too many books
She got movies inside her head
She wants me to walk out running
She wants me to crawl back dead
You need a different kinda man, babe...

The images and repetitions of "It Ain't Me, Babe" flow more smoothly than here. More noticeably, "Hero Blues" is in twelve-bar blues, a style and structure still unfamiliar to Dylan's 1964 audience. For "It Ain't Me, Babe," instead, Dylan leaves his listeners firmly anchored in the verse-and-refrain structure of most white popular music (including early Beatles) while he whirls the sense of the lyrics 180°, to "No, no, no."

As published in sheet music—a condition analogous to that of folksongs collected only on paper—"It Ain't Me, Babe" has three three-part stanzas, each with a three-line refrain. Each stanza's first segment, beginning "Go," rhymes *ABCB* and is backed by major chords. In each *AB* couplet the narrator commands Babe; in each *CB* he says what "I'm not." Then the guitar shifts to minor chords as the narrator shifts back to second-person pronouns to paraphrase what "You say you're looking for" in couplets rhymed *DEFE*. The guitar changes back to major chords for each final segment: a closing verse line *G* and then the refrain, in which the lead pronoun is "it." Within stanzas, the longest instrumental breaks follow the *B* lines.

In none of the six performances I analyze does anyone sing the exact melody as published for the *ABCB* and *DEFE* segments. (And far be it from me to do what musicologists have never done, to attach discursive meaning to melodic variations.) For the last verse line and refrain, however, all six do have much the same sung melody. The tune of the refrain, then, is one of the few nontextual attributes that remain constant from performance to performance—whatever the various emotional implications.

On paper the song's three *G* lines rhyme across stanzas, door/more/more, and also stand out from the rest of the melody as published. Most of the song falls within the vocal range of a fifth, its high and low notes defined by the drop from "me" to "Babe" that ends two lines of the refrain. Most sung lines go gently up, then down, then up, then down in melodic profile— all except each *G* line, which is mostly level, on a note one pitch higher than any before, until its last sung word, which climbs yet another pitch. The *G* end-rhymes thus occur on a higher pitch than anything in the song except for the first "No" in the refrain: after "me, Babe" drops a fifth, that "No" leaps to one pitch above "Babe."

Set apart by melody and interstanzaic rhyme, the three *G* lines interact with one another. The first names a participant in one of the more pointless sex-role rituals, the "Someone" who opens doors for her. But by nonlinear association with the "and more" that follows death in the second *G* line and with the "nothing more" that follows "life" in the last *G* line, "door" can seem a positive term, an escape route. There is more beyond dying, more beyond "a lover for your life," more beyond his window ledge, more beyond the door.

The higher pitch that links these images of life, death, and escape to each other also links them with the "No, no, no" of the refrains. The raised pitch of each *G* rhyme word can suggest hopefulness; then, after only a brief drop in melody for the statement "It ain't me, Babe," the highest pitch in the song could make "no" as positive sounding as are "more" and "door," and even more certain. In addition, the triple "no" concentrates the three negative refrain lines and the three stanzas of the song, each reiterating the others.

The lines of refrain build on each other's statements, their threefold incremental repetition suggesting, and expanding on, the twice-repeated line characteristic of twelve-bar-blues structure. Twofold incremental repetition, elsewhere, also echoes blues structure: "I'm not the one you want, Babe/ I'm not the one you need" in the first stanza; in the second, "Go lightly from the ledge… on the ground" and "Someone to close his eyes… heart." As in "Oxford Town," this pattern suggests black tradition without actually reproducing it. A listener nestles in familiar three-stanza strophic structure, waiting securely for the refrain to come back around on the guitar.

Other repetitions, besides the entire refrain, link stanza to stanza of text. Every *D* line, at the change to minor chords, is "You say you're looking for someone." The *or* sound of this "you're" and "for" gets picked up in the *G*-line rhymes (door/more/more) and in the "for, Babe" that ends every refrain. "Babe" appears outside the refrains too, linked by assonance with the repeated "You say" of *D* lines and "ain't" of refrains. Squished between "ain't" and "Babe," in every line of refrain, is the narrator's "me," its long *e* assonating with the speed/need rhyme that opens the song. And the *oh* of "No, no, no" rhymes with the very first word in each stanza, "Go."

Thus the central refrain line, "No no no, it ain't me, Babe," contains three of the five (orthographic) long-vowel sounds of English: *oh, oh, oh, ay, ee, ay*. What of long *i* and long *yew*, to complete the set? Named throughout, and by implication present in this line, are the "I" that is the narrator and the "you" that is Babe.

A typical listener to this song, of either gender, would identify with the narrator "I" rather than the rejected "you"—in various ways, depending on performance. In Dylan's 1964 studio version, I will show, a listener can interact with the song by joining "I" to drive out all the definite "you"s and indefinite "it"s that want her to be what she ain't. I had listened to that album cut hundreds, perhaps thousands, of times before the 1973 publication of *Writings and Drawings*. I can recall my surprise at seeing the lyrics printed for the first time: I had never thought of a male narrator and a female Babe. I knew all the lines and could probably have combined them in the order Dylan sang them, and I knew what the song meant—for sure I knew what it meant. And what looks on the page like an "emotional core" had almost nothing to do with what it meant.

The overall opposition throughout the text, between "I" and "you," is not resolved. The song ends with her still looking for that special someone despite the narrator's strong implications that she never will find any such "lover for your life." Stanza by stanza, the narrator on paper becomes less self-confident. In the first stanza, his *CB* statements of what "I'm not" are definite; also, by paraphrasing what "You say" into mutually exclusive pairs, he makes her expectations seem just plain unreasonable. The second-stanza paraphrase (*DEFE* segment) involves more complex oppositions, ones not impossible to the rational mind, and the third stanza simply lists her expectations, unpaired, hinting at childishness more than at Hollywood-romantic love.

The most notable binary irresolution apparent in the text involves syntactic structures that nudge two words into apparent polarity, regardless of their exact discursive meaning. The first such pair is "want" and "need." The song opens with the narrator's command to Babe: he tells her to go off on her own, make her own choice. As he shifts to say what "I'm not," then, the negative sound assonates particularly with "one you want," which in turn will reverberate with the frequent "someone" that she will not find, by phonetic implication, no matter how much she looks.

Incremental repetition here shoves "want" and "need" into opposition.

The sense implied by polarity resembles that in Dylan's line "Your debutante just knows what you need/But I know what you want" ("Memphis Blues Again," 1966), wherein needing suggests weakness and wanting suggests strength. And appropriately, backed by ominous minor chords, the next image in this first stanza forms a double opposition, "never weak but always strong," rhymed with the clearly polarized "right or wrong."

Because aural understanding is nonlinear, "want" and "need" seem mutually exclusive not only because of incremental repetition but also because they are juxtaposed to unmistakably oppositional pairs—sucked into their magnetic field, as it were. The same goes for the phrase "protect you and defend you," sandwiched in between the weak/strong and right/wrong images. The two verbs take on passive/active overtones, "protect" seeming a covering gesture and "defend" a striking out. Babe's expectation that she be both protected and defended seems as irrational as does her need for acceptance whether right or wrong.

Two more word pairs, in the second stanza, likewise seem oppositional by association with right/wrong and weak/strong and by incremental repetition: "Go lightly from the ledge, Babe/Go lightly on the ground" and "Someone to close his eyes for you/Someone to close his heart." The implied (and prepositional) contrast between "ledge" and "ground" makes the ledge seem precarious; the ground, farther from the narrator's bedroom, seems safe and solid. He again says, "I'm not the one you want, Babe," leaving her the stronger of the verb pair want/need. Instead of repeating his denial, though, he explains, "I'll only let you down," in an apology of sorts.

"Let you down," on the page, holds in tension two possible meanings—one metaphorical, the other literal. The narrator will let Babe down emotionally, by not fulfilling her expectations. But she has just been let down physically as well, from precarious ledge to solid ground.

A similar ambiguity occurs in the paired images, next, of "close his eyes" and "close his heart." Eye closing can be a literal, physical action; heart closing cannot. Furthermore, each phrase itself has two unresolved metaphorical implications. "Close his eyes for you" suggests a movie-star kiss, ethereal unsullied romance; the phrase equally suggests some wrongdoing of hers to which he should close his eyes. "Close his heart" remains even more dichotomized. Babe expects "Someone" to take her into his heart, closing it afterward to anyone else. But instead that someone's heart might well have closed to exclude her beforehand.

As the third stanza opens, unresolved tensions between literal and metaphorical implications of words become even more elaborate. Paired terms now overlap couplets. "Go melt back into the night," he first tells her—back with those nonrational powers of darkness, where she belongs. "Everything inside is made of stone," he goes on, "There's nothing in here moving." "Everything" and "nothing" seem to refer to the same "inside." Yet "made of stone" cannot refer literally to his bedroom—if everything inside it were made of stone, there would be no room at all—and so must refer to the narrator's metaphorical heart, his stony emotions. Because of the house walls in a listener's awareness, "stone" here is a metaphor straining toward, but being denied, physicality. Similarly, "nothing in here moving" wants to refer literally to the narrator's ever-present room, not to his romantic heart. Yet the next line, "anyway I'm not alone," makes remote the possibility that all is literally motionless inside his bedroom tonight. Again Dylan infuses new life into a cliché, in both imagery and the neatness with which "not alone" echoes the sounds of "No no no."

As the guitar again changes to ominous minor chords, in this third stanza, the narrator abandons his increasingly convoluted attempts to reason her out of romantic infatuation. Dialectical logic may help ward off hard rain, but it won't stop Babe. The someone of her final *DEFE* expectations would treat her like a child with skinned knees—and it wasn't so irrational, in those baby days, for someone to come comfort any of us. The final verse line, *G*, then gives "someone" the title "lover" and puts a limit not on his life (as in the parallel line of the second stanza) but on hers. And the refrain rejects her one more time—"Very brightly," says the sheet music.

In a few phrases, the printed text can be interpreted to suggest that the narrator may reject her for her own good. He tells her to choose her own speed; the ground seems more solid than his window ledge; he gives up on pure reason and allows some leeway for female images of darkness and childhood. A singer is under no obligation to develop these hints about the potential for strength in Babe; and among my six performances, only Dylan in the studio version does so.

The studio-version narrator demonstrates how to make it on your own. In this 1964 performance, Dylan's acoustic guitar marks regular measures, varying only slightly in volume and tempo. Between sung stanzas, he plays four to twelve measures in his distinctive harmonica style. The harmonica figure after the first stanza precisely imitates the sung phrase "looking for." After the second stanza, it sounds less like a voice but remains within the vocal range and melodic profile established. Finally, the harmonica closes the song with leaps in pitch, including a sustained high note just before the closing slight drop. Thus the entire performance, like each *G* line within it, leaves the listener at a high pitch of anticipation, not finality. The song need not be over; each listener can resolve in her own way the ominous sentiments expressed by the minor chords of Babe's romantic expectations. A listener is aided by the harmonica's gradual progression from voicelike inflections to its decidedly instrumental effects, leading her step by step away from culture-bound dependency on words.

During each sung stanza, however, the interaction of voice and guitar creates quite an opposite effect: a listener focuses attention on the words, for the voice is refusing to cooperate with the regular beat being encouraged by the guitar. Almost every sung line of the 1964 studio version begins before or after the accented beat of its measure. From the very beginning, from "Go away from" tucked in between two accented beats, Dylan's voice defies the guitar just enough to carry the listener along with the voice. Each sung line is a small adventure: the voice acts just a little differently from what musical regularity would lead the listener to expect. Furthermore, by such defiance, the voice gets what it wants: the listener's attention.

Throughout this performance Dylan's vocal inflections are speechlike and regular. The most noticeable manipulation of pronunciation is a tendency toward vowel reduplication in each *Nee-oh, nee-oh, nee-oh*. He articulates without slurring, as in the carefully pronounced *ing*s of "nothing in here moving." He seldom shifts pitches midword or bends, stretches, and truncates words as he does in other versions of it and in other songs on this album, such as "All I Really Want to Do."[5] Because a listener to this song in its immediate artistic context, its album, knows to what extent Dylan's voice could be choosing to defy conventional vocal limitations, she can more easily believe what the soothing voice implies: no matter how temptingly regular and secure your culturally expected roles may seem, you, the listener, can do just fine on your own, off the beats, away from the window, melted into the night. Be a little offbeat. I'll show you how.

In the 1964 concert version, Dylan and Joan Baez also keep a very regular beat going on their acoustic guitars. But the relationship of regular rhythm to sense of lyrics here differs extremely: this performance contradicts the text's rejection of sex-role stereotypes. Dylan and Baez perform in a romantic duet, with his voice strongly leading and hers meekly agreeing.

Now, Joan Baez does not have a weak or meekly agreeable voice. Her powerful soprano can be heard, often louder than Dylan's voice, in other duets they sing this Halloween night, 1964, at Philharmonic Hall in New York. One of her most dramatic vocal techniques is a pure vibrato, which Baez pitches a third or fifth above Dylan's voice. In the song just before "It

Ain't Me, Babe" on tape, "With God on Our Side" (1963), she sings vibrato at least once and often twice in every line. But throughout "It Ain't Me, Babe" she usually sings in unison with Dylan; when she does harmonize, she only occasionally produces a very soft vibrato (on the word "strong" in the fifth stanza, and in the last stanza on "nothing," "anyway," "fall," and "call"). None of these vibratos sounds self-confident: a female voice is allowing a stronger male one to lead her, protect her and defend her, pick her up every time she falls. She is in little danger of falling or being threatened in any way by irregularity, though, for his voice aligns exactly with the accented beats on the guitar.

Partly because the female voice seems here to have chosen this subordinate role and might therefore choose others, however, the duet does not sound sappily romantic. "It Ain't Me, Babe" becomes, instead, a playful and teasing love song. Dylan chuckles from time to time during the guitar lead-in and the singing; once, on the word "heart" in the second stanza, Baez almost laughs in response. After the third stanza, without even a breath break, they repeat the refrain; Dylan disrupts this potential intensity with a giggle after "No no no." The quickness and neatness with which they both shift to the additional refrain, both eliminating the "But" from "But it ain't me, Babe," makes the two voices seem a mutually responsive, happy couple at the end just as at the beginning.

Besides dropping "But," Dylan and Baez make other small changes in the lyrics (bracketed in Appendix A). Their second stanza, for example, begins "Go lightly from the ledge, Babe/Go lightly from the ground." That last phrase, replacing "on the ground," confounds the contrast between precarious ledge and solid ground; going "lightly from the ground" suggests an angelic gait, Babe bouncing effortlessly off into the night.

Very seldom can such slight textual variations, or even rather drastic ones, be interpreted to predict changes in performed meaning, however. The Turtles' elimination of an entire stanza helps simplify the sentiments expressed in their version; in the Rolling Thunder Review version, likewise, the interjected comment "Must be someone else!" adds to the shoulder-shrugging casualness. But such implications become clear only when one works backward from a known performance. To go the other way, from the dozens of collected textual variants of a folksong to implied performance styles and meanings, would be a shaky matter indeed.

So, the slight textual changes for the 1964 concert have almost no impact on its overall effect, that of a cheerful romantic duet with two guitars to mark the regular beat. The tempo is a bit slower than in the studio version, which, on a metronome, measures M.M. ♩ = 138, as compared to this M.M. ♩ = 132. Dylan and Baez speed up the instrumentally defined tempo together, during the final repeated refrain, again suggesting cooperative understanding: guitar/guitar coordination, like voice/voice and voices/guitars, stays all on the beat. Dylan plays harmonica after each stanza, but differently than in the studio: each figure features a simple high pitch, then low, then high, then low. It imitates the melodic profile of sung lines but makes no demands that a listener come to understand the harmonica for its own instrumental sake. In this way, too, this performance fulfills rather than challenges cultural expectations. Two voices, two guitars, and harmonica: all keep to the regular beat.

The beat becomes overwhelming in the Turtles' performance of this song. The tempo is fast, M.M. ♩ = 160. A bass and tambourine regularly, unmistakably mark measures. All variations in line length are eliminated. For example, instead of expanding the refrain from a three-measure line to three and a half to six (as on the sheet music), the Turtles make each refrain line three measures backed by six strong beats. They eliminate the entire third stanza, instead closing the song with "No, it ain't me you're looking for, Babe" and then "I said-a no, no, no, it ain't me, Babe," repeated five times and fading.

The regularity makes their performance easy to describe. During both *ABCB* segments, the tambourine is struck eight times per line; the lead singer vocalizes alone, rather softly. For both *DEFEG* segments the bass, plucked twice each time, marks eight beats alternately with the eight strong beats that the tambourine continues to mark. The lead vocalist sings more loudly than before; the other musicians harmonize, singing "a-a-ah" four times in each eight-measure line.

During the first refrain, the lead vocalist sings more loudly still and more harshly. The other singers exactly double their time, singing "a-a-ah" three times per three-measure line. The tambourine likewise doubles its time and thus merges with the bass so that both mark six beats per line. After the words of the first refrain end, the bass and tambourine continue loudly and double time for three more measures, then more softly return to former eight-times-per-line roles. During this clearly separated instrumental break between stanzas, the drum and lead guitar carefully fill the spaces between tambourine strokes with simple, repeated chord changes. Just before the vocalist begins the second stanza, the lead guitar plays the same figure that had opened the song. The second verse goes the same as the first. The second refrain differs somewhat: the instrumentation goes into the same double time, but the background vocalists do not go "a-a-ah." The tambourine stays loud and double time for the six extra sung lines, and fades along with the singer.

This performance carries a listener twice through three distinct steps, something like (1) statement, (2) intensity and complication, (3) rejection. The repetition of the three-part series itself, and the repetition over and over of the "no no no" lines, makes rejection seem inevitable, final. Instrumentation, voice, and the most obvious sense of the lyrics all carry the same message. The narrator seems cool, polished, certain that complete rejection is the solution, untroubled by regret or sympathy for Babe. The text alone would not express his glee, however, nor the way in which the unavoidable instrumental beat makes it even easier for a listener to join the narrator in carefree rejection. A listener hears the repeated lines but need not think about the sense of the lyrics nor about possible changes in her own attitudes. The beat goes on until the song fades away, complete unto itself.

The regularity of the beat matters also in Bryan Ferry's 1974 studio performance: its beat forms the white canvas behind a Jackson Pollock of sound run riot—but controlled riot. The tempo is very slow, M.M. $\mathbf{d}$ = 92-96. Remarkably various instruments appear and disappear, sometimes on but more often off what would be the accented beat in a measure. The vocalist, utterly bored, pronounces the familiar formula of words appropriate to this particular social ritual, the rejection of romance.

Amid the elaborate instrumentation occur brass fanfares—the organ imitating brass fanfares, actually, and at the opening the organ imitating a piano imitating brass. Partly because of these effects, this version calls up the image of a king efficiently conducting state business: he calms noble disputing noble, nation disputing nation, organ disputing guitar but with tense, unorganlike and unguitarlike sounds. At last this king notices a peasant woman who has been there all along, crying that she still loves him. He assigns her a child-support payment of £100 per annum. No, make that £95 and a royal apology for the heartbreak.

Other cuts on this same album show that Ferry's voice can express many moods other than acute ennui (though every mood seems at least tinged with sarcasm) and that his instrumentation, while always complex, need not produce this performance's effect of offbeat chaos kept barely under control. The instruments in other cuts at least agree on whether keyboard or guitar is to play the lead, but in "It Ain't Me, Babe" they never quite settle the issue. This cut also features many special effects on not-quite-identifiable instruments: there are arbitrarily placed plucks on what sounds like an amplified dulcimer but is probably a guitar string, in the first stanza, and also a "plonk" effect, probably a single organ key.

Ferry's organ in another guise—that of a not-so-resonating piano playing a trumpet fanfare—opens the song. Alone and dignified, it plays a chord twice, then takes a brief step upward to play a higher chord twice. It descends three solemn steps, then, but is interrupted by two sharp drumbeats and then Ferry's slow, deliberate, carefully articulating voice.

During the first *ABCB* segment, measures are marked by a very soft tambourine or cymbals and brush beat on the drums. The dulcimerlike pluck begins, but not yet loud or conspicuously offbeat. A brief organ upbeat leads into the first *DEFE* segment. The "plonk" effect starts in, apparently ready to replace the tambourine in marking measures. But after one line the "plonk" shifts offbeat, falling behind "always" instead of "strong." And a conflict begins between "plonk" and the plucked sound—no cat fight this, but a series of teeth-gritting declarations of the right to land as offbeat as I please, even on the same offbeat moment as you.

These two sounds cease before the refrain begins, as Ferry's voice deigns to express a slight vibrato on the high-pitched "door" that stretches without break into a very careful articulation of the words in the oh-so-familiar refrain, undistracted by instrumentation. Only in the refrains does Ferry sing the published melody. Drum rolls follow and finalize each "But it ain't me, Babe." The second line of each refrain has a soft fanfare ascending stepwise after "No no no" and a louder "brass" flourish at the end. The first and second refrains end in similar performances, the line phrased such that an added "that" increases the self-centeredness of the narrator. While the organ plays three descending "brass" flourishes, Ferry phrases, "It ain't... me... that you're looking for." Two of the fanfares surround "me"; the rest of the sentence is crammed together within the third. The organ descends stepwise, then, to lead directly into the next stanza.

The second stanza calms down. Offbeat plucks reappear, but they are not as loud and defiant, nor do they jostle other instruments. The organ plays organlike chords. Drum brushes keep the beat, whereas before they muffled it. A drumroll marks the transition from *ABCB* to *DEFE*. Ferry sings "You say you're looking for someone" with a break after "look" and a two-syllable, rising "ing." He does the same on the parallel line in the first and last stanzas, amid distractions from surrounding instrumentation, but his inflection can be heard far more clearly in this middle stanza.

In the last stanza, Ferry sings "stone" in a vibrato (the nature of stone to the contrary) and its rhyme word "alone" on a descending slide. He also stretches the word "time" in both *E* lines, doubling its diphthong onto two rising pitches, and his voice rises and falls within "fall" and "call." But the first two of these vocalizations, in particular, get buried behind elaborate instrumentation—for in this final stanza, at last, the organ does what it wants.

The organ echoes its stairstep descent from the second refrain with a quicker descent after the *A* line. Then it takes off, playing separate notes behind and between lines, quite scorning the beat—notes that go up and down a bit but usually up, higher and higher to peak behind "I'm not," then to descend behind "alone," forcing Ferry's otherwise imperturbable voice to descend with them. His organ playing finally breaks through his voice's cool, momentarily, but it does so by highlighting "I'm not," an expression that is both self-centered (like each refrain's "me") and also negative, like the "No no no" that every version of this song in some way makes central.

The emotion-piercing organ has done its work, though. This narrator is forced to admit that the words he is uttering are not an empty, ritualistic formula, not a Pledge of Allegiance or Hail Mary. Words have meaning; they affect the woman in the song. Ferry alters the song's last line into a gentler, less self-centered statement than in the two earlier refrains. The three "brass" fanfares are softer. Ferry phrases the line so that "me" is backed by only one of the three; "looking" goes with the second, and "for, Babe" has the third. Thus Babe finally gets some recognition, a bit of the fanfare, even though the closing organ riff recalls the opening one and thereby leaves the narrator fully in charge of all fanfares and other instrumental effects.

To go from Ferry's performance to Dylan's 1974 version is to go from molasses to red-hot pepper. Dylan's 1974 version actually moves slightly more slowly than in the studio, about M.M. ♩ = 120-32 as compared to M.M. ♩ = 138. But it seems much faster because of, as elsewhere in this L. A. concert, greater rhythmic density. The percussion marks at least two strong beats per measure, often quickening to drumrolls toward ends of musical lines. Percussion also defines the song's structure, adding cymbals after the *ABCB* segment of each stanza. Instrumentation has as much to say as do words in this version. Binary irresolutions of the text are affected by binary irresolutions in performance—between voice and instrumentation, or between two instruments doing gymnastic stunts during the extensive wordless musical spaces. Except in refrains, each line of words is followed by four or more accented beats of instruments alone. As in the 1974 "Like a Rolling Stone," recorded the day before, the Band does a tight performance. Each musician is aware of the others; voices, guitars, percussion, and keyboard all respond to one another's flourishes and changes. Never battling for control of a musical space, as in Ferry's version, the instruments either take turns or play together without dissension.

This cooperation becomes particularly dramatic at the song's closing. The organ, regaining instrumental dignity after some of its earlier acrobatics, coordinates tightly with the dense percussion that has structured the song. The pattern of descending organ chords concludes in a drumroll. And it seems that more than a song has proven its worth here: this closing processional seems the elated wedding vows of organ and drum, of European religious ritual music and African religious ritual music, of white and black culture combined in rock music to overthrow political oppression at this moment of Watergate-era euphoria.

Textual variations, again, offer only shadowy hints about the nature of this performance. In retrospect, one can see that expanding refrain lines to "No, no, no, it *still* ain't me, Babe" helps this version be a shout of victory ten years after. But that "still" might have been sung in a tone of agony or grumbling; even sung in chorus, it need not mean triumph. In another textual variation, both instances of "Go" that open the second stanza become "Move." The resulting "Move lightly from the ledge.... on the ground" seems a milder command because it no longer rhymes with "No, no, no." Babe's presumed action also creates a clearer opposition with this "nothing in here moving," and possibly, though with a subtlety not noticeable during a concert, the new "Move" nudges a pun out of the new "still" since now neither narrator nor Babe stands still in the still of the night. But far more obviously, in performance, Dylan hums into and slithers over the verb "Move," creating oral onomatopoeia such that Babe moves away quite easily.

Dylan's vocal effects are particularly dramatic elsewhere, too, playing instrumentlike games on a words-to-music spectrum for this version:

> sense of lyrics
> > sound of lyrics
> > > vocal flourishes
> > > > instrumental flourishes
> > > > > rhythm (percussion)

On line-ending words stretched into instrumental breaks, his voice cavorts with organ and guitar. Sometimes all agree to reinforce the sense of the words; other times they go their separate but equally merry ways. (See Appendix C for sketch.)

In the first stanza, organ and voice tend to imitate one another's pitch contours—especially on "door," for which both swoop up and then down.

The voice alone reinforces the speed/need rhyme, sinking dramatically on both words; the organ alone does a frothy up-and-down flourish after "strong," then swoops upward in mock hopefulness after "defend you." Hopeful anticipation is also implied by the rising vocal pitch that ends "You say you're looking for someone." This repeated line is sung the same way in the second stanza—whereas the last-stanza "someone," sung on a falling pitch, tells Babe to give up hope.

Only during the refrains does Dylan sing the melody as published, as Band members join in singing. The lead guitar makes the transition to the second stanza. In its *ABCB* segment the voice, keyboard, and guitar each imitate Babe's descent from ledge to ground—to a solid-seeming *grouwound*, rounded and wide. Oral onomatopoeia is even more noticeable on the rhyme word "down," then: the guitar repeats the descending pitches of the voice, and both their descents stand in sharp contrast to the keyboard riff that has just risen in anticipation after "want, Babe."

This emphatic "down" is reversed by the next segment, *DEFE*, during which voice and guitar bound upward, especially on the closing word, "heart." "Heart" is also very unlike its rhyme word, a low, growled "part." Thus, an instrumental/vocal heart leaps in joyous anticipation, once Babe has gotten down off that ledge.

As compared to the first stanza, in the second each instrument does not reinforce the voice so much as make a separate statement of its own—albeit in agreement. For example, a voice could not do chords like those with which the organ imitates the drop after "ledge, Babe" and "ground"—but the voice is content to slide down. Because voice and instruments seem more differentiated, the effect of their reunion in the second refrain is stronger than in the first.

In the third stanza, then, voice and various instruments go separate ways, displaying less interest than before in what the text is saying. The voice and guitar do imitate "stone," with low, gloomy pitches. But the potentially gloomy meaning of its rhyme, "alone," is contradicted by the frothy, carnival atmosphere of a lengthy keyboard flourish. More softly, the organ also defies the "nothing… moving" line, with a flourish that moves a great deal, and the word "fall," for which neither the organ nor Dylan's voice falls. The lead guitar, however, does then imitate "call," shouting out separate, rising tones.

On the verge of the last refrain, all the tensions between structural segments, between organ and guitar, between voice and instruments, between text and performance remain unresolved. But again, all elements reunite in the familiar refrain. Dylan sings the song's last "for, Babe" on a high pitch, not the low one that would give the melody a feeling of resolution, and at that high pitch the lead guitar takes over from his voice. Guitar and keyboard and drums all share a measure or so; then the guitar fades as the organ descends three times in fast but carefully harmonic chords, and a sustained, low organ chord and a drumroll together close the performance.

The overall effect of this version is of interlocking and writhing sets of tensions, each unresolved as it occurs within what would be a listener's linear experience of the performance, but of the whole mass resolved all at once in that psychological loophole that allows understanding of musical performance to be nonlinear. All these oppositions, all thereby resolved, together create the triumphant feeling of the 1974 performance.

The 1975 version instead creates a lackadaisical feeling—even though its tempo is the fastest of all the versions, about M. M. d = 184. This Rolling Thunder Review narrator need not express conflicting feelings of guilt or triumph toward Babe. Babe exists only in the words, and the words have long since lost out to the music.

The instrumentation clearly shapes the performance: whole lines of words are manipulated into the structures the music demands. Percussion keeps the beat fast throughout; most measures are marked also by a high organ chord. One structural alteration is in the relative length of sung lines. In other versions, each *ABCB* line takes up only a measure or so more musical space than does each *DEFE* line. Here, each *ABCB* line takes twice as long. That is, four musical beats back up "I'm not the one that you want, Babe" and vocal pause; four beats back up "I'm not the one that you need" and longer pause; and then only four beats back up the whole of "You say you're looking for someone not weak but always strong."

As another structural distinction, in this version, each refrain begins not at the first "But it ain't me, Babe" but instead at "No, no, no," where the other Rolling Thunder Reviewers join in singing.[6] Each refrain still lasts three lines, however, because each adds a final line with sinking melodic profile—"It ain't me that you're looking for." And the melody of these refrains, again, is one of very few elements in common with the five earlier performances.

This version may strike one first as a parody of the studio version— partly because the words are made so subservient to musical structures and partly because in the opening lines the musicians laugh, clap, hoot, and whistle. Parody certainly has a place in this world; rock music has kept itself healthy, these several decades, by never taking itself seriously for too long. The Beatles' white album from 1968, as the most obvious example, parodies somebody's style in almost every (or every?) song. And from 1978 comes an elaborate album and TV "documentary," masterminded by Eric Idle and Neil Innes, that follows the developments in songwriting and performing style throughout the career of the fabulous "Rutles" themselves. Where does influence stop and parody begin? Is "It Ain't Me, Babe" a parody of "She Loves You"? And what of an identically worded song that is understood as a parody of performance style alone? For example, a bootleg tape of the Beatles' "Help" clearly parodies both early-Beatles instrumentation and Bob Dylan's voice.[7] At a case like that and not, I would say, at a borderline parody like this performance of "It Ain't Me, Babe," someone else is welcome to launch the issue.

Most textual variations in this version, predictably, force words to fit into spaces being defined by music. The last *B* line in the song, for example, adjusts its syllables to the beat, producing a sort of comic Italian accent: *And-a any-a-way I'm-a not ay-lone.* The "Go" that opens both second-stanza commands is again altered, this time to "Step lightly from the ledge." It alliterates with "someone" instead of rhyming with "No, no, no"; more noticeably, though, the *Sssssstep* allows Dylan's voice to hiss its way into the stanza. For the third-stanza *G* line, a switch from "and" to "but" shifts discursive meaning slightly: "A lover for your life but nothing more." Babe's expectation seems somewhat more reasonable: if that's all she wants, if she would be content with *only* a lover for her life... then it still ain't this particular narrator, but "Must be someone else!"

That interjection, spoken rhythmically before the very last refrain line, makes a casually performed version even more so. The song, no longer as universal, becomes one man excusing and extricating himself from one woman's expectations. But this added line is only one among many distinguishable elements that make this performance sound nonchalant.

The sound track of Dylan's film *Renaldo and Clara* features another 1975 Rolling Thunder Review performance, similar to this one in fast tempo and in vocal/instrumental structuring, but tight. Here, instead, the performance gets off to a ragged start and remains loose. Musicians take few chances with dramatic riffs; what flourishes are played remain isolated, not responded to. After "ground" in the second stanza, for instance, the lead guitar rises in pitch, creating tension with the meaning of the word and with the glockenspiel, whose tones then descend after an up-swooping vocalization of "I'm." But the effect is isolated, seeming accidental. At the parallel spot in the third stanza, "stone" is followed by three solid drumbeats that perhaps imitate stone; then, "There's nothing in here that's-a moving" is punctuated by a glockenspiel descending more softly than before but with no apparent relationship to the word "moving" or to the drumbeats before.

The lead guitar and organ do coordinate a bit, during the familiar refrains. In the second refrain, guitar predominates in the instrumental measure after the first "But it ain't me, Babe"; then, organ takes charge after "No, no, no, it ain't me, Babe." In the third refrain, they neatly reverse roles. They agree also during the entire instrumental stanza that follows the last sung one. There, the spotlight belongs to the lead guitar, as in the eight-measure introduction to the song, while the organ adds only frills.

As the instrumental stanza reaches what would be "But it ain't me, Babe" if sung, Dylan's harmonica joins for the rest of the song. Since sung refrains have begun at a chorused "No, no, no," this all-instrumental stanza with its harmonica refrain shows more respect for textual divisions than did the sung stanzas. Dylan's harmonica, as usual, mediates between vocal and instrumental effects, but here the conflict has been so one-sided that the harmonica favors the underdog text. Only occasionally does Dylan's voice itself create instrumentlike effects. In the second stanza, for instance, his rising pitch on "I'm" leads without qualms to an absolute "not the one you want." His vocal phrasing, however, leaps right out and demands listener attention. As the song opens the first two lines are phrased differently than the second two, in equal musical spaces:

> Go away... from my window
> Leave... at your own chosen speed
> I'm not the one... that you want, Babe
> I'mnottheoneyou... neeeeeed

This vocal phrasing, setting apart imperative verbs, possibly reinforces the sense of the lyrics: "Leave" is a clear command, here, and "at your own chosen speed" a hypocritical afterthought (rather than helpful advice). But interaction is rare; words are manipulated in and around the musical beat as if they had no meanings of their own. Sometimes, without relating to the discursive sense of the words, the phrasing helps set two juxtaposed lines into aural tension with one another. Most of the other lines vary in vocal phrasing. All contribute to the overall effect that words don't matter and music does.

Thus, we arrive again at the issues of subjective judgment and the limits of analysis. To me, a typical member of Dylan's mass audience, it seems that vocal phrasing affects my responses to this version, but not to Dylan's 1974 one, and that vocal inflections and pitch changes on individual words are important in 1974 but not 1975. What if I went through each performance line by line, comparing inflections in one to inflections in the other, phrasing in one to phrasing in the other, hoping to show more precisely why I perceive the relative importance of these performance variables? I could do the same with instrumental flourishes, tempo, regularity of beat, vocal/instrumental proportions, and so on. I could then line up my other four versions on a chart of such performance variables and add on the *Renaldo and Clara* version, which differs from my 1975 one mostly on the axis of tight vs. loose performance. I could get at least six early performances of the song by Dylan on bootleg tapes[8] and perhaps as many as thirty-nine more versions from the 1974 tour and fifty-three more from the Rolling Thunder Review tour, plus all the cover versions released by other singers, and I could record street singers in Berkeley and buskers in the London tube and line up all their performances as well.

I can't imagine doing all this, even with computers. But then again, before Thomas Tyrwhitt and then the industrious Victorian editors, no one could really imagine lining up all fifty-five manuscripts of *The Canterbury Tales* and computing the variants. In that long process, unfortunately, editor-critics set the trend for regarding medieval manuscripts—and other works intended for oral performance—as texts meant for silent reading, with one definable meaning per line, instead of analyzing just how the words that an author assembles can allow various interpretations of his commentary and characters in various sociohistorical contexts. Because of the editors' painstaking work, though, we can go back to decide for ourselves which textual variants are "scribal error" and which might be, in fact, the remnants of different people's interpretations of how a character would talk. Analogously, using this half-century's advances in recording technology, perhaps somebody someday will want to undertake a thorough comparison of all the performance variables in even this one song.

Must be someone else....

Now, what of aesthetics? A "scientific" comparison of versions could ignore the issue, assuming that all affect a listener equally. But in practice, as I have said, aesthetic judgment cannot be separated from listener response: one mentally tunes out what one doesn't like, instead of responding. In the next two chapters, I will investigate the bases on which performers and listeners actually make aesthetic judgments. These six versions of "It Ain't Me, Babe" suggest that the literary effectiveness of printed lyrics will be a minor consideration and that a song is not automatically good, either, if its words and the performance of them unite toward the same effect. Of all these versions, the Turtles' straightforward, gleeful rejection most nearly expresses the sense of the text, and theirs is not the most artistically effective of these six.

But then again, the Turtles' is the only version that attained the proven mass popularity of Top Ten singles charts. The same record-buying and radio-listening audience, during the same month, September 1965, also chose the studio performance of Dylan's "Like a Rolling Stone."[9] That original "Like a Rolling Stone" still seems artistically complex and satisfying; the Turtles' "It Ain't Me, Babe" seems simplistic and dated. Yet in its sociohistorical context it meant a lot to its listeners. In '65 we still needed the beat, at least some of the time.

At any rate, while developing criteria for the close analysis and aesthetics of oral performance, I will be giving mass popularity the benefit of the doubt. Commercial interests, even when they try, seldom succeed in fooling the public into listening to trash. Certainly, record companies keep puffing along behind, trying to pin down a style long enough to exploit it (witness "punk"). In the early sixties Bob Dylan, more than any other recording artist, trampled the playing field for this continuing game of fox and geese with the capitalist system. And the continuing escape of rock musicians and their audiences, as a self-defined social group that has used mass technology rather than be somehow absorbed by it, can go to show how and why other folk groups cohere and, more particularly, how music functions in that cohesion.

A slogan of the sixties addresses this very issue: "The Man can't bust our music." Ah—a proverb in oral tradition, passed face to face in tense situations? Well, no. Perhaps a line from a rock song, then, functioning like proverbial wisdom even if never spoken aloud? Well, no. Well, actually, "The Man can't bust our music" headlined an advertising campaign by Columbia Records.

> *But it's alright, ma*
> *It's life and life only*
> *— "It's Alright, Ma," 1965*

VI

Improvements

[Jonathan Cott:] What is "Idiot Wind"?
[Bob Dylan:] It's a little bit of both [anger and sentimentality] because it
uses all the textures of strict philosophy, but basically it's a shattered
philosophy that doesn't have a title, and it's driven across with will power.
Will power is what you're responding to.[1]

L ong ago D. H. Lawrence said that no one should expect an artist to interpret his own work. Dylan in interview, treading as he often does the thin line between intensity and bullshit, here proposes an analysis that I will just let pass. Perhaps he put into it will power and a shattered philosophy, but what comes out of "Idiot Wind" (1974) is an intricate musical interweave of poetic images that evoke a breakup of lovers, the Watergate cover-up, the loneliness of the road, rejection of a celebrity's heroic role, religion, home, fire, death, blindness, and Woody Guthrie—who remains a hero, still someone to follow on the road through it all.

"Idiot Wind" is a song for the mid-seventies, as Dylan and his audience pieced together what all had happened, personally and publicly and politically—a sort of post-Watergate American dreaming. "Wind Imagery and U.S. Domestic Politics: The Role of Bob Dylan," who also supplied the sixties with "Blowin' in the Wind" and then "You don't need a weatherman/To know which way the wind blows." This slogan, from "Subterranean Homesick Blues" (1965), would not have so affected its mass audience and thereby national politics had it remained "don't be bashful/ check where the wind blows," as in a document available for only "Subterranean Homesick Blues" among Dylan's songs: its rough draft, reproduced facing page 160 of his *Writings and Drawings*. (See Appendix A.) "Idiot Wind" likewise exists in an unfinished state: as a bootleg tape of a rejected studio outtake with different lyrics and a decidedly less effective performance than in the cut released on *Blood on the Tracks*.

In both cases, as I here begin to distinguish artistic improvement from artistic variation, I can adapt the vocabulary of literary criticism to say how and why lyrics improve. Then, however, combining linguistic and musicological terms with approaches developed by record reviewers in *Rolling Stone* and elsewhere, I will show how textual and other improvements go to make each song more effective aurally, not textually— even in a very word-centered song like "Idiot Wind."

No one could accuse "Subterranean Homesick Blues" of word-centeredness. At a fast tempo, with few instrumental or breath breaks, Dylan ejects images of paranoia about sickness/crime/politics/dope/money/ authority figures, images of empty futures to follow ghetto/suburban (or black/white) upbringings, and, at the last, the image of a vandalized pump. On paper the lines can be analyzed for poetic and even, briefly, narrative connections. In performance, I defy anyone to remember the lines in sequence. Dylan apparently can't; for two decades he never performed the song anywhere captured on bootleg tape.[2]

Dylan parodies this characteristic, the jumpy line sequence, in the opening shot of *Don't Look Back*, the documentary film of his 1965 British tour. As the released "Subterranean Homesick Blues" plays, and as Allen Ginsberg talks to Bob Neuwirth among trash cans in the alleyway behind, Dylan slouches before the camera to flash a series of cue cards. Most show a key word of the line being sung, with aberrations like "District Attorney" for "Orders from the D.A.," "20 dollar bills" for "Wants eleven dollar bills," "Watch it" and "Here they come" for "Look out kid, you're gonna get hit," and "Dig yourself" after "Twenty years of schooling/And they put you on the day shift." Some cards suggest what oral performance does to words: "Pawking metaws" for "Watch the parking meters," "Suckcess" for "Try to be a success," "Manwhole" for "Jump down a manhole."[3]

Thus, the lyrics of this song—excepting for a moment the slogans that end three of the stanzas—offer little to fulfill a 1965 audience's cultural expectations that words should create linear pathways toward understanding. And the music, considered alone, is by no means complex. In Madison in the sixties, we used to say that "Subterranean Homesick Blues" would be our national anthem after the revolution. A multileveled contrast, in retrospect: whereas "The Star-Spangled Banner" has often been called unsingable for anyone without the range of a professionally trained voice, nearly the whole of "Subterranean Homesick Blues" can be sung on one note, C above middle C on the published sheet music. The only phrase repeated from stanza to stanza, "Look out kid," is the only place where the melody moves more than a third away from C above middle C. "Look out kid" is backed by a D7 guitar chord, and the next-to-last couplet in each stanza by an E7 chord; otherwise, the entire song is played on A7. An A7 chord calls for a C-sharp in the vocal line, yet the score shows C natural— a clearly performed blue note.

And the most direct precedent for this style is, indeed, the talking blues. A black tradition first recorded by whites, as has happened so often, talking blues came through Chris Bouchillon in the twenties and Robert Lunn, a Grand Ole Opry star of the thirties. Woody Guthrie made the genre political, as in "Talking Dust Blues," performed in rhythmic chant to lone acoustic guitar. Dylan's first two songs, released on his otherwise traditional 1962 album, are his "Song to Woody" and a "Talking New York" blues that ends with him heading out "for western skies. So long, New York. Howdy, East Orange." For "Subterranean Homesick Blues" Dylan speeds up the chant, chops up the narrative, adds in harmonica and drums and electric guitar, and offers up a few slogans to shout while running from one city hideout to the next.

Certainly, Dylan played electric rock before 1965, even releasing the single "Mixed Up Confusion" in December 1962. It is nonetheless tempting to assign a place in cultural history to the voicelike shriek of electric guitar that opens "Subterranean Homesick Blues," the first cut on the first side of the album that is bringing back home the black urban blues. In no other cut is the electric guitar quite as demanding, and the album's second side is mostly acoustic.

"Subterranean Homesick Blues" begins with the fast acoustic guitar-and-drum riff that will continue without letup through the song. The electric shriek punctuates the rhythm; then the electric guitar sings out, continuing behind the first few vocal lines, with more melodic expressiveness than in the human voice. Then it fades almost completely until midway through the third stanza. There, separated electric-guitar tones highlight the lines "Get jailed, jump bail/Join the army if you fail"—the culmination of a ghetto kid's adolescence, parallel to the fourth-stanza image of middle-class futility, "Twenty years of schooling/And they put you on the day shift." The electric guitar reemerges during this fourth stanza, highlighting the rhyme words that now occur with increasing frequency. These separate guitar tones merge and swell behind "The pump don't work/'Cause the vandals took the handles." In the fading instrumental measures that follow, electric guitar and harmonica together play a melody of a range such that a human voice could have carried it. But Dylan's voice, throughout the song, has declined its cultural obligation to sing.

· "Subterranean Homesick Blues" shows a particularly neat spectrum for the interaction of words and music. At the far "music" end are the absolutely regular acoustic guitar and drums. At the far "words" end is the sense of the lyrics, spat out in barely coherent bursts of paranoia and futility:

> sense of words
> > sound of words (esp. rhyme)
> > > vocal effects (esp. voice-forced rhyme)
> > > > harmonica and electric guitar
> > > > > rhythm instruments

Each term in the spectrum mediates between the effects of its more wordlike and its more musiclike neighbors; each element within itself has musiclike and wordlike traits. Furthermore, the performance exactly reverses cultural expectations concerning the proper roles of words and music. Music should be emotive; words should structure perceptions toward linear understanding. But here, already fragmentary words gradually lose control further to forced rhymes; by the last sung stanza, word sound has far more effect than word sense. And then electric guitar and harmonica finish the song in harmony, quite ignoring the voice that has chanted all those words in vain.

The mediating role of Dylan's voice is particularly apparent. Confined to a monotone, with no time for pitch changes, slides, stretches, growls, sneers, or reduplications, his voice shows some respect for the sense of the lyrics. He articulates very quickly but carefully. Not until the last stanza does he slur words much, such that "Don't steal, don't lift," for instance, sounds like *only only*. The couplet that follows, "Twenty years of schooling/ And they put you on the day shift," is clearly articulated like the stanza-ending slogans. A listener, straining to understand, focuses on the choppy, fast-rhyming words such that each clearly pronounced slogan stands out, demanding to be remembered and, perhaps, acted upon before it's too late.

Another mediating element is rhyme, which even in print links together, by sound, words that differ in meaning. During the fourth stanza the already profuse rhymes become even more frequent and even less confined to the expected spots for rhyme—to wit, ends and maybe middles of lines. The closing rhyme set, manhole/candle/sandals/scandals/vandals/ handles, shows the extent to which Dylan's voice can force rhyme out of what would be assonance/consonance in print. A rhyme scheme for this song would not show the internal rhymes, and each stanza would differ. Let me list the performed rhyme sets, stanza by stanza:

1. basement/medicine/pavement/government
    laid off/bad cough/paid off
    kid/did
    when/again/friend/pen/ten

2. foot/soot/put/but
    anyway/many say/they/early May/D.A./stay away/which way
    [picking up on alleyway/basement/pavement from the first stanza]
    kid/did
    toes/no bows/those/hose/nose/clothes/know/blows

3. well/well/bell/tell/sell
    hard/hard/fired/army
    braille/jailed/bail/fail
    kid/hit
    losers/users
    cheaters/theaters/leaders/meters
    girl/whirlpool/looking/fool/follow

4. born/warm
    pants/romance/dance
    dressed/blessed/success
    gifts/lift/shift
    kid/hid
    jump/bum/gum/pump
    manhole/candle/sandals/scandals/vandals/handles

A vowel/consonant progression like girl/whirlpool/looking/ fool/follow, forced toward rhyme in performance, may suggest the narrator's control over language or else—as in "your... curse hurts but what's worse" from "Just Like a Woman"—a narrator's submission to certain sounds. In addition, as cited in reference to "Like a Rolling Stone," sociolinguistic studies suggest that an orally rhymed insult may both give extra power to an attacker, by showing control of language, and ritualize the exchange, by distancing the attacker from responsibility for hurt caused by those rhymed words.

The "Subterranean Homesick Blues" narrator carries these tendencies to an extreme. As the voice manipulates far more rhymes than the English language has, the narrator distances himself thoroughly from the song. He stands back and watches the flashes of action, perhaps from a rooftop, periodically shouting advice. But he leaves the rhymes themselves in control of the song.

A narrative "I" appears only in the second line, "I'm on the pavement." But throughout, the narrator continues to warn "you," the kid, against the "they" who lurk through the lyrics, keeping it all hid except during drug busts and the day shift. The forced rhymes put Dylan's voice in cahoots with the music end of the words-to-music spectrum, and thereby put those who issue warnings against the chaotic world of the lyrics potentially in control of it. Any government that can be forced to rhyme with "medicine" can someday be subdued.

Dylan's artistic development of these rhymes, and of other patterns that remain assonance and consonance and alliteration (such as please/please/steal, in the last stanza), appear in the rough draft of "Subterranean Homesick Blues." (See Appendix A.) This typescript shows that the song's clusters of imagery began in much the same sequence as they ended up—the man demanding money, the bust, the get-sick-get-well biography, then the get-born-keep-warm biography. The segment most shifted, from middle to opening, is the pavement/government/medicine passage. The completed song adds "basement" to these three rhymes, thus plunging the opening scene immediately underground and justifying (or inspiring) the title.

The last-stanza "Jump down a manhole" is not yet there in rough draft, nor is the suggested homeyness of "Light yourself a candle"—a closing scene reminiscent of Ralph Ellison's *Invisible Man* or Jack Kerouac's *Subterraneans*. The kid, apparently besieged, is told to "get down/drop down/make it out the back door/or else quit laying on the floor before you get your back sore." Below "floor" Dylan has typed "(closet)"; for the finished song, he has found the kid an even safer hideout, below firing range.

On the typescript, apparently as an afterthought, is the skeleton of the slogan so powerful that the Weather Underground took its name and indeed apparently lifestyle from it: "You don't need a weatherman/To know which way the wind blows" began as "don't be bashful/check where the wind blows/rain flows." It is one of three "bashful" lines, along with "don't be bashful if you see they wanna try you" and "don't be bashful but please be careful," but neither word appears in the finished song. These abstract adjectives give way to concrete visual images—carefulness becomes "Walk on your tiptoes," for example, and lack of bashfulness turns into "Don't follow leaders."

Besides abstractions, two similes disappear before the finished song: "a voice come sounding like a passenger train" and "mailman coming down the chimney like santa claus." Even their ideas are eliminated, although the two characters resurface in "On the Road Again" on this same album ("I ask you who's in the fireplace and you tell me Santa Claus.... The mailman comes in and even he's gotta take a side"). A simile tends to slow down a line and call attention to the comparison, as in "Like a Rolling Stone." The concentration of verb-centered metaphors in "Subterranean Homesick Blues," with no similes or extended comparisons of any sort, helps create the feeling of rush, of image piled on threatening image too fast for a listener to sort out but still not so overwhelming that "you" can't escape by shouting slogans, ducking underground, and controlling the threatening words with music, monotone, and mocking rhymes.

The rough draft includes several tightly rhymed lines appropriate to the paranoia and deadpan humor of "Subterranean Homesick Blues"—for instance, "it's nowhere, all bare/they just pay you fare there/t (sick) the smog/thick fog/they tell you that it's fresh air." The song could well have gone on for another stanza. But it stays at two minutes and seventeen seconds, shorter even than the three-minute standard for radio singles. The briefness of the whole performance helps create its feeling of hurry. A listener experiences threats to her money, health, dope, and freedom, and then two entire futile childhoods and adolescences climaxed by a dive back underground. The song is a two-minute dash from basement to manhole.

Some of the finished song's patterns of imagery do appear in rough draft, then; others are suggested, added, or eliminated. But there from the start are the sounds of words, their rhyme and alliteration, and also the poetic meter. Even without musical beat as reinforcement, the lines pound out very regular trochees and dactyls, reversing to anapests for "Look out kid" couplets (where voice also shifts pitch, and guitar changes chords). From the typescript we can only assume—but safely—that Dylan began from musical sound, along with meter and rhyme, and that the sense of the lyrics emerged more gradually, adapted and improved to fit the sound he heard in his mind (as quoted earlier, "the sound of the street with the sunrays.... Words don't interfere with it. They—they—punctuate it").[4]

Words, themselves besieged in this song, cling to enough textual meaning to guide listeners not only through the song but also through real life—with those four clearly articulated, sloganlike lines. "You don't need a weatherman/To know which way the wind blows" has punctuated several Modern Language Association presentations, although I have seldom heard it quoted aloud in less formal situations. "Don't follow leaders/Watch the parking meters" much resembles a traditional proverb, with its rhyme and bipartite structure (witness "Haste makes waste" and many others). But neither it nor "Twenty years of schooling..." nor the closing "pump" lines would normally be spoken out loud as proverbial advice or chanted like a slogan ("2, 4, 6, 8, organize and smash the state").

Lines from rock songs, heard over and over, need not be repeated aloud to affect a listener's behavior. And they need not make readily paraphrasable sense, certainly. Take, for example, "The pump don't work/'Cause the vandals took the handles." When I ask people for favorite Dylan lines, they frequently say this one, usually along with "But I don't know what it means or why I like it." Within the text, the line's ambiguity could be summarized as, Are the vandals us or them? If them, the line expresses despair at a ruined pump. If us, the line becomes a call to destructive action.

In this performance, I will show, rhymes and voice and instrumentation clear away the chaos set out in most of the lyrics to make this final line a threat against the system, like the earlier slogans. The enemy is us, said Pogo. So too can be the vandals, once a listener accepts that music has as much to say as do words, or more.

But in real life, outside this one performance context, a line like this one cannot, should not, be pinned to one meaning. Dylan has particular skill in creating images that can float up to articulate "What oft was *Thought*, but ne'er so well *Exprest*."[5] For example, on Picnic Point in Madison, Wisconsin, is an old pump that used to work. One morning, a bit thirsty, I came around the bend of the path to discover that the pump handle had been stolen. No mundane thought like "Who broke the pump?" had the slightest chance to enter my mind. Or again, some years later, I was hiking from Mount Tamalpais down to the Pacific Ocean. I topped the last rise and thought, "Oh no, I can't stand it" because "The beach is deserted except for some kelp," which is the worst line Bob Dylan ever wrote.[6]

The opening stanza of "Subterranean Homesick Blues," unlike the other three, ends with no slogan; its closing lines instead tell of a threat to the kid, a demand for more money than he has earned. The problem is precise. The solution has yet to be elaborated, though, and the motivation for the demand is kept well hidden. But the opening four lines, with forced end rhymes, have already set out patterns of imagery that will continue through the song.

The opening scene has political implications. "Mixing up the medicine" could also suggest a dope pusher or a mad doctor in the basement, but the immediate "government" makes Johnny also a mixer of homemade bombs, remedy for the ills of the state. These three possible identities for "Johnny" continue, merged. Medicine even becomes literal for the ghetto babyhood, in "Get sick, get well." And although neither Johnny the mixer nor the first-person thinker reappears as such, their habitats remain—basement and pavement.

In the second four lines of the first stanza, the sinister man in the trench coat suggests equally a gangster and a Bogart-style tough cop, organized crime and the state both demanding a payoff. "Badge out" suggests a cop, not necessarily an honest one. "Laid off" hints at the futility of growing up to become what "they" expect in the later two biographies. And juxtaposed to this image of unemployment, "Badge out" is understood aurally also as "bad job," for a listener need not choose one sense or the other. Continuing the medicine imagery, the trench-coated man wants to be paid off for his bad cough. Insurance compensation for job-related tuberculosis or black lung? Perhaps, out of context. But because this scene of confrontation is understood nonsequentially with the next scene, in which a man clearly demands money from the "you" he confronts, the trench-coated man seems to be blaming his disease on his hapless victim.

That victim, as the first "Look out kid" couplet makes clear, is "you," the kid. Most of the song features second-person advice to the kid, bad advice from others and good from the benevolent narrator. This narrator is not attacking "you," as in nonlove songs; instead he is warning and offering advice, such that a listener would tend to identify with the second-person kid.

The narrator first advises "you" to duck down the alleyway and look for a new friend. (Perhaps Allen Ginsberg, in the opening scene of *Don't Look Back*, is acting out this line.) But what seems a way out of the pavement world is not: the kid escapes the trench coat only to come up against a differently garbed authority figure who also wants money. A coonskin cap like his was worn by two morally ambiguous denizens of the fifties television set: Davy Crockett—a child's hero, once noble and patriotic and free, now as sinister as a gangster or cop—and senator Estes Kefauver, who was supposedly investigating organized crime in televised hearings.

The scene switches, but the paranoia remains. In a fairly straightforward narrative half-stanza, Maggie runs in to tell of a bust "they" are planning. The bust is certain, their motivation unclear: are they after dope, crime, politics? The pun on "plants in the bed" stands alone in the song. The pavement world has no place for gardens, even in the heat of early May— except for a healthy crop of parking meters. Now the narrator's advice changes. Ducking down an alleyway didn't work, so the narrator advises "you" to stick around the pavement but to make yourself inconspicuous so that "they" can't tell how strong you really are.

In this stanza the rhymes try to disguise themselves as the ordinary end rhymes of ordinary written poetry. But gradually they become conspicuous in their strained inconspicuousness. Seven of the last eight lines end in a pure *ohz* rhyme; in the final "know which way the wind blows," the rhymes also overwhelm the previous long-*a* rhyme set, which includes "they" itself. Watch the plain clothes, the rhymes advise, as well as the easier-to-spot wearers of trench coats, coonskin caps, and any uniform, even a fireman's. By the last stanza's "Don't wear sandals," "you" can learn from their miscalculations about clothing disguises. And in this windstorm, this force of nature that penetrates even the caverns of the city, it's obvious what must be done: so don't be bashful, please be careful, dig yourself, and don't think some weatherman knows more about what's happening than you do.

Dylan chants the first eight lines of each of these two stanzas, seemingly without taking a breath. Each stretch is subdivided not by pauses but by the rhymed syllables. "Look out kid" stands out because of the melody, meter, and chord change, and also because of vocal pauses before and after. The remaining eight lines return to a chant, but a lighter chant that allows breath breaks. It also allows a drop in the melody line, corresponding to the E7 chord change, so that each penultimate couplet is chanted on B instead of C above middle C.

This less dense chanting continues into the third stanza. In the half-stanza of parental advice, the rhymes begin to cluster two or more to a line, begin to take over the lyrics instead of lining up where poetic structure would expect them to stay. Dylan's voice seems to speed up—not because he is singing more words in the space of a musical line but because he is packing together more separate scenes, more active verbs that advise the kid how to live a monotonous life. These commands take the kid only a bit past adolescence in working-class life: through the "ink well" and "bell" of school, through trying hard at one job and then another, to the equally grim alternatives of jail and the army. The syntax leaves both alternatives possible, not mutually exclusive: if you fail to jump bail, you end up in both jail and the army.

This third-stanza "Look out kid" couplet is followed by a five-line ghetto street scene, intricately cross-rhymed into a whirlpool of related phonemes.

The verbs "Hanging around" and "Looking for," no longer imperative, tell what happens to six-time users and fools. "Looking for a new fool" echoes "Looking for a new friend," from the first stanza's thwarted escape attempt, and this girl is out to victimize someone, as were the men in the alleyway. But the seeker is no longer the kid, now more streetwise.

This five-line flash of cheaters, con artists, gamblers, and prostitutes suggests an alternative to the pavement world of the government—but one that evades laws and restrictions instead of setting out to destroy the authorities who decree those laws. "Don't follow leaders/Watch the parking meters," coming hard after, rejects this already tried underworld. A listener must depend not on precedents but on her own perceptions of what's wrong with authority figures and with the symbols of power they erect along every street.

As in the Beatles' later "Lovely Rita, Meter Maid," parking meters here suggest political power at its pettiest and most irritating. You may lurk underground all you want, scheming to smash the state, but you've still got to run out with a coin every hour or face the consequences. Syntax (a comma splice) keeps positive/negative implications at bay. "Don't follow leaders": that's clear advice. But what relationship is then implied between it and "watch the parking meters"? But instead? or else? and also? and also don't? Should you watch out for parking meters, which might contain hidden mikes, cameras, time bombs? Should you watch them to figure out how the enemy operates? (Time is money....) Should you watch to learn how you and others might line up, omnipresent but inconspicuous, ready to take over the pavement world before time runs out?

A listener to this stanza has an extra four beats to contemplate alternative interpretations, five instrumental measures instead of four. The harmonica plays a random insertion, as it does between other stanzas—this time accompanying the rhythm instruments for about two of the five measures. Then, the fourth stanza sets out another biography that again extends just past adolescence. Images suggest a law-abiding, middle-class upbringing with your own pediatrician, dancing lessons, birthday parties, church, and of course twenty years of schooling. This set of privileges—which to a ghetto kid might seem to promise a better life than army or jail—leads not to the sarcastically said *suck*-cess but to the entrapment of the day shift.

After the fourth-stanza "Look out kid" couplet backed by the emerging electric guitar, Dylan's voice becomes lighter and less dirgelike. The kid can control his environment, down in the manhole, by lighting a candle; likewise, the singer controls the sense of the words more and more, with forced, two-syllable rhymes. The *andle* rhymes start to become as conspicuous as were the *ohz* rhymes in the second stanza. But they have learned from the mistakes of their predecessors. They hide for a couplet behind a parody of parental nagging, "Don't wanna be a bum/You better chew gum." The rhymes have learned from their own history and learned something also from "they"—to "keep it all hid," to keep them guessing about the extent of Rhyme Power. And power it is, enough to draw the disguising *um* rhyme into the closing slogan as "pump"—now in cahoots with another and yet another *andle* rhyme. "They" thought we must have run out of *andle* rhymes by now, the closing couplet crows, but here we still all are. Underground.

In rhymes as well as structure and instrumentation, this final image suggests not despair at a ruined pump but instead a simple, practical way to prevent it from pumping out any more monotonous bursts, monotonous lines, monotonous lives. Well-meant parental advice is just as sinister as are trench-coated figures who demand payoffs and tap phones. All must be rejected. And the vandals are us.

It is startling to see how literally members of the Weather Underground seem to have been enacting this two minutes and seventeen seconds of imagery. The sociopolitical implications are unprecedented, of a nationwide audience, all of whom know—know for absolutely certain, having heard so over and over—that you don't need a weatherman to know which way the wind blows, that your sons and your daughters are beyond your command, and that there are no truths outside the gates of Eden.[7]

"Subterranean Homesick Blues" would not have embedded itself so deeply in several million consciousnesses had it featured a refrain of "Don't be bashful but please be careful." The changes that Dylan made in lyrics before finishing the song, however, fall at only one end of the words-to-music spectrum. His aesthetic intentions in creating the song certainly also include phonetic, vocal, instrumental, and rhythmic effects. More about artistic decisions and improvements, thus, can be postulated from a rejected performance than from a draft of the words alone.

The rejected studio outtake of "Idiot Wind" at first had little company.[8] Until about 1980 Dylan had recorded live in the studio, intentionally releasing cuts that are not polished performances. (An example is the laughter and "All right, take two" that opens "Bob Dylan's 115th Dream," 1965). Because he would seldom rerecord a cut, few outtakes made their way into the ever-vigilant bootleg-tape underground. From the 1962-1963 *Freewheelin'* sessions come seventeen tracks that were not used on the album. But only "Corrina, Corrina" is a rejected performance of a later released song; the rest are songs that did not appear on the album. From the 1966 *Blonde on Blonde* sessions survive six cuts performed with the Band, which does not accompany Dylan on the album. Two of these cuts are fragmentary earlier versions of released songs: "Medicine Sunday" became "Temporary Like Achilles," and "(Seems Like a) Freeze Out" became "Visions of Johanna." But not until *Blood on the Tracks* do several outtakes survive that are full length, with similar words but different sound than in the performances released instead.

In September 1974, *Blood on the Tracks* was recorded in Columbia Studios, New York City, with the musicians credited on early prints of the album. Too late to change the credits before the scheduled release date, Dylan rerecorded five of the cuts in Sound 80 Studios, Minneapolis. The four outtakes besides "Idiot Wind" are interesting in several ways. For example, in the outtake "Tangled Up in Blue," the narrator starts out as a third-person pronoun. He switches to "I" at the narrative point where his life reintersects with the woman's, after their respective periods on the road, at "She was working at a topless place, and I stopped in for a beer." In the released version the narrator is first-person from the start. And in the Rolling Thunder Review performance in the film *Renaldo and Clara*, Dylan gives the pronouns yet another twist, to tell the start of the story from the woman's viewpoint.

Of the five outtakes, though, "Idiot Wind" is the most changed in overall sound and most improved as a performance. Another version of "Idiot Wind," in the Rolling Thunder Review concert on *Hard Rain*, relates to the released studio version as a reinterpretation, not as a better or worse performance. A close comparison of these three "Idiot Wind" performances—the released studio version, a released concert version, and a rejected studio outtake version—should bring us a bit closer to defining the aesthetics of rock, or anyhow of Dylan.

The lyrics of the more recent concert version differ slightly from those of the studio release. The words of the earlier outtake differ extensively, as transcribed separately in Appendix A. It seems a shame to have lost some of the earlier lyrics, especially

> You close your eyes and part your lips
> And slip your fingers from your glove
> You could have the best there is
> But it's gonna cost you all your love
> You won't get it for money

Dylan has said that a lot of lines come to him "that would be better off just staying on a printed page and finishing up as poems."[9] Perhaps these outtake lines are among them. At any rate, before showing how its lyrics and performance have been altered and the song thereby improved, I will first describe the released studio version, for convenience termed the standard version.

In "Idiot Wind," many of the same elements interact that had made "Subterranean Homesick Blues" such an anthem for the mid-sixties, ten years before. Imagery intertwines personal life with political—but on country roads rather than city streets, with quite different priorities. Paranoia and defiance permeate each song, but "they" disappear after the first stanza of "Idiot Wind" as the narrator thereafter confronts his "Sweet lady" face to face. Rhyme, voice, and instrumentation go to enhance the sense of the lyrics in "Idiot Wind," not to help destroy it. And the narrator, instead of dodging from basement to manhole, takes seven minutes and forty-five seconds to look around his life and piece together the fragmentary scenes.

The end-rhyme scheme of "Idiot Wind" is flawless; the standard-version instrumentation is regular and unobtrusive, always supporting the lyrics. It is thus a song whose words have more impact than does its music, on a listener's response, but it does not thereby become a poem. Much of its effect comes from Dylan's articulation of those words—from the way he growls "heart" or swallows "love" or grits "teeth." In addition, the scenes change without syntactic links, and the poetic images develop nonsequentially, unlike even a very impressionistic poem.

"Subterranean Homesick Blues" has four eighteen-line stanzas, with refrains suggested only by irregular harmonica riffs after the sloganlike end couplets. "Idiot Wind," far more slowly, glides also through only four stanzas, each made up of an eighteen-line verse and a seven-line refrain. Instrumentation and rhyme divide each verse into four-line segments, with an isolated line in the middle that rhymes with an isolated line at the end of each. Each verse end-rhymes *ABCB, DEFE, G, HIJI, KLML, G*. Each refrain develops the images of "idiot" and "blowing" by incremental repetition. Until the closing refrain, the first and last four refrain lines stay the same, only the middle refrain couplet changing its images of emptiness. For the final refrain other lines change too, such that the previous second-person accusation becomes a first-person-plural acceptance of blame.

Except for a few tense shifts and plurals, all rhymes could work in print. Even when Dylan's pronunciation changes a word, as in the third verse when he sings not "apart" but *apaarrr*, he then rhymes it not with "heart" but with *haarrr*. These unstrained, careful rhymes, as compared to all the voice-forced rhymes in "Subterranean Homesick Blues," suggest a narrator attempting not to manipulate the world of the lyrics but to understand how and why its language works the way it does.

The musical structure coordinates with the rhyme scheme. The melody repeats such that each eighteen-line verse is divided into two musical halves. Within each nine-line half-verse, the *ABCB* and *HIJI* lines pass slowly, their end rhymes clear, because of the instrumental break after each rhyme word. In contrast, the *DEFEG* and *KLMLG* lines of each half-verse flow together without instrumental interludes. The *DEFEG* and *KLMLG* segments are further kept structurally distinct from the *ABCB* and *HIJI* segments because of the organ, which regularly plays a high and then a low chord behind each of the *DEFE* and *KLML* lines.

The words and music of the standard "Idiot Wind" begin simultaneously, with no instrumental introduction. For two lines Dylan's voice rushes ahead of the musical beat, suggesting the narrator's attempt to escape the someone who's "got it in for me." The drum, the basic rhythm instrument, marks off two-measure segments, often coordinating closely with the vocals. In the instrumental break after the first *G* rhyme word, "lucky," the organ swells to join the drum, marking the song's first structural segment.

These first nine lines tell what "they" say about the narrator. In everyday speaking we make distinctions among a definite "they," an indefinite but unthreatening "they," and what has been termed "the paranoid they"—like those hiding throughout "Subterranean Homesick Blues." The numerous "paranoid they"s in the first half-verse of "Idiot Wind" would start to sound silly in speech or print. But sung, the pronoun remains unobtrusive; its effect builds by repetition until the narrator is surrounded by hostile and gossiping "they"s.

In this brief story, details sketch out the outlaw/hero/con artist/stud image that "they" enviously fantasize about a famous person. Such a superman can casually shoot Gray, whose name suggests a bland, boring husband, and take Mrs. Gray to Italy, whose national reputation adds to the narrator's romantic appeal. The emotional power of this theme—seduction of a woman immediately after her husband's death—is shown by its centuries-long existence as a folktale sometimes known as "The Matron of Ephesus."[10] The theme here intensifies in that this woman, like Hamlet's mother, hastily marries her husband's murderer. Perhaps Mrs. Gray even helped with the murder, but she gains only the narrator's company as he takes her to Italy to let her die there. She and then the narrator inherit a fantasy-laden million bucks, symbol of success. I did it, the narrator shrugs, with just luck—luck, the antithesis of hard work in the American dream. But despite this sarcastic disclaimer—which Dylan renders as *I can't HELP it… IF… I'm luckeeeee*—the story implies that his success has come from romance. Sexual romance, a little… but more the romance of the hero that American popular culture creates over and over—Stagolee, Billy the Kid, Capone, Bogart, Dylan.

Other lines in this first half-verse literally describe a rock star's public life—"They're planting stories in the press," for example, though the next line's "cut it out" puns about the newspaper. Such literalness would fall flat without the accompanying evocation of the fantasy hero. The power of that hero image broadens the verse to lament not just stardom but also the dilemma of anyone who finds herself idealized and expected to live up to another's fantasy.

This explanation provides a bridge to connect the media-hero imagery with the broken-relationship imagery in the first verse. The song itself has no such bridge. After two more couplets of what "they" think and do about the narrator, the scene switches to "you." "Even you yesterday," Dylan sings softly and breathily. The alliteration of "yesterday" and "years" adds to the proliferation of "you"s, repeated in this *KLML* segment until the narrator is again surrounded, engulfed by this pronoun as he was a few lines earlier by "they." The last verse line reveals the pronoun's identity, with long-drawn-out *es*: "Sweet lady."

The line "You had to ask me where it was at" again shows Dylan foregrounding a cliché. A dictionary defines "where it's at" as "1. Where the exciting, trend-setting, successful, or satisfying events, people, ideas, etc., are. 2. Where the ultimate truth lies; where the unvarnished facts are."[11] In slang the phrase is present tense. The past tense of Dylan's line implies that the asker regards "where it's at" as some permanent state that the narrator has been steadily in for all these years. Even in present tense, the phrase would suggest that the sweet lady idealizes him; in past tense, it shows her inability to understand how little he likes being where it's at.

The slow "Sweet lady" and then a rich organ chord signal the start of the first refrain. Careful listening reveals that what at first sounds like "the idiot wind" is in fact *ihyidiot wihind* throughout, most clearly in the second refrain. The extra syllables make the oral phrase onomatopoetic: its five short-*i* sounds reverberate with *d-t-d* like gusty wind through a flap, whistling with the middle *w* sound.

Visual images of this sweet lady, like those of the sad-eyed lady of the lowlands, show mostly parts of her face, beginning here with her mouth.

The midrefrain couplet contains two powerful visual images of "blowing," set apart by the "Idiot wind" before and after. Dylan holds the notes for "mou" and "sou," the latter somewhat longer, pronouncing neither final *th*. He increases the assonance of "you move your mouth" and slurs the sounds that the words do not share, so that the phrase becomes something like *ya moo vya mowowow*. Word sound reinforces sense: although a silent reader might never notice, the consonant-diphthong combination *mow* forces a pronouncer, in fact, to move her mouth through a wider arc than does almost any other combination.

In this couplet a third major pattern of imagery appears, with no more rational a transition than there was to the second, "Sweet lady" pattern. The transition comes by means of the aurally evoked wind, which now refers to both her empty talk and the lonely traveler heading south. A scene of southern backroads, with the wind, suggests dust and emptiness. In the blues, furthermore, men usually head north toward fantasized fame and fortune, and head back south after they have failed.[12] Thus, heading south means a return to home and emotional security—usually symbolized as a woman. Dylan's juxtaposition of face and road imagery in this couplet works not only because of wind but also because of the all-forgiving and all-nurturing Woman that his sweet lady had apparently once meant to him. There is still only resentment in the narrator's attitude and Dylan's voice, though—still no recognition that this blues-tradition female is as fantasized as is the heroic male he refuses to be.

The words of the last three lines are identical and the performances similar, in the first three refrains—except that all vocal inflections become more emphatic in the second refrain, making it seem more hostile than the others. Dylan always renders "idiot" as *ihyidiot*, even midline for each "You're an idiot, babe." "Teeth" he usually draws out for four syllables; on the second syllable his vocal pitch shoots very high, then descends while overlapping most of the drum-riff interlude. To pronounce "teeth" aloud, one's lips must draw back as if to sneer, leaving the teeth exposed—to the wind, as it were—for the duration of the vowel. Dylan does not repeat this rendering for the rhyme "breathe": he stretches its vowel only a little, staying on the same note but sinking in volume, and cuts off the word with a burst of breath, an articulated *th*.

The narrator begins the second verse by switching from his resentful focus on the mouth, teeth, and breath of "you" back to a picture of "I." He is confused, out of control: if the fortune teller had said that lightning would strike for sure, he would feel less disoriented. Dylan's exclamatory tone isolates "beware," making danger seem certain but still undefinable. His voice becomes louder on the rhyme lines and softer on the lines between, imitating the "peace and quiet" the narrator names and the confusion he feels. And then, again without a syntactic tie, comes a clear, powerful, five-line vision of the lone soldier on the cross—who is, on one level, Woody Guthrie.

An early poem of Dylan's ends:

> And your feet can only walk down two kinds of roads
> Your eyes can only look through two kinds of windows
> Your nose can only smell two kinds of hallways
> You can touch and twist
> And turn two kinds of doorknobs
> You can either go to the church of your choice
> Or you can go to Brooklyn State Hospital
> You'll find God in the church of your choice
> You'll find Woody Guthrie in Brooklyn State Hospital
> And though it's only my opinion
> I may be right or wrong
> You'll find them both
> In the Grand Canyon
> At sundown [13]

Guthrie's autobiography inspired Bob Zimmerman to leave Minnesota and begin his own singing career.[14] *Bound for Glory* is full of fight scenes; it opens with a free-for-all that spills out a boxcar door until Woody gets tossed off the train along with the fighters. Calling him a soldier instead of a scrapper glorifies him, as does the cross and its implication that Woody died for our sins. His lingering death is described by Mrs. Guthrie now,[15] and presumably also when the young Dylan used to visit them, as a "losing battle" against Huntington's Disease.

The image does not end with Woody, however. Jesus Christ was no lone soldier, but medieval artists and writers found ways to add courage in battle to Christ's accumulated character assets (as he freed the righteous from hell or overturned money-changers' tables). The same has come to folk heroes like Cuchulainn and Charlemagne: whatever his historical exploits, a hero lives on in oral tradition weighted by a snowballing mass of transferred traits and stories. The "lone soldier on the cross" suggests not only Woody Guthrie but also any rightfully glorified hero, such that the image stands in clear contrast to the sleazy con-artist hero of the first stanza.

When *Blood on the Tracks* was released, my household in Santa Cruz was losing a war against an eviction-bent landlord. With no thought for how the lines relate to the rest of "Idiot Wind," we promptly made a sign for our bulletin board of "In the final end he won the war, after losing every battle." Dylan had done it again, had given us yet another sloganlike bulwark against whoever tries to control our lives. As in many proverbs, this couplet encompasses two mutually exclusive terms, winning and losing, and thereby provides a focus for unstated tensions.

As my household used the line, "he won the war" meant "we will win the war." We didn't. But a more numerous "we" were nonetheless winning a war after losing every battle. Dylan wrote this song not long before September 1974, probably during Watergate summer. Again, most members of his audience would not have admitted rationally that the end of the draft and the war in Vietnam and the hard reign of Richard Nixon had done anything far-reaching to overthrow the capitalist system—but the need to celebrate was there. And these "won the war" lines of "Idiot Wind," set apart in the standard version by sharp drumbeats, suggest the mass community's covert cry of triumph.

This slogan raises listener responses so high that the fall to the roadside is very harsh. Dylan comes down hard on both substantive syllables of "daydreaming." Daydreaming is not quite mutually exclusive of waking up, but is askew enough to show the narrator still confused after his vision. His waking vision, in contrast to the "lone soldier" dream, evokes the pain of a hangover or knockout headache. Dylan howls "stars" as *starrrr*, holding it longer than its rhyme word, "are." Hard drumbeats add to the pain.

In the *KLMLG* segment, then, the narrator hurls his most direct accusations at the sweet lady, predicting her death with a vicious curse. "Cover up the truth with lies" directly evokes Watergate. The ditch in this scene reinforces road imagery elsewhere, for throughout the song (as in Woody Guthrie's *Dust Bowl Ballads*) roads are lonely, windswept, possibly dangerous, certainly not beckoning to fun and freedom. The eyes of the corpse reverberate with the sweet lady's facial features elsewhere. The bloody saddle—an image that Dylan combines with a road image to entitle the album *Blood on the Tracks*, "tracks" suggesting both railroads and footprints of the wounded—recalls Gray, slain so casually by the fantasy hero. It also suggests menstrual blood, an aspect of the mysterious power of the Female that echoes other of the narrator's attitudes toward his sweet lady: her holiness in the last verse, for example, and the narrator's patient waiting for her while the seasons run their cycles.[16]

In performance, this powerfully worded curse does not stand out. Dylan's voice becomes soft and breathy for "I love best" and a bit louder for "in the ditch"; he also pronounces the word "around" as a circle, mouthing its *ow* diphthong. But compared to the venomous voice that Dylan can use —and does use as nearby as the next refrain's "You're an idiot, babe"—his voice remains steady and unemphatic, as does the instrumentation. The curse sounds less resentful than it looks on paper—automatic, almost sad.

By the rhymed couplet of the second refrain, the rotting corpse in the ditch has turned into one of the more pleasant possible images of death, flowers on a tomb. The next line brings the sweet lady back to life, in the secure home that billowing curtains suggest. In this refrain Dylan exaggerates the drawn-out, sneering pronunciation of *ihyidiot* and the four-syllable, four-pitch "teeth." His vocal bitterness purges the narrator's resentment and enables him to begin rationalizing.

As the third stanza opens, the organ comes into prominence, backing up the narrator as he shifts blame away from the sweet lady and onto uncontrollable forces of gravity and destiny. After "apart" and "heart" the organ holds a chord over the usual drum riffs. Dylan leaves off the *t* and growls the final *rrr* of each *B*-line rhyme, blending it into the organ chord. His growl makes good aural sense out of the lion, which in print seems an arbitrary image of masculinity. The narrator now gives the sweet lady some credit for trying in the relationship: he blames not her but "it"—as impersonal as gravity and destiny—for failing to change his heart. He is not ready, quite yet, to accept responsibility for changing his own heart.

The wheel-of-fortune imagery in the *DEFEG* lines again suggests Watergate. Throughout "Idiot Wind" the narrator's attitude toward the sweet lady tends to be primary, with images that evoke his feelings sometimes taken from national politics. Here political flashes focus into a rather direct description of an American leftist's feelings during Watergate summer, when a government that had long been a solid symbol of evil suddenly split into bad guys and self-righteous good guys. The passage could also tell how Nixon himself felt. But it is not just historical commentary. With the oppositions of good/bad and top/bottom, the lines evoke the mental and emotional chaos of other situations, including a love affair going bad. And, like the not quite opposites of waking up and daydreaming, like the fortune teller's tentative but alarming warning, the concept of "a little upside down" is even more confusing than if everything were clearly upside down. The organ imitates "upside down" with a high, looping run.

The "you" with corrupt ways, like the "you" on top and bottom, can be understood as both Nixon and estranged lover. But the concept of blindness shifts the scene back to the face of the sweet lady. Corruption and blindness recall her corpse rotting in the ditch; now her face comes back to life, with eyes that can see but should not be trusted. Dylan's voice exclaims all three words "eyes don't look," making sure a listener notices those shifty eyes.

An organ chord pulls the scene abruptly away from her face to a third-person vision of corrupted religion. The seventh day and the wearing of black as clergy and in mourning suggest religious ritual—empty ritual, though, because this priest is unmoved by fire, whether of sacrifice or purgation or just wanton destruction. The burning building recalls the "smoke pouring out of a boxcar door." But, in spite of *Bound for Glory*, the boxcar image gives more an impression of hobo cooking than of destruction. Thus this priest couplet implies the corruption of the ideals of the lone soldier on the cross and thereby the fragility of the narrator's vision of the rightful hero. In conjunction with the Watergate imagery, the priest passage suggests some ultimate death-bearing authority—capitalism itself, perhaps—unmoved by what superficially appears to be a climactic event. In addition, the priest's stone face affects how a listener experiences the sweet lady's face: her shifty eyes perhaps cover up some deeper hardness of heart.

This priest passage acts as a sort of catalyst for negative imagery, tying together death and authority and ceremony and fire and face. But it is not essential to what would be poetic development on paper nor dependent on the rest of the song for its impact. In its position it provides a third-person break between two more literal comments about the narrator's love relationship.

The organ adds to the sinking feeling of the next couplet. While the narrator waits, apparently stood up for a date with the Eternal Female whose fertility marks the cycle of seasons, four organ chords descend as down stairsteps. The images of "running boards" and "cypress trees" suggest a scene out of Faulkner, perhaps—anyhow, a scene that reverberates with the "backroads heading south" and that ends with Dylan's slowly drawn-out *oh* of "slowly" and *um* of "autumn."

Without the instrumental break that usually separates verse from refrain, Dylan plunges ahead—imitating the narrator's impatience after the long, slow autumn. And now the wind has shifted; in the couplet it blows, not around her face, but around the narrator's skull. "Like a circle" suggests whirlwind, confusion; in Dylan's pronunciation, it also suggests "sucker round my skull," perhaps a sinister, clinging snake. The next line—the only one in its position without "blowing"—in a few words again evokes the entire confusion of American politics.

Woody Guthrie's song "Grand Coulee Dam" glorifies the U.S. government, in the guise of the New Deal, for providing flood control, electricity, industrial goods, and, most important, jobs for the people. Its imagery shows American government at its most benevolent—bringing the crashing waters of the Columbia under control, useful and still beautiful.[17] Dylan's mention of the Grand Coulee Dam calls up an idealization of government parallel to the idealization of Woody himself as hero. The geographical sweep of Dylan's line echoes Guthrie's best-known song, "This land is your land... from California to the New York island." But the spiritual sweep is vaster still from that political attitude, possible in the thirties, to the present-day Capitol—especially to a Capitol sinking as distinctly as Dylan's voice does on the final syllable.

The last three lines seem milder than in previous refrains. "Teeth" is three syllables, not four, as Dylan's voice sinks evenly instead of shooting up and then down in steps. This inflection so much resembles the pitch change on the last syllable of "Capitol" that it and "teeth" become aurally related to one another as well as to their rhyme words, "skull" and "breathe." Again, the face of the sweet lady gets linked to what's wrong in Washington.

The narrator then leaves politics behind for a quite literal, personal fourth verse. Dylan's voice is very soft and breathy on the first line; with "touch the books," he returns to normal volume. A looped organ run behind the word "read" further highlights this fresh image of loneliness. The male narrator is left behind, the woman gone away—a role reversal from the much more common blues theme of man leaving home and woman, and a situation set up elsewhere in *Blood on the Tracks*. The image "I can't even touch the books you've read" shows a lover left alone in what was once home. Books would not mean home in the blues; the evocation works for the particular sociological subgroup that makes up Dylan's audience—young, white, and overeducated. (Sometime between a couple's moving in together and the marriage ceremony, for example, comes a degree of commitment symbolized by their combining books, getting rid of duplicate copies.)

The narrator's humiliating crawl past her door sets up a contrast with his following her down the road to ecstasy, contrast in both his posture and the home/road imagery borrowed so extensively from the blues. Dylan heightens the home/road contrast by making the road momentarily sound exciting and adventurous: "down the tracks" seems to bristle with exclamation points. "Road to ecstasy" he sings more calmly, but the image is enlivened by sharp drumbeats after.

The line "And all your raging glory" continues this verse's extreme focus on "you," the sweet lady. Dylan draws out the "your," not the phrase "raging glory" that a silent reader would notice. After "very last time" he pauses, imitating the finality, and then goes on to exclaim "free!" An organ chord and sharp drumbeats punctuate the exclamation.

The image of the "howling beast" on the borderline suggests maybe jealousy but more certainly whatever monster it is that destroys relationships. The organ becomes more prominent here, with a long chord to introduce the straightforward, sad statement that concludes the verse. The organ plays the same four stairstep chords with which it had backed up the waiting lines that ended the third verse, but here it does the stairstep faster, twice over, once behind "you'll never... rise above" and again behind "And I'll never... kind of love." The descent imitates the sinking sadness of the lines, culminating in a "love" that Dylan chokes in like *luv*. The incremental repetition highlights the reciprocal thoughts that the two lines express. The final line has more words than does any other in its position, and in it Dylan's phrasing sets apart both "feel" and "sorry." The fourth verse begins with the narrator's inability to feel her and ends with his ability to feel sorry about his inability. The narrator has learned how to feel, but nonetheless has lost his sweet lady.

In the closing refrain, the change in personal pronoun shows the narrator's new awareness of reciprocal feelings and shared blame. In the first two refrains "you" were wrong, in the third "I" was confused, and here in the fourth "we" are both cold, unprotected by what ought to cover one person adequately. The letters and the dusty shelves pick up on the image of books as home. And the narrator and sweet lady are still *ihyidiots*, even together.

"It's a wonder we can even feed ourselves," as a closing, hints at mothering and nurturing. The parallel line in other stanzas, "It's a wonder that you still know how to breathe," suggests, of course, death. This switch from not-breathing to not-being-fed is the same shift of imagery as in the third refrain, from "tomb" to "room," death to home. Here, as so often elsewhere, death and motherhood combine into a powerful poetic image.

The death threat is a vicious line made milder, in all three refrains, by Dylan's tone of regret: each time he sneers "teeth," and then he does not fulfill the aural expectation that "breathe" too will be sneered. No listener has experienced death, not-breathing. She can only imagine it, fearfully, as does the narrator in early verses. However, every listener does have subconscious memories of the time when she could not feed herself, when she did need another person as this narrator once needed his sweet lady and she him.

Dylan's soft and mellow harmonica comes in to accompany the band through an entire refrain and fade-out. Here as elsewhere, especially because of the final mothering image, Dylan's voicelike harmonica seems to imitate an infant learning to talk, whose highest aspiration is to sound like a human voice, who has no desire whatsoever to rush off proving what an instrument can do that a voice cannot.

In contrast to the voice-centered, word-centered nature of this standard "Idiot Wind," the concert version released on *Hard Rain* features Dylan's voice as one among many instruments. True, his voice continues throughout the song, whereas musical instruments instead take turns in the spotlight. In the first stanza guitar and tambourine are most noticeable; the piano takes over in the second and continues through much of the third. A glockenspiel enters at the third verse, then also highlights the *ABCB* lines of the fourth. The drum predominates throughout the fourth verse and refrain, it and again the tambourine becoming louder toward the end.

Besides this variety of instruments, and besides the occasional raggedness of an unedited performance, the most marked difference between the standard version and this one is the distinctive percussion riff that fills the musical spaces between many sung lines. It is a two-measure, syncopated riff, its rhythm x♩ ♪♩ x♪ x♩♩o . Its fourth beat is marked by a chord change on guitar and usually by a shivering tambourine stroke (i.e., one produced by sideways wrist motion). This riff is usually repeated twice after each *B* line and more often in the longer instrumental breaks between verse halves, between verses and refrains, and between stanzas. Each of these instrumental gaps predicts what will happen during the next sung line. That is, a *B*-rhyme line of lyrics, accompanied by a G guitar chord, is followed by two instrumental riffs—the first changing G to C-minor, the second back to G and again to C-minor—and then by the next sung line, accompanied by a C-minor chord.

Instrumental gaps are active to start with, because of the chord changes in this repeated riff, and are further enlivened by instrumental flourishes. In the first stanza, for example, a loud electric-guitar figure follows each line "I can't help it if I'm lucky" and "People see me all the time." The change after "lucky" seems to rise in pitch; that after "time" seems to fall. Thus these two consecutive lines, though not a poetic couplet, are made by instrumentation into an incrementally repeated couplet in binary opposition. After the "sweet lady" line that ends the first verse, three quickly ascending guitar pitches imitate a climb upward into the "Idiot wind."

In the second stanza, fast repeated piano chords come in at the *HIJI* lines such that the instrumentation continues to pound at the narrator, who has just been awakened by sharp drumbeats after "losing every battle." In the concert version, his painful visions show not a "chestnut mare"[18] but a "smoking tongue," which new image combines fire and face imagery. The "Blood on your saddle" curse that follows, however, makes less complex poetry than in the standard version: "One day you'll be in the ditch" becomes, in concert, "One day you'll be in the grave," no longer linked to the road imagery.

Other changes in concert may affect the sense of the lyrics. For example, the standard "I haven't known peace and quiet" seems more peaceful than does the concert "I haven't known about peace and quiet now," packed into the same musical space. The most extensive textual changes come in the *BCB* lines of the last verse, which become in concert "I can't even touch the clothes I wear/Every time I come into your door/You leave me standing in the middle of the air." The lyrics are then the same as in the standard version until "I think I finally see," in place of "now I'm finally free." "I can't even touch the books you've read," eliminated in concert, elaborated the home/ road imagery, as did "crawl past" and "free." And the concert narrator's "I finally see" somewhat blurs the blindness/vision imagery, since all along he has been seeing what the bloody-socketed sweet lady does not.

"Your corrupt ways have finally made you blind," the third-stanza line that refers neatly to both Nixon and the sweet lady, is in this concert version highlighted by loud glockenspiel tones during and after. The glockenspiel returns briefly and more softly in the fourth verse, as do guitar and piano flourishes, before sharp tambourine strokes and loud drumming, including cymbal crashes, finish the song. The last verse of the outtake lyrics, I will show, methodically resurrects each of the song's major patterns of poetic imagery. In this concert version, instrumentation creates a similar effect: during the final verse each instrument says one more time that no one of them is the most important, that each will take its turn. And because of the distinctive instrumental riff, whose chord change seems to be predicting a line to follow even at the close of the song, it seems that all these congenial instruments will continue their cooperative progress though the words are over and done with.

Dylan's voice, pronouncing those words, tends to echo the patterns set out by instrumentation. For example, two of the distinctive instrumental riffs follow each *B*-line rhyme word, and for each, beginning with *preyess* and *gueyess*, Dylan emphatically makes the rhyme two syllables. Also, he frequently up-swoops his vocal pitch within words, particularly line-end words; such a rising pitch gives an unsettled feeling that more will follow, as do the chord changes in those instrumental riffs.

Dylan's unusual vocal phrasing particularly stands out in this concert version because at least one other singer joins in during each refrain. While that voice aligns with the musical beat, Dylan's voice usually strays far from both the voice (or voices) and the beat. In the first "Blowing every time you move your mouth," for example, when the other vocalist arrives at the *m* of "mouth," Dylan is already well into mouthing its reduplicated *ow* diphthong.

For the last line of every refrain—the "breathe" lines and then "feed ourselves" at the end—the other vocalist(s) and all instruments stop. Dylan sings each line a cappella, coming down hard on every other syllable, "It's a *wonder that* you *still* can e-ven buh-*reeethe.*" This vocal effect could be termed sarcastic iambic pentameter, done with little regard for the sense of the lyrics. With his voice, thus, Dylan can choose to exaggerate or ignore normal English-language rhymes and other vowel/consonant sounds. His voice in this concert version does what it damn well pleases among potentially regularizing influences. When a vocal effect does relate to the sense of the lyrics, it often seems sarcastically overdramatic: for example, he seems to sob during "I can't feel you anymore."

Dylan's unpredictable voice interacts with the instrumentation throughout this concert version, for instruments trade off flourishes and backup rhythms in no particular order. The lyrics likewise shift around scenes and images of lovers, politics, publicity, heroes, roads, homes, books, faces, fires, tombs, rooms, and wombs—connected by gusts of the idiot wind. The word-centered studio performance seems to unify these themes; all are part of one narrator's consciousness as he tries to sort out his life. This instrument-happy concert performance, instead, makes the scenes in the lyrics even less connected than they look in print. But disunity doesn't matter, it's alright ma, because the narrator is part of a congenial community of instruments that feel just as chaotic as he does but that will help him past this personal crisis just as the feeling of group solidarity has helped him past so many others. Insofar as a listener identifies with each narrator, a listener to the *Blood on the Tracks* version feels rather sorry for herself. But what listener could feel sorry for herself out there cheering a Rolling Thunder Review concert in Fort Collins, Colorado?

A listener to the rejected studio outtake version feels sorry for the organist. After every single line that contains the word "wind" or "blowing," twenty in all, the organ does a wind imitation, *woo-oooo-o*. It imitates wind also after the narrator daydreams "about the way things sometimes are."

The organ also overdoes the descending stairsteps of chords, like those that back up "I waited for you on the running boards" and a few other appropriately down-spirited lines of the standard version. In the outtake descending organ chords back up lines much more frequently, sometimes detracting from the sense of the words. For instance, such chords behind "losing every battle" make losing, rather than winning, primary. The dream slogan is not as high-spirited, so the narrator does not fall with a crash to wake up on the roadside. Or again, an organ swell behind the third-stanza *DEFEG* segment, vaguely imitating "Now everything's a little upside down," is less effective than the looping organ run that imitates "upside down" in the standard version simply because dramatic organ flourishes are so commonplace in the outtake.

The drum defines the basic rhythm in the standard version; in the outtake the drum stays well in the background, leaving the acoustic guitar almost alone to begin and end the song, to make transitions between structural segments, and to define a regular musical beat—with which Dylan's voice could possibly be setting up tension. Only occasionally and gently, though, does his voice indulge in unusual phrasing or inflection. The overall effect of this outtake performance is of softness, gentleness, a calm steady emotional state throughout.

The outtake lyrics differ extensively from the standard ones. (See Appendix A.) These earlier lyrics express consistent resentment toward the sweet lady, the only hint of reconciliation or shared blame coming in the switch to first-person-plural pronouns for the last refrain. In spite of the harsher words, however, the musical and vocal performances make the outtake a gentle, nonthreatening love song. This clash in tone could conceivably have produced an overall effect, of confusion between love and exile, home and death, similar to the unresolved tension between the lyrics and the performance of them in "Shelter from the Storm." (The released "Shelter" was recorded at the same New York sessions as was the outtake "Idiot Wind.") But the outtake misses this artistic possibility and mostly seems monotonous.

The guitar opens the song with a few measures of the riff that will both back up and follow sung lines throughout. Dylan sings each of the four opening lines ahead of the musical beat, here too suggesting the narrator's paranoia and his attempt to escape.

The entire first outtake verse and refrain have lyrics not changed. In the "man named Gray" story, Dylan's voice exclaims the word "died" and pauses afterward. The fantasy hero thus seems crueller: the key word "lucky," which Dylan's phrasing links to "inherited" in the standard version, here is connected to the seduced woman's death. For the phrase "where it was at," Dylan uses the soft, breathy tone otherwise used for professions of love.

The line "Sweet lady" has no stretched vowels as in the standard version; the following guitar part swells in volume, however, and leads into Dylan's louder voice on "Idiot wind." Dylan reduplicates the vowels of this and other "Idiot wind"s, but less emphatically and less consistently than in the standard version.

The lyrics of the second verse are much altered: the narrator in the outtake lyrics is more in control of his situation. Instead of running into a fortune teller, he takes the initiative to seek out a prediction. The personification of "peace and quiet" here, creating a clearer visual image, also implies that the narrator is out seeking peace and quiet. And that picture is then made fuzzy by the indefinite "it," which refers to his state of mind but seems also to equate "peace and quiet" with "living hell."

The outtake's "lone soldier on the hill" suggests a World War I hero; the move from "hill" to "cross" gives him two more millennia of heroic meaning. Whereas the standard version's "smoke" and "boxcar" suggest companionship, the possibility of heroic hobo society, the outtake rain isolates the lone soldier. Rain is an isolated image in the song, too, muddying the idiot wind that everywhere else seems dry and dusty and biting.

Because a listener's spirits are not buoyed up by the sinking "losing every battle" slogan, next, she does not fall hard and fast to the roadside. The "hoofbeats pounding in my head" create more immediate pain than does the isolated "chestnut mare" image that replaces them. But the "your" that refers to that chestnut mare connects the headache directly to the sweet lady; in the outtake the juxtaposition of glorious-hero vision and painful-lady vision is less striking. The curse lines in the outtake, as in the standard, have little impact in inflection or instrumentation.

The third verse begins with an unemphatic shift of blame onto impersonal forces. The only word that Dylan stretches is "enough"; the outtake thus lacks both the anguish and the lion's growl of *apaarrr* and *haarrr*. The organ swell behind the "upside down" lines, next, becomes louder behind "bottom" but fades quickly so that the usual guitar riffs follow the words.

Dylan changes the lyrics of the last half of this third verse, leaving only the priest image relatively intact. In the replaced ceremony lines, the narrator does not focus on her changed face. Instead, a whole new scene is sketched. The "bags" suggest unwanted burdens that she leaves him, in contrast to the narrator's own light luggage later, when he packs up his uniform. The outtake priest, juxtaposed to this ceremony passage, waltzes around instead of sitting stone-faced—a vivid character change in two words. The narrator switches back to the sweet lady to say that she cannot be trusted; this blunt statement has less poetic impact than does the standard version's glimpse of her shifty eyes. And by converting the outtake "quickly" to "slowly," Dylan reproduces the cycle of seasons in the love relationship, adding to the ritualistic overtones of the passage. The outtake image of the narrator left behind with all her bags, but no more her and not even any help, expresses somewhat the same feeling of sinking hopes as does the standard version's image of waiting by cypresses, backed by descending organ chords. The waiting image has the poetic advantage, though, since it is linked to the "backroads heading south" and thence to the ever-present wind.

The couplet of the third refrain has also been altered drastically, in only a few words. The wind in the outtake version shifts only from her mouth to her jaw; the image neither suggests a whirlwind of confusion nor anticipates the narrator's gradual acceptance of blame. The use of "Capitol" instead of the outtake "Mardi Gras" has enriched the song's meaning considerably. The revision focuses the Watergate imagery, and it not only echoes Woody Guthrie's most famous line but also reevokes his heroic nature and expands that attitude onto New Deal politics. (Dylan's outtake "From the Grand Coulee Dam to the Mardi Gras" simply puts specific names to Guthrie's "From the redwood forests to the Gulfstream water.") The distance from the Grand Coulee Dam to the Capitol implies a spiritual distance, a political discrepancy, a once-praiseworthy government gone bad, the fall and breakup of the American dream. "Mardi Gras," the romantic but arbitrary image in the outtake, resurfaces in one of the other cuts rerecorded in this session, "Tangled Up in Blue," in which one scene switches from Los Angeles to New Orleans.

The fourth verse, its lyrics totally changed for the standard version, contains several memorable lines. In particular, the triplets that end "struck me kinda funny" and "You won't get it for money" seem succinct, emotion-packed images for a relationship going bad. By changing this verse to a more gentle and direct statement, one of regret, Dylan has chosen to sacrifice flashes of aphoristic cynicism to the song's overall emotional development.

But I have been saying all along that a song, unlike a poem, affects its audience not by linear development but instead by letting a listener experience the emotions it evokes without transition in time or rationality. Until one begins analyzing the printed lyrics, one does not notice that the standard "Idiot Wind" narrator is cruel at the beginning, has a heroic vision, gradually admits his own confusion, and becomes gentle and sorrowful at the end. A listener instead simultaneously experiences all these emotional states, plus those of Watergate, Italy, cypresses, and so on, for a song can create in a listener a mixture of feelings within a moment of time—within the pulsation of an artery, as William Blake says.[19]

The development of emotional mood during the course of the standard "Idiot Wind" makes it work better in print than does the outtake. But because these are songs, not poems, the overall emotional effectiveness of the two versions might have remained constant. The added gentleness in the revised lyrics could have been balanced, in a listener's comparative experience, by the outtake's gentler instrumentation throughout. The poetic inferiorities of outtake lyrics, considered independent of performance, are minor—a few isolated images and muddied effects. Overall, the artistic fault of the outtake is in the tired monotony of its instrumentation and of Dylan's voice.

The last verse of the outtake picks up on and expands each of the earlier strands of poetic imagery, so that a listener experiences each emotion one more time before the narrator's abrupt switch to first-person-plural acceptance of blame in the refrain. The first line of the verse uses a cliché that could have acquired a Dylanesque twist had he used "fell" instead of "jumped" in the next line: "We pushed each other a little too far/And one day just fell into a raging storm." This image would pick up on "gravity" earlier... but mine is not to rewrite rejected Dylan lines. The "raging storm" (which becomes "raging glory" later in the standard fourth verse) suggests the idiot wind itself and perhaps the "raindrops" of the second outtake verse. The hound dog, baying in the outtake, turns into the revised "howling beast" and the phrase "hounded by your memory." The uniform he packs up is in contrast to the bags she left behind and also recalls the second stanza's lone soldier. In the *DEFEG* lines, syntax sets into opposition "word" and "excuse," implying something like truth vs. hypocrisy; this oppositional effect increases as a listener experiences the clearer love vs. money contrast that ends the verse.

The terms "double-crossed" and "lost my mind" say in ordinary, dead metaphors what scenes earlier in the song said by implication: "double-crossed" tells how the narrator felt after the ceremony, and "lost my mind" puts him back in the ditch hallucinating. The ladykillers and dice recall the "lucky" narrative of the first verse and perhaps her bloody corpse. In performance Dylan breaks this line firmly before "behind my back," which phrase he ties to the next line's "imitators steal me blind." This complaint literally, with a reawakened cliché, describes a rock star's life, as did the first-verse images. In the standard version, blindness becomes an attribute of the sweet lady and Nixon and the corpse in the ditch, simultaneously; this outtake line's blinding of the narrator as well is less effectively integrated into previous imagery patterns.

The last half of the fourth outtake verse focuses on the sweet lady, reminding us that the song's imagery patterns go together to express the narrator's feelings about her. The details are carefully chosen—her eyes and lips, instead of flyridden and idiot windblown, now become unmistakably seductive. Most of the song has pictured her face; the stripping of her hand in this passage makes narrator and listener suddenly aware of the rest of her body. In the standard version, the last image of the sweet lady names her holiness; her appeal is romantic and mothering, as well, but never as overtly sexual as in the outtake. In the *MLG* lines of the last outtake verse, her sexuality turns into a mirror image of female prostitution: love and money, in structural opposition, imply that she would pay money for "it."

The text, although not Dylan's voice particularly, suggests a sneering, egotistical narrator. For this last *KLMLG* segment, however, Dylan's voice expresses more than it has throughout the song. He misses the beat for the "You" that begins the *K* and *M* lines; his voice rushes to catch up with the music, imitating the narrator's distraction as he stares at her closing eyes and parting lips. Dylan sings the seductive "glove" line softly and breathily, and uses a similar tone for "all your love"; then, cynically, he uses the same breathiness for "money."

The organ's wind imitation continues unabated through the last refrain. Dylan's phrasing helps the organ with its too-clear message, for his vocal pause after the last "Blowing" leaves the wind, not the shared blame, primary for a listener. He ends the lyrics abruptly: "feed ourselves" is run together, Dylan's voice dropping quickly in pitch to end the completely articulated word before its musical beat. The guitar continues its usual pattern. Dylan's harmonica comes in also, for an entire half-verse and a refrain, complete with wind imitation. Several times the harmonica plays the end of the melody of "The answer is blowing in the wind"; for the instrumental refrain, though, it returns to a close reproduction of the sung melody of "Idiot Wind." Everyone playing seems sleepy.

I have pointed out some specifics as to why this outtake "Idiot Wind" is artistically inferior to both the *Blood on the Tracks* and concert versions. Beyond the kind of poetic considerations I have suggested in connection with this and with the rough draft of "Subterranean Homesick Blues," what generalizations can be made about artistic improvements in performance?

Paul Griffin's wind imitations are a drawback. Is direct instrumental imitation of the lyrics always artistically boring? No—there is plenty on *Blonde on Blonde*, which Dylan considers his most successful studio album, and especially on the exuberant 1974 concert album. Overdone instrumental imitation is bad—but how much is overdone? In the outtake "Idiot Wind," the lyrics express bitterness and the music, reconciliation. But instead of mismatch, the effect might have been of unresolved tension, as in "Shelter from the Storm." In this outtake, Dylan's voice is relatively uninteresting. But in "Subterranean Homesick Blues," vocal monotony creates major artistic effectiveness.

"To Generalize is to be an Idiot," says Blake.[20] Much more evidence is needed to even begin consideration of the aesthetics of performance, or the aesthetics of rock, or even just the aesthetics of Dylan, from the performer's point of view. Somewhat more evidence is available on aesthetic standards from the audience's point of view, however, as I show in my next chapter.

As different as "Subterranean Homesick Blues" and "Idiot Wind" are in tempo and in relative positions on a words-to-music spectrum, their wind-related imagery patterns occur within texts that both can be analyzed for the characteristics of successful songs: pronouns that can encompass a listener, extensive rhyme and other vowel/consonant patterns, nonsequential development of ideas and images, and so on. In neither song, however, are binary oppositions in the text—allowing flexibility in performance—a striking feature. It could be said that "Subterranean Homesick Blues" does not in fact allow various meanings in performance: for years, Dylan never sang it in public, and cover versions tend to change text and structure drastically.[21]

Disconcertingly, however, "Idiot Wind" can project at least two aesthetically successful meanings in performance, and the scattering of non-quite-oppositional images in its text ("daydreaming," "a little upside down," and so on) creates just one effect among many. Even more disconcertingly for one of my theses, Dylan has eliminated several oppositional images in improving the outtake text for release.

Yet binary oppositions do play the roles I have analyzed elsewhere: in imitating the "Hard Rain" narrator's struggle toward rational understanding, in portraying love-song women as irrationally appealing, in making "Just Like a Woman" a jagged weapon and "Like a Rolling Stone" a personal victory for each listener, and in allowing "It Ain't Me, Babe" so many possible resolutions. Does successful literature intended for oral performance somehow use more binary oppositions than does other literature? Or is it inertia that has kept most literary critics from seeking paradigmatic structural patterns as such in what is intended for silent reading? Is unresolved ambiguity more characteristic of songs than of spoken literature? Would distinctions appear between works intended for oral delivery and for silent reading by the same author?

Yes, and how many seas must a white dove sail
Before she sleeps in the sand?
The answer, my friend, is blowing in the wind
The answer…
                    —*"Blowin' in the Wind," 1962*

VII

Aesthetics

[Happy Traum:] Pete Seeger told me the John Wesley Harding album is great to skate to. He said some records are good to skate to and some aren't, and that's a good one.
[Bob Dylan:] I'm awfully glad he feels that way about it.[1]

The vocabulary and techniques of literary criticism developed gradually. In fifth-century-B.C. Athens, the ability to write began slowly to shift from a workers' craft and memory aid to a privilege of the upper classes.[2] Twenty centuries later, the invention of printing began allowing standardized texts that an individual might afford to buy and read silently. After five more centuries, now, critics do agree on many terms and conventions—Chaucer certainly uses a simile to call the miller's wife in the "Reeve's Tale" "as digne as water in a dich"—although they still find arguments aplenty over what a text can mean.

Over the same stretch of centuries (and further back in other cultures, notably Indian) scholars have less decisively tried to portray music as abstract marks on a page, like spoken language, and also have tried to use words to describe how music can convey meaning. The invention of sound-recording equipment shook up any incipient conformity to a set methodology for analysis of music, which so blatantly differs from any notated score. As recently as 1966, Charles Keil despaired at ever coming to understand how music conveys meaning. "Musicologists go one way, anthropologists another," he says, "and the critics continue to tell us what they do and don't like."[3]

But beginning in 1966, critics did start putting onto paper descriptions of how songs—words and music together—convey meaning. They did so not in English or music departments but rather in periodicals directed at the particular sociological subgroup united by recorded music and by, very often, college education. Paul Oliver tells how records have helped develop and spread music that began in oral tradition:

> Through the blues record the lower-class Negro was able to hear the voice of his counterpart from a thousand miles away; hear him and feel a bond of sympathy which no other medium could impart.... Newspapers could only reach the literate, radio stations beamed locally only; records... could be played again and again, repeating their message in every playing.[4]

So, other social groups have defined themselves partly through recorded music; others, such as the British aristocracy, have taken higher education for granted. But not until the sixties did the two characteristics merge in a mass audience.

Two excerpts from interviews with musicians can spotlight this American subculture's boundaries. Both Brownie McGhee and Elvin Bishop learned to play the blues from records as well as from other musicians; McGhee is older and black, Bishop younger and white. McGhee says, "I graduated in Kingsport, Tennessee—Douglas High—in June, 1936. I didn't finish schooling till I was twenty-one, but... I was just lucky enough to strive for an education." Bishop says, "After I got out of high school, I was lucky—I got a National Merit Scholarship. So I could go to school anywhere I wanted.... I wrote down on my application either Northwestern or the University of Chicago, cause I knew that was where the blues thing was." Or, as Dylan keeps on saying, "Somebody got lucky, but it was an accident."[5]

Those who have sought to separate high from popular culture, folk from fine art, have used two main criteria: fine art has more internal complexity, and it appeals to an educated audience. Dylan's words and music, regarded separately, would be neither complex nor effective; together, in performance, they say a lot to an academic or nonacademic audience. Fine-art theories, about the aesthetics of words or music alone, offer more warning than help in analysis. They would form the farthest rim outward of a sort of spiral away from Dylan's particular fusion of poetrylike words and ever-changing music. Moving inward, then, theories become increasingly applicable—about the aesthetics of folklore and popular culture, of rock music in general, and of Dylan and the Beatles in particular.

At the center of this spiral I place eighteen reviews of Dylan's 1968 album, *John Wesley Harding*, from which I cull the aesthetic standards and analytic techniques actually used by listeners.[6] To describe my own perceptions so far, I have lifted terms from musicology and linguistics, adapted questions asked by folklorists and cultural anthropologists, and from literary criticism have taken a framework and set of assumptions most akin to the "reader-response" approach, regarding myself as ideal listener. Such an interdisciplinary merger is rare in academia. But record reviewers have anticipated nearly all my techniques and conclusions.

For example, I have assumed that comparing different performances of the same song will help develop ways to describe aural effects. Greil Marcus, telling of Dylan's 1974 tour, does the same:

> At first the music hit in explosions, and then resolved itself into textures—Garth's organ flowing delicately over a solo from Robbie that was pure anarchy while Dylan's wild howls cut across both. Then, when you thought you had a grip on the music, that you had heard what they had to say with it, they came back with something tougher—like "All Along the Watchtower."
>
> It had me riveted. It was a jagged, growling blast; the Band reached roughly for the melody and Dylan shouted past it. They made the recorded version—quite likely the best thing Dylan has done since *Highway 61 Revisited*—seem tentative and weak, as if, down there in Nashville in the late Sixties, Dylan had hedged his bet. In fact, six years later, he was raising the stakes.[7]

Journalists writing about *John Wesley Harding* refer comfortably to "fine-art" genres of literature and music; they also propose theoretical constructs concerning the interaction of words and music, and concerning the distinction between listener and reader response. First, though, let me pinpoint the issue of academic/nonacademic analysis by describing the three cited articles that are not reviews of *John Wesley Harding* but instead interpretations—that is, translations of the songs' rich imagery into bland, reductionist statements.

The impetus behind such interpretation is expressed by now-retired Dylanologist Alan J. Weberman in an interview in *Broadside*. He believes that Dylan, writing in code, or "irony," even in his first album, presents a "systematized ideology, a complete world view" involving revolutionary politics. "If you can't find the irony that doesn't mean it isn't there," explains Weberman earnestly. "It means only that you can't find it. Next, once he has decided on a symbol he tends to use it pretty consistently."[8] Weberman's misuse of academic terminology and technique is easy to criticize or to satirize, as Michael Gray does: "Example: when Dylan uses the word 'lady' he means 'oligarchy'. So pushing our brains and letting insight dawn, we have *Lay, Oligarchy, Lay, Sad-Eyed Oligarchy of the Lowlands* and so on."[9]

Now, few commercial publications have aimed for an elite, educated audience as clearly as did the *Saturday Review of Literature*. Yet there sociologist Steven Goldberg develops a premise parallel to Weberman's—that Dylan's albums document his personal life, in this instance his growing awareness of the One and the "mystic way." *John Wesley Harding*, "Dylan's supreme work… is his solution to the seeming contradiction of vision and life."[10] Goldberg, interpreting Dylan to readers who presumably review literature every Saturday, stops short of Weberman's literalness: he only implies that, say, Bob Dylan was once stuck inside of Mobile with the salvation blues again. But the motivation remains the same as Weberman's, to translate meaning-packed music and images into a bland and abstract set of biographical symbols.

A third interpretation differs from these somewhat in that it translates only *John Wesley Harding*, not Dylan's entire corpus. In the "1968" chapter of *Bob Dylan*, Anthony Scaduto moves away from the interviewing and documentation that his career in crime reporting had prepared him for, to indulge in some interpretation. To him, *John Wesley Harding* "is Dylan's version of the Bible, songs written as parables describing the fall and rebirth of one man—Bob Dylan."[11] Scaduto's song-by-song interpretations do not strain as far as do Weberman's or Goldberg's, for several reasons. First, thematic unity within an album is a possible artistic goal, whereas coded thematic unity throughout a career decidedly is not. Second, Scaduto conscientiously bases his theory on a brief comment of Dylan's: "I went into *John Wesley Harding* with that knowledge in my head…. that I was writing about myself in all those songs."[12] And third, Scaduto documents the biblical imagery that does help unify the album artistically. But Scaduto, like the other interpreters, cannot stop at aesthetic appreciation; he plunges onward until images become biography and "Dylan understands that in spreading the Word as a prophet, he has become as false as the idols of Babylon."[13]

These three pieces tell little about Dylan's art but much about popular response to it: they parallel the kind of oral discussions that accompanied release of this album. Such "folk commentary" is occasionally documented.[14] For example, *Rolling Stone* reports that "Frankie Lee and Judas Priest" was widely interpreted to refer to Dylan's feud with his manager, Albert

Grossman, and Jon Landau notes that "Dear Landlord" "has been thought to represent all manner of authority—everyone from his manager to the government." Michael Gray, in his "Theories—Anyone Can Play" chapter, relates the "Thief to Boss Theory": in early songs Dylan represents himself as a thief, outside the system; he gathers wealth and power until he becomes a master thief and then, during the course of *John Wesley Harding*, a master or boss. Each song on the album can be interpreted as either the old, honest-outlaw Dylan looking back, or the new, worldly Dylan mocking his public. Furthermore, in the two songs before the cheerful cop-outs that end the album, the old Dylan describes the new Dylan in "I Pity the Poor Immigrant"; then the new Dylan describes the old Dylan in "Wicked Messenger." The intricacy of such a theory suggests that such formulations were not entirely in vain for each audience member. Pointless speculation provides practice for the thinker's mental competition elsewhere—as does the educational process itself.

Reviews of the album are written for and by the educated. In the sixth issue of *Rolling Stone*, a periodical founded for the then-emerging counterculture, Gordon Mills reviews *John Wesley Harding* with reference to Samuel Daniel's sonnets, St. Augustine's *Confessions*, Bach's and Mozart's biographies, Franz Kafka's *The Trial*, Peter Watkins's *The War Game*, and Arthur Rimbaud's "miniature masterpiece, *My Bohemian Existence*."[15] Mills first praises the album for its musical qualities, though, as "a brilliant electronic adaptation of rural blues and country and western sounds"; he also points out how each song's meaning is partly conveyed by instrumentation—by a "swaying" or "delicate rippling" harmonica, by "the tapping chords of a bass guitar." Throughout, he analyzes the lyrics in such terms as "the concept of everyday Good and Evil," "spiced crispness [as in] Elizabethan verse," "elegant restraint," and, referring to "Frankie Lee and Judas Priest," a "too real, even surrealistic, dialogue between two opposed parties [that] attains a steam-hammer urgency."

In the *Rolling Stone* issue before this one, Ralph J. Gleason's "preliminary report" on the album contains no such literary references except to the "Yeatsian overtones" of "All Along the Watchtower."[16] Gleason, the Grand Old Man of rock-music criticism until his death in 1975, there describes the album's overall serenity, the instrumentation, and Dylan's voice, which is "fuller and warmer.... He holds notes much longer now than he used to." He sees the songs as "deceptively simple": Dylan "takes cliches from all of pop music and changes all their faces so that he ends up implying the[ir] use...[resulting in] a marvelously subtle turn which transforms a possible cliche into a new statement." Gleason fuses musical and verbal meanings to call "I Dreamed I Saw St. Augustine" a "moral dilemma conceived in rock 'n roll and r&b rhythms and played as a C&W tune." Furthermore, Gleason articulates how a listener experiences and comes to understand a record album:

> The point about Dylan's work, and it's a point that really applies only to the Beatles and Dylan, is that the more you listen to the music, the more bits and pieces and thoughts and fragments float up. You start out being impressed and grooving behind one or two or three tracks and then slowly (or sometimes in a blinding flash) other tracks move up into your consciousness and the outline and then the implications of their story take over.

Writing in the fifth and sixth issues of a publication directed at the mass audience of a "popular-culture" genre, these two reviewers do not hesitate to refer to "fine-art" literature and music nor to formulate theoretical statements about their aesthetic responses. Gleason is more clearly writing for an in-group, though, for he makes points by quoting lines from other Dylan songs. Of those who decry Dylan's latest style shift, for example, Gleason says that "they still don't know it takes a train to cry. And so they're stoning him again when he's trying to go home."[17]

Other reviews of *John Wesley Harding* do the same with Dylan lines. Most extensively, Michael March constructs a "fiction interview" in which he and Dylan supposedly discuss the album, often in lines from Dylan songs. In this format, in the short-lived rock magazine *Fusion*, March passes no value judgments. He does give briefly an insight that other reviewers develop: the album is both religious and political, for they are one and the same.

Two other reviewers use the same Dylan line to express their own thoughts concisely. To describe the style shift from earlier albums, both Paul Nelson and Jon Landau say that *John Wesley Harding* empties the ashtrays on a whole other level, which line in "The Lonesome Death of Hattie Carroll" (1964) tells how the kitchen maid earned her living.

Paul Nelson had been praising and defending Dylan's music for some time. The pages of *Sing Out!* document the battle, harshest in 1965-1966, between defenders of white rural acoustic-guitar tradition as the only pure folk music and advocates of the new electric-rock sound. Recognizing the split in his readership by 1968, Nelson documents the (white rural) folk melodies he hears in *John Wesley Harding*—"Engine 143," "The Lily of the West," "I Dreamed I Saw Joe Hill," "Frankie Silvers." And Nelson, like

Gleason, articulates the process of coming to understand an aurally experienced record album. While listening to it four times through, he says, he began to realize that Dylan has added to simple and straightforward folk tunes a complex philosophy: "It is as if Jean-Paul Sartre were playing the five-string banjo and confining himself to stating all of his theories in words of under four letters." Nelson promises to write more in the next issue because "what happens on fifth, sixth, and seventh hearings is even more amazing.... The 'folk' album *really* takes a curious turn, and becomes a 'folk' album in a completely different sense of the word." But later issues of *Sing Out!* do not continue Nelson's review.

Jon Landau is more comfortable within his medium—the fifteenth issue of the rock magazine *Crawdaddy!* Grounded firmly on this latest album, Landau expands his analysis to encompass Dylan's career. Although refraining from biographical interpretation, he does set up a chronological schema for artistic development (the myth or mask that Dylan cyclically presents), in support of which he has to strain some songs and ignore others. Such a framework resembles those in several unpublished dissertations on Dylan[18] but differs in that Landau deals with performed words and music and vocal inflections, not just with words on paper. "All Along the Watchtower" may seem incongruous, Landau says,

> if one confines oneself to just the lyrics. Rather than see the song as something to be interpreted, I tend to see it as an evocation of a mood, created primarily by the way Dylan sings his words. Suppose he sang "There must be some way out of here" softly, in 3/4 time. Supposing he was laughing while he sang it. That would change the meaning, such as there may be, drastically. But now suppose he scatted in place of using words, and that he did the scatting precisely as he sings the words. You'd probably respond quite similarly, except your response would be less specific due to the lack of words to focus on.

Besides analyzing his own mental processes as a responsive listener, Landau notes that Dylan's "genuine detachment from his work... allows him to do several things at once without seeming to contradict himself." He also remarks on false dichotomies involving fine vs. folk art and high vs. popular culture, but then simply attributes to Dylan a move from pop to classical artistry.[19]

At about the same time as Landau's piece, Ellen Willis published a similarly expansive analysis, focusing on *Blonde on Blonde* to describe vocal, musical, and verbal effects. She remarks only briefly on *John Wesley*

Harding, in sociohistorical context, as a statement of reaction against the hard and arty rock that groups had been vying to overproduce. By reconciling himself with his past and "even—warily, ambivalently—with his arch-enemies, the landlords of the world," she says, Dylan is continuing to declare his rebelliousness, this time against "the *Sgt. Pepper* straitjacket." Willis, as compared to other reviewers, comes at the album with analytic tools swiped from the social sciences rather than the humanities.[20]

Another reviewer who sees the album as a reaction to rock-music excesses, Robert Christgau, tells *Esquire* readers that *John Wesley Harding* may "stand as the funniest album of the year. Even if it failed as music (it doesn't), it would succeed as strategy." Calling it Dylan's most impersonal record, Christgau emphasizes that "Dylan has learned the value of understatement.... Diction is spare, traditional (almost all the songs function as parodies), and abstract. Everything is so careful that a well-placed detail of linguistic self-indulgence carries the weight that a whole stanza used to, so the familiar sense of unreality prevails, reinforced by the fact that many of the songs seem to end in the middle."

Consciously or not, Christgau is here echoing what *Village Voice* reviewer Richard Goldstein had said three months earlier. Goldstein, too, points to the economy of Dylan's diction—"His songs, once epics of qualification, have become declarative statements"—and to the unfinished effect of such songs as "All Along the Watchtower," whose atmosphere "is charged with the imminent arrival of something inevitable, absolute, and evil.... [The song's] details rush us toward an apocalypse which never happens (except, perhaps, off camera)." He describes verbal and musical parody: "Dylan confronts a cliche the way a butcher eyes a chicken." The two critics do differ. Christgau considers Dylan's harmonica "occasionally intrusive" whereas Goldstein praises it unreservedly: "The indiscriminate harmonica fills on his first albums have become sharp, distinct statements. And his voice... is now a sturdy, sustaining instrument." Goldstein also remarks on the need for analytic criteria for a new, aural art: "Once we have abandoned the idea of 'poetry,' [these songs' barren imagery] works incognito, bringing a mood of profound apprehension to this album."

These reviews so far appear in periodicals aimed to some degree at the sociological subgroup that makes up Dylan's audience. The same sorts of insights occur, more briefly, in general-interest publications. Among all eighteen reviewers, only two refrain from passing aesthetic judgments on the new album. Michael Wood, in the British *New Society*, uses the album's release as a takeoff for a brief review of Dylan's career. And *Variety*'s interest is clear from the headline: "Dylan, Back On Pop Scene, Gets Instant Gold Disk." Only one reviewer condemns the album: Charles Fager compares it unfavorably to *Blonde on Blonde* but quickly adds, "Either that, or the new songs' meaning went completely over my head."

Although writing for *Christian Century*, Fager barely mentions the biblical imagery that is pointed out in general-interest publications—*Time*, *Life*, and the *New York Times*. The *Time* reviewer, for example, says that several songs form "a sorrowing series of meditations on the Christian ethic, outlined in a language that is [deceptively] simplistic." These reviewers also assume readers' familiarity with "fine-art" literature (e.g., Shelton calls Dylan "a gardener of the flowers of evil") and terminology (e.g., Aronowitz: "He used to telegraph an entire novel in a single song. Now his novels have become parables, allegories and morality plays.") All the reviewers at least mention the music as well as the words.

For the most articulate and thorough analysis of the aural effects of *John Wesley Harding*, however, we must look to early issues of the rock-music magazine that predates *Rolling Stone*, *Crawdaddy!* Its first issue came out in January 1966; its editor, publisher, and at first only writer was seventeen-year-old Paul Williams. Introducing the compilation of his early writings, *Outlaw Blues*, Williams says with well-deserved immodesty that "since no one had fooled around with this particular social function [i.e., record reviews] before, I was pretty much able to create my own forms."[21]

Reviewing *John Wesley Harding* just after its release in January 1968, Williams describes his analytic techniques for understanding the artistry of this particular record. *John Wesley Harding*, he says, is accessible in its simple-seeming language and music, and intentional because of Dylan's "self-awareness, the artist knowing what he wants to do, and why, and just churning it out."[22] Williams describes how this "tricky combination" of intentionality and accessibility produces tension in a listener's mind, tension that is not there in words alone or in any other component alone but in the overall aural effect of the album. You listen to it, says Williams, and "any time you happen to say to yourself, 'I wonder why he did that,' you really feel obliged to work at figuring it out. 'Cause you know he did it on purpose.... you can't help absorbing all the words and getting involved in their implications.... [and] subjective questions." He lists the questions he and two friends asked themselves about "All Along the Watchtower," and the mental processes by which he came to realize what makes the narrative so ominous and the opening line ("There must be some way out of here") "so incredibly successfully claustrophobic": the song's time sequence has been disrupted so that the narrative's "ends have been twisted, and taped together.... [like] a moebius strip."

Interviewed in *Sing Out!* ten months later, Dylan contrasts his songs on *John Wesley Harding* to the traditional ballad:

> See, on the album, you have to think about it after you hear it, that's what takes up the time, but with a ballad, you don't necessarily have to think about it after you hear it, it can all unfold to you. These melodies on the *John Wesley Harding* album lack this traditional sense of time. As with the third verse of the "Wicked Messenger," which opens it up, and then the time schedule takes a jump and soon the song becomes wider. One realizes that when one hears it, but one might have to adapt to it. But we are not hearing anything that isn't there; anything we can imagine is really there. The same thing is true of the song "All Along the Watchtower," which opens up in a slightly different way, in a stranger way, for here we have the cycle of events working in a rather reverse order.[23]

So Dylan put in there, indeed, and Williams figured it out.

By the next *Crawdaddy!*, February 1968, Williams has worked such insights into a general theory of "How Rock Communicates," with quotations from Marshall McLuhan, Susanne K. Langer, and more.[24] But his theoretical stance toward Dylan's art in particular comes in July 1966, just after the release of *Blonde on Blonde*. There Williams says that "art is not interpreted but experienced" and that the "sensitive critic must act as a guide, not paraphrasing the songs but trying to show people how to appreciate them."[25] It is possible that, by age eighteen, Williams had already read Susan Sontag's "Against Interpretation":

> The aim of all commentary on art now should be to make works of art— and, by analogy, our own experience—more, rather than less, real to us. The function of criticism should be to show *how it is what it is*, even *that it is what it is*, rather than to show *what it means*.[26]

But even if he did know this essay, Williams's exact and detailed commentary transmutes and develops, rather than simply applies, Sontag's ideas:

> "Inside the museums," he sings, "infinity goes up on trial." It doesn't *mean* anything; but you know what a museum feels like to you, and you can see the insides of one, the particular way people look at things in a museum, the atmosphere, the sort of things that are found there. And you have your image of a trial, of a courtroom: perhaps you don't try to picture a lazy-

eight infinity stepping up to the witness chair, but there's a solemnity about a trial, easily associable with the image of a museum. And see how easily the feeling of infinity slips into your museum picture, endless corridors and hallways and rooms, a certain duskiness, and perhaps the trial to you becomes the displaying of infinity on the very walls of the museum, like the bones of an old fish, or maybe the fact that museums do have things that are old in them ties in somehow... there's no *explanation*, because the line (from "Visions of Johanna," by the way) *is* what it is, but certainly the line, the image, can turn into something living inside your mind. You simply have to be receptive... and of course it is a prerequisite that you live in a world not too unlike Dylan's, that you be aware of museums and courtrooms in a way not too far different from the way he is, that you be able to appreciate the images by having a similar cultural background.... This is true of most literature, in a way; and of course Dylan has his elements of universality as well as his pictures of the specific.[27]

Paul Williams is the last nail in the coffin that Dylan has built around the fine-art/popular-art dichotomy. Writing as a teenager, for his contemporaries, focusing on the details of the "popular culture" they understand and experience, Williams came up with the rudiments of a theory of art criticism as valid as those emerging from scholars' reams of "high-culture" evidence. Steven Goldberg, in contrast, wrote about Dylan's supposed mysticism and "poetry of salvation" as a professor of sociology at C.U.N.Y., with papers "in various scholarly journals" to his credit. And it is the pomposity of Goldberg's writing style, not the validity of his premise, that distinguishes his analysis from that of A. J. Weberman, who dropped out of college to devote a decade of his life to ferreting out and stashing and communicating, to anyone who would listen, every bit of information he could about Bob Dylan. It is Weberman whose work, like James Boswell's, will interest future scholars, for with pack-rat instinct Weberman assembled a Dylan archives of bootleg tapes and ephemeral literature, of just the sort of primary material that historians and others may someday want.[28]

Williams's "Understanding Dylan" is the best brief analysis of Dylan's particular artistry; Michael Gray's *Song and Dance Man* is the best and only book-length one. Gray sets important precedents for an analysis of Dylan's work. He examines the traditions it developed out of, especially rock and roll, and (white rural) folk music. He offers the first and what suffices as the last word on "Dylan and the English Literary Tradition," pointing out that the fine- vs. folk-art distinction is recent in literary history.[29] He analyzes both released and unreleased songs. He sometimes talks about the interaction of words and music and about Dylan's vocal inflections. But

Gray, failing to face the problem of aesthetics, judges the songs by standards for written poetry or by personal preference: "while *The Times They Are A-Changin'* has been castrated, and will be altogether buried by changing times, *When the Ship Comes In* is bound to last."[30] Here and elsewhere Gray succumbs to the critic's temptation to decree what art the masses ought to prefer instead of analyzing how and why a simple-seeming song does in fact appeal to its listening audience.

Gray's value judging makes even more difficult the task he finds thrust upon him in his closing chapters, that of keeping up with an artist in progress. Although Dylan's recent releases (in 1972) had nowhere near the popular impact of his mid-sixties albums, Gray discusses them in almost as much detail. Dredging deep into *Self Portrait*, he finally finds that this derivative album, analyzed, is just as "trite, rutted and simplistic" as it sounded the first time through. "Dylan, of course," perceives Gray, "would say that if we didn't screw ourselves up with this useless desire to divide things into good and bad, our problem would not exist. For me at least, screwed up or not, it just isn't that easy."[31] He thus becomes aware of slippery aesthetic standards at the end of his book on Dylan.

A more general book on rock music remains weak for an opposite reason: a too rigid set of aesthetic definitions. With the premise that "distinguishing between folk, fine, and popular art has become extremely difficult in the 1960's," Carl Belz compiles valuable sociohistorical data for *The Story of Rock*. His theories on art get bogged down, though, in the very fact that he considers the distinctions invalid but continues to employ the three terms anyhow, as plug-in categories. In the course of the book, gradually, "folk art" comes to mean rock music, "popular art" to mean easy-listening ("middle-of-the-road") music, and "fine art" to mean any in which the artist is conscious of his intentions. To Belz, *John Wesley Harding* shows a "clear inclination toward fine art"; the acoustic-guitar simplicity of style signals Dylan's "conscious return to an idiom that he initially practiced unconsciously."[32]

Bob Dylan wrote "The Lonesome Death of Hattie Carroll" while he was twenty-two—not while he was unconscious. Belz's book is worthwhile for other than its theory, particularly for its annotated bibliography of fourteen other books on rock music.[33] From there, I endorse Belz's estimation of a book with the promising title *The Aesthetics of Rock*. Richard Meltzer intends that this book's "incoherency, incongruity, and downright self-contradiction" parallel his experience of rock music.[34] As rock never does, though, Meltzer conveys resentment at some unnamed target almost wholly in meaningless,

Latinate, polysyllabic abstractions, keeping well hidden his apparently immense knowledge gleaned from record collecting and from associating with rock musicians. Frustratingly, also, in more lucid moments he starts to raise valid issues, as in a paragraph that begins to define the unique sociological context for experiencing rock music.[35]

As I spiral outward from *John Wesley Harding* reviews, scholarship becomes less and less relevant to Dylan's particular kind of rock music. As Gleason says, Dylan and the Beatles are in a class by themselves. Musicologist Wilfrid Mellers's *Twilight of the Gods: The Music of the Beatles* is the most detailed study ever done of the interaction of words and music, because philosophers of fine art tend to assume that music swallows words.[36] With the premise that "there is no valid way of talking about the experiential 'effects' of music except by starting from an account of what actually happens in musical technique, the terminology for which has been evolved by professional musicians over some centuries,"[37] Mellers continually has trouble making the songs fit such terminology. The Beatles slide around and shift pitches or sing quite off any proper note; the instrumentation is often indescribable. Mellers can push at the bounds of fine-art vocabulary to describe the interaction of words and music within a Beatles line:

> The words "feeling" and "reaching" are enacted by a tension between flat seventh in the instrumental part, sharp seventh in the vocal line; and on the word "you" a declining melisma swings us wildly and wonderingly from a D major to an F major triad which then immediately rocks back to G.[38]

But Mellers, commenting on Dylan, avoids detailed, atomistic analysis of the interaction of words and music. He speaks of the pentatonic or ragtimey feel of a Dylan tune and of its ironic or catalytic interaction with the sense of the words, but he never tries to use classical terminology for individual lines or notes.[39]

Musicologist Richard Middleton dedicates his *Pop Music and the Blues* to Wilfrid Mellers. But he assumes from the start that rock music and "the blues are not generally notated or notatable. Readers are advised to *listen* to some blues, and to check the discussion to come... against what they hear."[40] His analysis of the Beatles only briefly incorporates notation; his analysis of Dylan, not at all.[41]

I have emphasized throughout that fine-art standards for written poetry do not apply to Dylan's lyrics; Mellers's and Middleton's experiences show that fine-art musical terminology is equally inappropriate. Words and music cannot be wrenched apart and shooed off to their respective academic disciplines. And folklorists, trained in anthropology, for some decades have emphasized the inappropriateness of passing any aesthetic judgment on what one collects, especially if influenced by European fine-art standards. The folklorists who have begun to investigate aesthetic standards held by folk artists and audiences—including Michael Owen Jones and Henry Glassie—insist on the varieties of aesthetic experience, on the need for detailed contextual data on each individual's preferences. Only a few folklorists have tried to systemize such evidence. For example, Robert Jerome Smith did an experiment in folklore aesthetics: he recorded two stories in oral circulation on campus, divided each into constituent events, and had students listen and mark each event according to their responses on a pleasant/ unpleasant scale. Thus emerged contour graphs of hearers' affective responses.[42]

But let's face it: when King Lear dies, everybody is going to mark "unpleasant." Such a means of objective testing for aesthetic value is sure to share the problems that have plagued philosophers of music since Pythagoras. "The attempt to explain and understand music as a succession of separable, discrete sounds and sound complexes is the error of atomism," snaps Leonard B. Meyer unsympathetically.[43] Analyzing a song as the sum of its affective parts is, of course, even less likely to work for rock than for classical music.

I am at the outermost concentric ring around a study of the artistry of *John Wesley Harding*, having gone from the aesthetics of Dylan to the aesthetics of rock to "folk" aesthetics to fine-art aesthetics. The seemingly promising ring that I have skipped over, that of popular-culture studies, also offers few guidelines. An article entitled "The Aesthetics of the Popular Arts" contributes nothing. In it, Abraham Kaplan articulates the defensive stance of the elite establishment, his style marked by frequent use of the word "mere": popular art replaces aesthetic perception with mere recognition, replaces aesthetic response with mere reaction, and so on.[44]

In contrast, John G. Cawelti understands and appreciates popular art, in an article similarly entitled. But his is a plug-in paper: he suggest applying to Beatles songs the methodology developed by the auteur school of film criticism. He urges the popular-art critic to "examine the entire body of work for recurrent stylistic and thematic patterns [which build tension and fulfill expectations], rather than [undertaking] the isolated analysis of the individual work in its unique totality."[45] But as I have shown for Dylan, and as one could show for the Beatles, isolated analysis of the individual song's unique details is precisely the proper starting point. Examining the entire body of work leads straight toward a morass of strained chronological schemata, pointless generalizations, and pretentious mush.

In *Popular Culture and High Culture*, sociologist Herbert J. Gans argues extensively "that if people seek aesthetic gratification and that if their cultural choices express their own values and taste standards, they are equally valid and desirable whether the culture is high or low."[46] So-called high culture has advantages over the four other taste cultures that Gans defines: a small absolute advantage in that it can provide a somewhat wider emotional and geographic outlook, and an enormous practical advantage in that "high culture standards are explicit... codified... [taught] often as the only set of aesthetic standards in existence. The standards of the other taste cultures are rarely discussed and taught, and are thus implicit, uncodified, and for all practical purposes invisible."[47] Gans is interested in media other than records, however; he hints that his criteria might not apply to recent popular music.[48]

Gans is right: the *John Wesley Harding* reviews show that journalists writing for the rock-music subculture constantly and comfortably articulate, discuss, teach, and make explicit the standards by which they judge artistic merit. To discuss the album they raise at least briefly the same issues that I have been developing full-length: the merger of black and white musical traditions, interaction of vocal and instrumental effects with sense of lyrics, differentiation of listener from reader response, variation in performance, the question of author's intention, the identification (or not) of the listener with the narrator in the lyrics, the judicious use of pronouns and negatives and oppositions, foregrounding of clichés, remarkable rhymes, disruption of narrative time sequences, aphoristic use of individual lines, and the effects of musical variety and verbal thematic unity throughout an album—in *John Wesley Harding* encompassing images of courts and justice, freedom and chains, outlaws and honest men, hands and arms and feet and garments and gold, heaven and homes and entrapment, gifts and messages, glass and blindness and vision and revelation, roads and friends, death and time and eternity, whores and lovers and mothers and babies, all combined in the album to recreate the atmosphere of America in 1967 without once saying "Vietnam" and to evoke the power of Judeo-Christian mythology without once saying, "This is the only way out of here."

In separate, atomized disciplines, academia is far less than the sum of its parts, for no one set of time-tested analytic conventions can deal adequately with a new phenomenon. But precedents can be found and adapted, by those who seek. So let me just say to those who would claim that academia already has all the answers and to those who would claim that academia necessarily stifles all the important questions,

> *You're right from your side*
> *I'm right from mine*
> *We're both just one too many mornings*
> *And a thousand miles behind*
> > —*"One Too Many Mornings," 1964*

Heu mater, haec vero clausula sit?

Appendix A

Texts and Recording Information for Performances Discussed

When no lead singer is given, assume Bob Dylan. All music publishers are ASCAP. A question mark means that this musician is credited on the album but may or may not be playing on this cut.

Main text given is for first performance of the song discussed. Variant lines, to the right, refer to text published in *Writings and Drawings* only for "Sad-Eyed Lady" and "Subterranean Homesick Blues." Otherwise, variant lines refer to other performances, coded in brackets before their respective recording information. Spelling follows written English, except where spelling out (e.g., "going to" for pronunciation "gonna") would give false idea of timing. Titles of songs are spelled as published. All Dylan songs reproduced by permission of Ram's Horn Music, Warner Bros., Inc., and Dwarf Music.

Chapter I

"Oxford Town" (copyright 1963, Warner Bros., Inc.): Studio version from *The Freewheelin' Bob Dylan* (Col. CS 8786). Recorded April 1962-April 1963, released May1963. Producer, John Hammond.

Oxford town, Oxford town
Everybody's got their heads bowed down
Sun don't shine above the ground
Ain't a-going down to Oxford town

He went down to Oxford town
Guns and clubs followed him down
All because his face was brown
Better get away from Oxford town

Oxford town, around the bend
He come to the door, he couldn't get in
All because of the color of his skin
What do you think about that, my friend?

Me and my girl and my girl's son
We got met with a tear-gas bomb
I don't even know why we come
Going back where we come from

Oxford town in the afternoon
Everybody singing a sorrowful tune
Two men died 'neath the Mississippi moon
Somebody better investigate soon

"The Ballad of Oxford, Mississippi," by Phil Ochs (copyright 1962, by author): Not recorded. Text from *Broadside* [N.Y.], no. 15, November 1962. Reproduced by permission of Appleseed Music, Inc.

Note to second edition:

Permission to quote this song was denied, by some L.A. conglomerate that has somehow seized control of Phil Ochs' songs.

"A Hard Rain's A-Gonna Fall" (copyright 1963, Warner Bros., Inc.): Studio version from *The Freewheelin' Bob Dylan* (Col. CS 8786). Recorded April 1962-April 1963, released May 1963. Producer, John Hammond.

[Textual variants for:] Studio version by Bryan Ferry (vocals and keyboard), from *These Foolish Things* (Atl. SD 7304). Recorded June 1973, released 1974. With John Porter (guitars, bass), Eddie Jobson (violin, keyboard, synthesizer), David Skinner (piano), Roger Ball and Malcolm Duncan? (saxophones), Henry Lowther? (trumpet), Robbie Montgomery and Jessie Smith (vocals). Producers, Bryan Ferry, John Porter, John Punter.

Oh, where have you been, my blue-eyed son?
And where have you been, my darling young one?
    [Where have you been, my darling young one?]
I've stumbled on the side of twelve misty mountains
I've walked and I've crawled on six crooked highways
    [Walked and I've crawled on six crooked highways]
I've stepped in the middle of seven sad forests
    [Stepped in the middle...]
I've been out in front of a dozen dead oceans
    [Been out in front...]
I've been ten thousand miles in the mouth of a graveyard
And it's a hard, and it's a hard, it's a hard, it's a hard
    [It's a hard, and it's a hard, and it's a hard, and it's a hard]
It's a hard rain's a-gonna fall
    [And it's a hard rain's a-gonna fall]

Oh, what did you see, my blue-eyed son?
And what did you see, my darling young one?
[What did you…]
I saw a newborn baby with wild wolves all around it
[I saw a newborn baby with wild wolves around it]
I saw a highway of diamonds with nobody on it
[Saw a highway…]
I saw a black branch with blood that kept dripping
[Saw a black…]
I saw a room full of men with their hammers a-bleeding
[Saw a room…]
I saw a white ladder all covered with water
[A white ladder…]
I saw ten thousand talkers whose tongues were all broken
I saw guns and sharp swords in the hands of young children
And it's a hard, it's a hard, it's a hard, and it's a hard
[And it's a hard, and it's a hard, and it's a hard, ha-hard, hard]
It's a hard rain's a-gonna fall
[And it's a hard rain's a-gonna fall.]

And what did you hear, my blue-eyed son?
And what did you hear, my darling young one?
[What did you…]
I heard the sound of a thunder that roared out a warning
I heard the roar of a wave that could drown the whole world
[Heard the…]
I heard one hundred drummers whose hands were a-blazing
[Heard the one…]
I heard ten thousand whispering and nobody listening
[Heard ten…]
I heard one person starve, I heard many people laughing
[Heard one person starve, many people laughing]
I heard the song of a poet who died in the gutter
[Heard the…]
I heard the sound of a clown who cried in the alley
And it's a hard, it's a hard, it's a hard, it's a hard
[And it's a hard, and it's a hard, and it's a hard, hard, hard, hard]
It's a hard rain's a-gonna fall
[And it's a hard rain's a-gonna fall]

Oh, what did you meet, my blue-eyed son?
   [Oh, who did you meet, my blue-eyed son?]
And who did you meet, my darling young one?
   [Who did...]
I met a young child beside a dead pony
I met a white man who walked a black dog
I met a young woman whose body was burning
   [I met a young girl whose body was burning]
I met a young girl, she gave me a rainbow
   [A young girl, she gave me a rainbow]
I met one man who was wounded in love
I met another man who was wounded in hatred
   [Another man who...]
And it's a hard, it's a hard, it's a hard, it's a hard
   [And it's a hard, and it's a hard, and it's a ha-ha hard]
It's a hard rain's a-gonna fall
   [And it's a hard rain's a-gonna fall]

And what'll you do now, my blue-eyed son?
   [Oh, what'll you...]
And what'll you do now, my darling young one?
   [What'll you...]
I'm a-going back out before the rain starts a-falling
I'll walk to the depths of the deepest dark forest
   [Walk to the...]
Where the people are many and their hands are all empty
Where the pellets of poison are flooding their waters
Where the home in the valley meets the damp dirty prison
And the executioner's face is always well hidden
   [Where the executioner's...]
Where hunger is ugly, where the souls are forgotten
Where black is the color, where none is the number
   [Where black is the color and none is the number]
And I'll tell it and speak it and think it and breathe it
   [And I'll tell it and think it and speak it...]
And reflect from the mountain so all souls can see it
   [And reflect it from...]
Then I'll stand on the ocean until I start sinking
   [Then I'll stand in the ocean...]

But I'll know my song well before I start singing
And it's a hard, it's a hard, it's a hard, and it's a hard
    [And it's a hard, it's ha-hard, and it's a ha-ha-ha-ha-ha-ha hard]
It's a hard rain's a-gonna fall
    [And it's hard rain's a-gonna fall]
    [And it's a hard, and it's a hard, and it's ha-ha hard]
    [And it's a hard rain's a-gonna fall]
    [And it's a hard, and it's a hard, and it's a so-oh-oh-oh ha-ha hard]
    [And it's hard rain's a-gonna fall]

Chapter II

"She Belongs to Me" (copyright 1965, Warner Bros., Inc.): Studio version
from *Bringing It All Back Home* (Col. CS 9128). Recorded January 1965,
released March 1965. With musicians not credited, probably including Bruce
Langhorne (guitar). Producer, Tom Wilson.

She's got everything she needs, she's an artist, she don't look back
She's got everything she needs, she's an artist, she don't look back
She can take the dark out of the nighttime and paint the daytime black

You will start out standing, proud to steal her anything she sees
You will start out standing, proud to steal her anything she sees
But you will wind up peeking through her keyhole down upon your knees

She never stumbles, she got no place to fall
She never stumbles, she got no place to fall
She's nobody's child, the law can't touch her at all

She wears an Egyptian ring that sparkles before she speaks
She wears an Egyptian ring that sparkles before she speaks
She's a hypnotist collector, you are a walking antique

Bow down to her on Sunday, salute her when her birthday comes
Bow down to her on Sunday, salute her when her birthday comes
For Halloween buy her a trumpet, and for Christmas give her a drum

"Sad-Eyed Lady of the Lowlands" (copyright 1966, Dwarf Music): Studio
version from *Blonde on Blonde* (Col. C2S 841). Recorded October 1965-

March 1966, released May 1966. With Wayne Moss, Charlie McCoy, Kenneth Buttrey, Hargus Robbins, Jerry Kennedy, Joe South, Al Kooper, Bill Aikins, Henry Strzelecki, Jaime Robertson (no instruments given). Producer, Bob Johnston.

[Textual variants as published in *Writings and Drawings*, pp. 222-23.]

With your mercury mouth in the missionary times
And your eyes like smoke and your prayers like rhymes
And your silver cross, and your voice like chimes
Oh, who do they think could bury you?
    [Oh, who among them do they think could bury you?]
With your pockets well protected at last
And your streetcar visions which you place on the grass
And your flesh like silk, and your face like glass
Who could they get to carry you?
    [Who among them do they think could carry you?]
Sad-eyed lady of the lowlands
Where the sad-eyed prophet says that no man comes
My warehouse eyes, my Arabian drums
Should I put them by your gate
    [Should I leave them by your gate]
Or, sad-eyed lady, should I wait?

With your sheets like metal and your belt like lace
And your deck of cards missing the jack and the ace
And your basement clothes and your hollow face
Who among them can think he could outguess you?
With your silhouette when the sunlight dims
Into your eyes where the moonlight swims
And your matchbook songs and your gypsy hymns
Who among them would try to impress you?
Sad-eyed lady of the lowlands
Where the sad-eyed prophets say that no man comes
    [Where the sad-eyed prophet says...]
My warehouse eyes, my Arabian drums
Should I put them by your gate
    [Should I leave them by your gate]
Or, sad-eyed lady, should I wait?

The kings of Tyrus with their convict list
Are waiting in line for their geranium kiss
And you wouldn't know it would happen like this
But who among them really wants just to kiss you?
With your childhood flames on your midnight rug
And your Spanish manners and your mother's drugs
And your cowboy mouth and your curfew plugs
Who among them do you think could resist you?
Sad-eyed lady of the lowlands
Where the sad-eyed prophets say that no man comes
    [Where the sad-eyed prophet says...]
My warehouse eyes, my Arabian drums
Should I leave them by your gate
Or, sad-eyed lady, should I wait?

Oh, the farmers and the businessmen, they all did decide
To show you where the dead angels are that they used to hide
    [To show you the dead angels that they used to hide]
But why did they pick you to sympathize with their side?
How could they ever mistake you?
    [Oh, how could they...]
They wished you'd accepted the blame for the farm
But with the sea at your feet and the phony false alarm
And with the child of the hoodlum wrapped up in your arms
    [And with the child of a hoodlum...]
How could they ever have persuaded you?
    [How could they ever, ever persuade you?]
Sad-eyed lady of the lowlands
Where the sad-eyed prophets say that no man's come
    [Where the sad-eyed prophet says that no man comes]
My warehouse eyes, my Arabian drums
Should I leave them by your gate
Or, sad-eyed lady, should I wait?

With your sheet-metal memory of Cannery Row
And your magazine husband, who one day just had to go
And your gentleness now, which you just can't help but show
Who among them do you think would employ you?
Now you stand with your thief, you're on his parole

With your holy medallion in your fingertips now that fold
   [With your holy medallion which your fingertips fold]
And your saintlike face and your ghostlike soul
Who among them could ever think he could destroy you?
   [Oh, who among them do you think could destroy you?]
Sad-eyed lady of the lowlands
Where the sad-eyed prophets say that no man comes
   [Where the sad-eyed prophet says…]
My warehouse eyes, my Arabian drums
Should I leave them by your gate
Or, sad-eyed lady, should I wait?

"Shelter from the Storm" (copyright 1974, 1975, Ram's Horn Music): Studio version from *Blood on the Tracks* (Col. PC 33235). Recorded September-December 1974, released January 1975. With Tony Brown (bass). Engineer, Phil Ramone.

'Twas in another lifetime, one of toil and blood
When blackness was a virtue, the road was full of mud
I came in from the wilderness, a creature void of form
Come in, she said, I'll give you shelter from the storm

And if I pass this way again, you can rest assured
I'll always do my best for her, on that I give my word
In a world of steeleyed death and men who are fighting to be warm
Come in, she said, I'll give you shelter from the storm

Not a word was spoke between us, there was little risk involved
Everything up to that point had been left unresolved
Try imagining a place where it's always safe and warm
Come in, she said, I'll give you shelter from the storm

I was burned out from exhaustion, buried in the hail
Poisoned in the bushes, blown out on the trail
Hunted like a crocodile, ravished in the corn
Come in, she said, I'll give you shelter from the storm

Suddenly I turned around and she was standing there
With silver bracelets on her wrists and flowers in her hair

She walked up to me so gracefully and took my crown of thorns
Come in, she said, I'll give you shelter from the storm

Now there's a wall between us, something has been lost
I took too much for granted, I got my signals crossed
Just to think that it all began on a noneventful morn
Come in, she said, I'll give you shelter from the storm

Well, the deputy walks on hard nails and the preacher rides a mount
But nothing really matters much, it's doom alone that counts
And the one-eyed undertaker he blows a futile horn
Come in, she said, I'll give you shelter from the storm

I've heard newborn babies wailing like a mourning dove
And old men with broken teeth stranded without love
Do I understand your question, man, is it hopeless and forlorn?
Come in, she said, I'll give you shelter from the storm

In a little hilltop village they gambled for my clothes
I bargained for salvation and she gimme a lethal dose
I offered up my innocence and got repaid with scorn
Come in, she said, I'll give you shelter from the storm

I'm living in a foreign country, but I'm bound to cross the line
Beauty walks a razor's edge, someday I'll make it mine
If I could only turn back the clock to when God and her were born
Come in, she said, I'll give you shelter from the storm

"Isis" (copyright 1975, 1976, Ram's Horn Music): Studio version from *Desire* (Col. PC 33893). Recorded July-October 1975, released January 1976. With Rob Stoner (bass, vocals), Scarlet Rivera (violin), Howard Wyeth (drums), Vincent Bell? (bellzouki), Dom Cortese? (mandolin). Producer, Don DeVito; engineer, Don Meehan.

I married Isis on the fifth day of May
But I could not hold on to her very long
So I cut off my hair and I rode straightaway
For the wild unknown country where I could not go wrong

I came to a high place of darkness and light
The dividing line ran through the center of town
I hitched up my pony to a post on the right
Went into a laundry to wash my clothes down

A man in the corner approached me for a match
I knew right away he was not ordinary
He said, "Are you looking for something easy to catch?"
I said, "I got no money." He said, "That ain't necessary"

We set out that night for the cold in the north
I gave him my blanket and he gave me his word
I said, "Where are we going?" He said we'd be back by the fourth
I said, "That's the best news that I've ever heard"

I was thinking about turquoise, I was thinking about gold
I was thinking about diamonds and the world's biggest necklace
As we rode through the canyons, through the devilish cold
I was thinking about Isis, how she thought I was so reckless

How she told me that one day we would meet up again
And things would be different the next time we wed
If I only could hang on and just be her friend
I still can't remember all the best things she said

We came to the pyramids all embedded in ice
He said, "There's a body I'm trying to find
If I carry it out, it'll bring a good price"
'Twas then that I knew what he had on his mind

The wind it was howling and the snow was outrageous
We chopped through the night and we chopped through the dawn
When he died I was hoping that it wasn't contagious
But I made up my mind that I had to go on

I broke into the tomb, but the casket was empty
There was no jewels, no nothing, I felt I'd been had
When I saw that my partner was just being friendly
When I took up his offer I musta been mad

I picked up his body and I dragged him inside
Threw him down in the hole and I put back the cover
I said a quick prayer and I felt satisfied
Then I rode back to find Isis just to tell her I love her

She was there in the meadow where the creek used to rise
Blinded by sleep and in need of a bed
I came in from the east with the sun in my eyes
I cursed her one time then I rode on ahead

She said, "Where you been?" I said, "No place special"
She said, "You look different." I said, "Well, I guess"
She said, "You been gone." I said, "That's only natural"
She said, "You gonna stay?" I said, "If you want me to, yes"

Isis, oh Isis, you're a mystical child
What drives me to you is what drives me insane
I still can remember the way that you smiled
On the fifth day of May in the drizzling rain

Chapter III

"Just Like a Woman" (copyright 1966, Dwarf Music): Studio version from *Blonde on Blonde* (Col. C2S 841). Recorded October 1965-March 1966, released May 1966. With Wayne Moss, Charlie McCoy, Kenneth Buttrey, Hargus Robbins, Jerry Kennedy, Joe South, Al Kooper, Bill Aikins, Henry Strzelecki, Jaime Robertson (no instruments given). Producer, Bob Johnston.

[Textual variants for:] Concert version from *Before the Flood* (Asy. AB 201). Recorded 14 February 1974 in Los Angeles Forum, released June 1974. Engineers, Phil Ramone, Rob Fraboni, Nat Jeffrey.

Nobody feels any pain
Tonight as I stand inside the rain
Everybody knows
That Baby's got new clothes
       [Baby's got new clothes]
But lately I see her ribbons and her bows
Have fallen from her curls
She takes just like a woman, yes she does
       [She takes just like a woman]

She makes love just like a woman, yes she does
    [And she aches just like a woman]
And she aches just like a woman
    [And she wakes just like a woman]
But she breaks just like a little girl
    [Yeah, but she breaks just like a little girl]

Queen Mary, she's my friend
Yes, I believe I'll go see her again
Nobody has to guess
That Baby can't be blessed
Till she finally sees that she's like all the rest
    [Till she sees finally…]
With her fog, her amphetamine and her pearls
    [In her fog, with her amphetamine and her pearls]
She takes just like a woman, yes
    [She takes just like a woman]
She makes love just like a woman, yes she does
    [And she wakes just like a woman]
And she aches just like a woman
But she breaks just like a little girl

It was rain from the first
    [It was raining from the first]
And I was dying there of thirst
So I came in here
And your longtime curse hurts
But what's worse
Is this pain in here
I can't stay in here
Ain't it clear that

I just can't fit
    [I just don't fit]
Yes, I believe it's time for us to quit
When we meet again
Introduced as friends
Please don't let on that you knew me when
I was hungry and it was your world

Ah, you fake just like a woman, yes you do
    [You take just like a woman]
You make love just like a woman, yes you do
    [And you ache just like a woman]
Then you ache just like a woman
    [And you make love just like a woman]
But you break just like a little girl

Chapter IV

"Like a Rolling Stone" (copyright 1965, Warner Bros., Inc.): Studio version
from *Highway 61 Revisited* (Col. CS 9189). Recorded mid-June 1965, single
released late June 1965, album released August 1965. With Mike Bloomfield
(guitar), Al Kooper (organ), Paul Griffin (piano), Bobby Gregg (drums),
Harvey Goldstein or Russ Savakus (bass). Producer, Tom Wilson.

[Textual variants *N65* for:] Concert bootleg, from Newport Folk Festival,
Newport, Rhode Island, 25 July 1965. With Al Kooper (organ), Mike
Bloomfield (guitar), Barry Goldberg (piano), Jerome Arnold (bass), Sam
Lay (drums).

[Textual variants *M66* for:] Concert bootleg, probably from Manchester,
England, spring 1966. (This cut is on a bootleg record called *The Royal
Albert Hall Concert 1966*.) With the Hawks: Rick Danko (bass), Garth
Hudson (keyboard), Richard Manuel (drums or keyboard), Robbie
Robertson (guitar), Mickey Jones (drums).

[Textual variants *L74* for:] Concert version from *Before the Flood* (Asy.
AB 201). Recorded 13 February 1974 in Los Angeles Forum, released June
1974. With The Band: Robbie Robertson (guitar), Garth Hudson
(keyboards), Levon Helm (drums), Richard Manuel (drums or keyboards),
Rick Danko (bass), all but Hudson also vocals. Engineers, Phil Ramone,
Rob Fraboni, Nat Jeffrey.

Once upon a time you dressed so fine
You threw the bums a dime in your prime, didn't you?
People'd call, say beware, doll, you're bound to fall
You thought they were all kidding you
You used to laugh about
Everybody that was hanging out
Now you don't talk so loud
Now you don't seem so proud

About having to be scrounging your next meal.
    [M66, L74: About having to be scrounging around for your next meal]
How does it feel?
How does it feel?
To be without a home
    [N65, M66: To be on your own]
    [extra line N65, M66, L74: With no direction home]
Like a complete unknown
Like a rolling stone

You've gone to the finest school all right, Miss Lonely
But you know you only used to get juiced in it
Nobody's ever taught you how to live out on the street
And now you're gonna have to get used to it
    [M66, L74: And you find out now you're gonna...]
You said you'd never compromise
With the mystery tramp, but now you realize
He's not selling any alibis
As you stare into the vacuum of his eyes
And say, "Do you want to make a deal?"
    [L74: And say, "Would you like to make a deal?"]
How does it feel?
How does it feel?
To be on your own [L74: To be without a home]
With no direction home
A complete unknown [N65, M66, L74: Like a complete unknown]
Like a rolling stone [L74: Just like a rolling stone]

You never turned around to see the frowns on the jugglers and the clowns
When they all did tricks for you
    [N65: When they come down to do...]
    [M66, L74: When they all came down to do...]
You never understood that it ain't no good
You shouldn't let other people get your kicks for you
    [N65: You can't let other people get...]
You used to ride on the chrome horse with your diplomat
    [N65, M66, L74: You used to ride the chrome horse...]
Who carried on his shoulder a Siamese cat
Ain't it hard when you discover that

He really wasn't where it's at
After he took from you everything he could steal
    [N65: After he's taken from you everything...]
    [M66, L74: After he's taken everything he can steal]
How does it feel?
How does it feel?
To be on your own [L74: To be without a home]
With no direction home
Like a complete unknown
Like a rolling stone [L74: Just like a rolling stone]

Princess on the steeple, and all the pretty people
    [N65: Ah you've gone to the steeple, and all...]
They all drinking, thinking that they got it made
    [N65: Drinking, thinking that they...]
Exchanging all precious gifts
    [N65: You better take your diamond ring and things]
    [M66, L74: Exchanging all precious gifts and things]
But you better take your diamond ring, you better pawn it, babe
    [N65: Better take it down and you're gonna pawn...]
    [M66, L74: But you better take your diamond ring down and pawn...]
You used to be so amused
At Napoleon in rags and the language that he used
Go to him now, he calls you, you can't refuse
When you ain't got nothing, you got nothing to lose
You're invisible now, you got no secrets to conceal
    [L74: You're invisible, you got no secrets...]
How does it feel?
How does it feel?
To be on your own [L74: To be without a home]
With no direction home
Like a complete unknown
Like a rolling stone [L74: Just like a rolling stone]

Chapter V

"It Ain't Me, Babe" (copyright 1964, Warner Bros., Inc.): Studio version from *Another Side of Bob Dylan* (Col. CS 8993). Recorded June 1964, released August 1964. Producer, Tom Wilson.

[Textual variants *B* for:] Concert bootleg, from Philharmonic Hall, New York City, 31 October 1964. With Joan Baez.

[Textual variants *T* for:] Studio version by the Turtles, from *It Ain't Me Babe* (White Whale WW-111). Released 1965? Howard Kaylan and Mark Vollman (vocals), Al Nichol and Jim Tucker (guitars), Chuck Portz (bass), Don Murray (drums). Producers, Lee Lasseff, Ted Feigin.

[Textual variants *F* for:] Studio version by Bryan Ferry (vocals and keyboard), from *Another Time, Another Place* (Atl. SD 18113). Recorded spring 1974, released 1974. With John Porter (guitar), Paul Thompson (drums), John Wetton (bass); also featuring nineteen more musicians, four vocalists, brass and string arrangers. Producers, Bryan Ferry, John Punter; engineer, John Punter.

[Textual variants *74* for:] Concert version from *Before the Flood* (Asy. AB 201). Recorded 13 February 1974 in Los Angeles Forum, released June 1974. With The Band: Robbie Robertson (guitar), Garth Hudson (keyboards), Levon Helm (drums), Richard Manuel (drums or keyboards), Rick Danko (bass), all but Hudson also vocals. Engineers, Phil Ramone, Rob Fraboni, Nat Jeffrey.

[Textual variants *75* for:] Concert bootleg, from the first Boston Music Hall concert, 21 November 1975. With the Rolling Thunder Review, including some or all of: Scarlet Rivera (violin), Joan Baez and Bob Neuwirth (vocals, guitars), T-Bone Burnette, Jim McGuinn, Steve Soles, Mick Ronson (all guitars), Dave Mansfield (dobro, steel guitar, mandolin, violin), Rob Stoner (bass), Howie Wyeth and Luther Rix (drums), Ronee Blakely (vocals).

Go away from my window
Leave at your own chosen speed
I'm not the one you want, Babe
    [75: I'm not the one that you want, Babe]
I'm not the one you need
You say you're looking for someone
Who's never weak but always strong
    [B, F, 74: Never weak but always strong]
    [75: Not weak but always strong]
To protect you and defend you
Whether you are right or wrong
Someone to open each and every door
But it ain't me, Babe
No, no, no, it ain't me, Babe

[74: No, no, no, it sure ain't me, Babe]
It ain't me you're looking for, Babe
[T: Well, it ain't me you're looking for, Babe]
[F: It ain't me that you're looking for, Babe]
[extra line 75: It ain't me you're looking for]

Go lightly from the ledge, Babe
[74: Move lightly from the ledge, Babe]
[75: Step lightly from the ledge, Babe]
Go lightly on the ground
[B: Go lightly from the ground]
[74: Move lightly on the ground]
[75: Step lightly on the ground]
I'm not the one you want, Babe
I'll only let you down
[B, F: I will only let you down]
[T: I'll only leave you down]
You say you're looking for someone
Who'll promise never to part
[B, F, 74: Who will promise never to part]
Someone to close his eyes for you
[T: Someone to close his eyes to you]
Someone to close his heart
Someone who will die for you and more
[74: Someone who will die for you and maybe more]
But it ain't me, Babe
[74: But it still ain't me, Babe]
No, no, no, it ain't me, Babe
[74: No, no, no, it sure ain't me, Babe]
It ain't me you're looking for, Babe
[F: It ain't me that you're looking for, Babe]
[extra line 75: It ain't me you're looking for]
[T: Well, it ain't me you're looking for, Babe]
[T ends here, after the extra lines:]
[No, it ain't me you're looking for, Babe]
[I said a no, no, no, it ain't me, Babe]
[I said a no, no, no, it ain't me, Babe]
[I said a no, no, no, it ain't me, Babe]
[I said a no, no, no, it ain't me, Babe]
[I said a no, no, no, it ain't me, Babe]

Go melt back in the night
    [B, F, 74: Go melt back into the night, Babe]
    [75: Melt back into the night, Babe]
Everything inside is made of stone
    [74, 75: Everything inside here is made of stone]
There's nothing in here moving
    [F, 74, 75: There's nothing in here that's moving]
And anyway I'm not alone
You say you're looking for someone
Who'll pick you up each time you fall
    [B, 74, 75: Who'll pick you up every time you fall]
To gather flowers constantly
    [74, 75: Someone to gather flowers constantly]
And to come each time you call
    [B, 74, 75: And to come every time you call]
A lover for your life and nothing more
    [74: A lover for your life and don't want (?) more]
    [75: A lover for your life but nothing more]
But it ain't me, Babe
    [74: And it still ain't me, Babe]
    [75: It ain't me, Babe]
No, no, no, it ain't me, Babe
    [74: No, no, no, it sure ain't me, Babe]
It ain't me you're looking for, Babe
    [extra lines B: It ain't me, Babe]
    [No, no, no, it ain't me, Babe]
    [It ain't me you're looking for, Babe]
    [extra lines 75: (spoken) Must be someone else!]
    [It ain't me you're looking for]

Chapter VI

"Subterranean Homesick Blues" (copyright 1965, Warner Bros., Inc.): Studio version from *Bringing It All Back Home* (Col. CS 9128). Recorded January 1965, released March 1965. With musicians not credited, probably including Bruce Langhorne (guitar). Producer, Tom Wilson.

    [Textual variants as published in *Writings and Drawings*, p. 160.]

    Separate transcription: Rough draft as published in *Writings and Drawings*, beside p. 160.

man in a coonskin cap in the pigp n wants 11dol ars bills a i only g
i stumble downtown

man wants   pay off

a voice com. sounding like a passenger train
look out kid, it's something you did
god nows when but you're doing i again
better duck down the doorway/ loo ing or a new friend
man in a coonskin cap кипих   does a back bend/
here comes maggie/ strutting down the кипих fifth street
mag ie comes fleetfoot/ face full of black soot
talking that the heat put/plants in the bed/ but
the phone's tapped anyway/maggie says that many say
they mu t bust in early May/ orde s from the da
look out kid/ it dont matter what you did
nxbe c reful that they sell yuh/ r else try t ell yuh
they nly try t tail you if they anna nail
knexxnnxikxxkxxkxdmxrx   dont be bashful but please be car ful
mailman coming down the chimney l ke sata claus

dont be bashful if you see they nn try you
keep a c ean nose
an eyes u n the
plai clothes

careful if they tail you/they onl   wann ill you

walking down payxxixxxxx/ hinking out the govt/
daddy's in the dimestore/ fxxt kxximxxkgetting 10 cent medicine
man in the trench coat/ badge out/laid off
wants t et paid off/ naxkingxxxan nxxixbxxxxff
says he's got a bad cough, wants t get aid off

get sick/ get well/ hang around the ink well
ri g bell/ hard t tell if anything is gonna sell
try hard/ get barred/ get back/ et stale
jxxp et nailed/ jump bail
join the army if you fail
look out id you gonna get hit
by teachers, preacher, 6timelov s hanging round threatres

get born/ keep warm/xaxixxxkm sh rt pants, romance
learn t dance/ ixxxxxxxdk get bl ssed/ try t be a success
please ne plea e him/ buy gifts/ dont steal/ dont lift
2- years of school an   put y u on the day shift
   look out kid/ ixxt they ot it ll hid
xkxkxxixxxkkxxixxxxnxkx xixixxxkixx kxkxxkxxxxxkkxkx
k it's nowhere, all bare/ they just pay you f re there
in t the smog/thick fog/they tell you hthat it's fresh air
   (sick)
get down/ drop down/ make it out the back door
or else quit laying on the floor before you get your back re
                        (closet)

 in a k ik /

dont be bashful/ check where the txx wind blows/rain flows
keep a clean nose an be careful of the plain clothes

Johnny's in the basement
Mixing up the medicine
I'm on the pavement
Thinking about the government
A man in a trench coat [The man in the trench coat]
Badge out, laid off
Says he's got a bad cough
Wants to get it paid off
Look out kid
It's something you did
God knows when
But you're doing it again
You better duck down the alleyway
Looking for a new friend
The man in the coonskin cap
In a pig pen [In the big pen]
Wants eleven dollar bills
You only got ten

Maggie comes fleet foot
Face full of black soot
Talking that the heat put
Plants in the bed but
The phone's tapped anyway
Maggie says that many say
They must bust in early May
Orders from the D.A.
Look out kid
Don't matter what you did
Walk on your tiptoes
Don't tie no bows [Don't try "No-Doz"]
Better stay away from those
That carry around a fire hose
Keep a clean nose
Watch the plain clothes
You don't need a weatherman
To know which way the wind blows

Get sick, get well
Hang around a ink well

Hang bell, hard to tell [Ring bell, hard to tell]
If anything is going to sell
Try hard, get fired [Try hard, get barred]
Get back, write braille
Get jailed, jump bail
Join the army if you fail
Look out kid
You're gonna get hit
But losers, cheaters [But users, cheaters]
Six-time users [Six-time losers]
Hanging around the theaters [Hang around the theaters]
Girl by the whirlpool
Looking for a new fool
Don't follow leaders
Watch the parking meters

Ah, get born, keep warm
Short pants, romance, learn to dance
Get dressed, get blessed
Try to be a success
Please her, please him, buy gifts
Don't steal, don't lift
Twenty years of schooling
And they put you on the day shift
Look out kid
They keep it all hid
Better jump down a manhole
Light yourself a candle
Don't wear sandals
Try to avoid the scandals
Don't wanna be a bum
You better chew gum
The pump don't work
'Cause the vandals took the handles

"Idiot Wind" (copyright 1974, 1975, Ram's Horn Music): Studio version
from *Blood on the Tracks* (Col. PC 33235). Recorded 27 or 30 December
1974 at Sound 80 Studios, Minneapolis, released January 1975. With Chris

Weber (twelve-string guitar), Ken Odegard (guitar), Greg Inhofer (keyboards), Bill Peterson (bass), Bill Berg (drums).

[Textual variants for:] Concert version from *Hard Rain* (Col. PC 34349). Recorded 23 May 1976 in Hughes Stadium, Fort Collins, Colorado, released September 1976. With Rolling Thunder Review, including some or all of: Scarlet Rivera (violin), Rob Stoner (bass and vocals), Steven Soles (guitar and vocals), Howard Wyeth (piano and drums), T-Bone Burnette (guitar and piano), Gary Burke (drums), David Mansfield (guitar). Producers, Don DeVito, Bob Dylan; engineer, Don Meehan.

Separate transcription: Studio outtake bootleg, from Columbia A&R Studios, New York City, mid-September 1974. With Tony Brown (bass), Paul Griffin (organ).

Someone's got it in for me
They're planting stories in the press
Whoever it is I wish they'd cut it out quick
But when they will, I can only guess
They say I shot a man named Gray
And took his wife to Italy
She inherited a million bucks
And when she died, it came to me
I can't help it if I'm lucky
People see me all the time
And they just can't remember how to act
    [I guess they just can't remember how to act]
Their minds are filled with big ideas
    [Their minds are filled with false ideas]
Images, and distorted facts
Even you, yesterday [And even you, yesterday]
You had to ask me where it was at
I couldn't believe after all these years
You didn't know me any better than that
Sweet lady
Idiot wind
Blowing every time you move your mouth
Blowing down the backroads heading south
    [Blowing on down the backroads...]
Idiot wind
Blowing every time you move your teeth

You're an idiot, babe
It's a wonder that you still know how to breathe

I ran into the fortune teller
Who said beware of lightning that might strike
    [She said beware there's some lightning that strikes]
I haven't known peace and quiet
    [I haven't known about peace and quiet now]
For so long I can't remember what it's like
    [For so long I don't even remember what it's like]
There's a lone soldier on the cross
Smoke pouring out of a boxcar door
You didn't know it, you didn't think it could be done
    [He didn't know it, he never thought it could be done]
In the final end he won the war
    [But in the final shot he'd won the war]
After losing every battle
I woke up on the roadside
Daydreaming about the way things sometimes are
    [Daydreaming about the way things really are]
Visions of your chestnut mare
    [Visions of your smoking tongue]
Shoot through my head and are making me see stars
You hurt the ones that I love best
And cover up the truth with lies
One day you'll be in the ditch
    [One day you'll be in the grave]
Flies buzzing around your eyes
Blood on your saddle
Idiot wind
Blowing through the flowers on your tomb
Blowing through the curtains in your room
Idiot wind
Blowing every time you move your teeth
You're an idiot, babe
It's a wonder that you still know how to breathe
    [It's a wonder that you still can even breathe]

It was gravity which pulled us down
And destiny which broke us apart

You tamed the lion in my cage
But it just wasn't enough to change my heart
    [But it wasn't enough to...]
Now everything's a little upside down
As a matter of fact, the wheels have stopped
What's good is bad, what's bad is good
You find out when you reach the top
You're on the bottom [You are on the bottom]
I noticed at the ceremony
Your corrupt ways had finally made you blind
    [That your corrupt ways...]
I can't remember your face anymore
    [I can't recall your face anymore]
Your mouth is changed, your eyes don't look into mine
    [Your mouth is changed and your eyes...]
The priest wore black on the seventh day
And sat stone-faced while the building burned
I waited for you on the running boards
Near the cypress tree while the springtime turned
Slowly into autumn
Idiot wind
Blowing like a circle around my skull
From the Grand Coulee Dam to the Capitol
Idiot wind
Blowing every time you move your teeth
You're an idiot, babe
It's a wonder that you still know how to breathe

I can't feel you anymore
I can't even touch books you've read
    [I can't even touch the clothes I wear]
Every time I crawl past your door
    [Every time I come into your door]
I been wishing I been somebody else instead
    [You leave me standing in the middle of the air]
Down the highway, down the tracks
Down the road to ecstasy
I followed you beneath the stars
Hounded by your memory
And all your raging glory

I been double-crossed now
For the very last time and now I'm finally free
     [For the very last time and I think I finally see]
I kissed goodbye the howling beast
On the borderline which separated you from me
You'll never know the hurt I suffered
Nor the pain I rise above
And I'll never know the same about you
Your holiness or your kind of love
And it makes me feel so sorry
Idiot wind
Blowing through the buttons of our coats
Blowing through the letters that we wrote
Idiot wind
Blowing through the dust upon our shelves
We're idiots, babe
It's a wonder we can even feed ourselves

"Idiot Wind," outtake version

Someone's got it in for me
They're planting stories in the press
Whoever it is I wish they'd cut it out
But when they will I can only guess
They say I shot a man named Gray
And took his wife to Italy
She inherited a million bucks
And when she died it came to me
I can't help it if I'm lucky
People see me all the time
And they just can't remember how to act
Their minds are filled with big ideas
Images and distorted facts
And even you yesterday
You had to ask me where it was at
I couldn't believe after all these years
You didn't know me any better than that
Sweet lady
Idiot wind

Blowing every time you move your mouth
Blowing down the backroads heading south
Idiot wind
Blowing every time you move your teeth
You're an idiot, babe
It's a wonder that you still know how to breathe

I threw the I Ching yesterday
It said there might be some thunder at the well
Peace and quiet's been avoiding me
For so long it seems like living hell
There's a lone soldier on the hill
Watching falling raindrops pour
You'd never know it to look at him
But at the final shot he won the war
After losing every battle
I woke up on the roadside
Daydreaming about the way things sometimes are
Hoofbeats pounding in my head
At breakneck speed and making me see stars
You hurt the ones that I love best
And cover up the truth with lies
One day you'll be in the ditch
Flies buzzing around your eyes
Blood on your saddle
Idiot wind
Blowing through the flowers on your tomb
Blowing through the curtains in your room
Idiot wind
Blowing every time you move your teeth
You're an idiot, babe
It's a wonder that you still know how to breathe

It was gravity which pulled us in
Destiny which broke us apart
You tamed the lion in my cage
But it just wasn't enough to change my heart
Now everything's a little upside down
As a matter of fact the wheels have stopped

What's good is bad, what's bad is good
You find out when you've reached the top
You're on the bottom
I noticed at the ceremony
That you left all your bags behind
The driver came in after you left
He gave them all to me and then he resigned
The priest wore black on the seventh day
And waltzed around while the building burned
You didn't trust me for a minute, babe
I've never know the spring to turn
So quickly into autumn
Idiot wind
Blowing every time you move your jaw
From the Grand Coulee Dam to the Mardi Gras
Idiot wind
Blowing every time you move your teeth
You're an idiot, babe
It's a wonder that you still know how to breathe

We pushed each other a little too far
And one day just jumped into a raging storm
A hound dog bayed behind your trees
As I was packing up my uniform
I figured I'd lost you anyway
Why go on, what's the use
In order to get in a word with you
I'd'd had to come up with some excuse
And that just struck me kinda funny
I've been double-crossed too much
At times I think I've almost lost my mind
Ladykillers load dice on me
Behind my back while imitators steal me blind
You close your eyes and part your lips
And slip your fingers from your glove
You could have the best there is
But it's gonna cost you all your love
You won't get it for money
Idiot wind

Blowing through the buttons of our coats
Blowing through the letters that we wrote
Idiot wind
Blowing through the dust upon our shelves
We're idiots, babe
It's a wonder we can even feed ourselves

Appendix B

Dylan's Albums 1961–1976

Bob Dylan, March 1962 (Col. CS 8579, CL 1779)
Side 1: You're No Good; Talkin' New York; In My Time of Dyin'; Man of
Constant Sorrow; Fixin' to Die; Pretty Peggy-O; Highway 51.
Side 2: Gospel Plow; Baby, Let Me Follow You Down; House of the Risin'
Sun; Freight Train Blues; Song to Woody; See That My Grave Is Kept
Clean.
[Dylan wrote only "Talkin' New York" and "Song to Woody."]

The Freewheelin' Bob Dylan, May 1963 (Col. KCS 8786, CL 1986)
Side 1: Blowin' in the Wind; Girl from the North Country; Masters of War;
Down the Highway; Bob Dylan's Blues; A Hard Rain's A-Gonna Fall.
Side 2: Don't Think Twice, It's All Right; Bob Dylan's Dream; Oxford
Town; Talkin' World War III Blues; Corrina, Corrina (trad.); Honey,
Just Allow Me One More Chance (from H. Thomas); I Shall Be Free.

The Times They Are A-Changin', January 1964 (Col. KCS 8905, CL 2105)
Side 1: The Times They Are A-Changin'; Ballad of Hollis Brown; With
God on Our Side; One Too Many Mornings; North Country Blues.
Side 2: Only a Pawn in Their Game; Boots of Spanish Leather; When the
Ship Comes In; The Lonesome Death of Hattie Carroll; Restless
Farewell.

Another Side of Bob Dylan, August 1964 (Col. CS 8993, CL 2193)
Side 1: All I Really Want to Do; Black Crow Blues; Spanish Harlem Incident;
Chimes of Freedom; I Shall Be Free No. 10; To Ramona.
Side 2: Motorpsycho Nitemare; My Back Pages; I Don't Believe You; Ballad
in Plain D; It Ain't Me, Babe.

Bringing It All Back Home, March 1965 (Col. CS 9128, CL 2328)
Side 1: Subterranean Homesick Blues; She Belongs to Me; Maggie's Farm; Love Minus Zero/No Limit; Outlaw Blues; On the Road Again; Bob Dylan's 115th Dream.
Side 2: Mr. Tambourine Man; Gates of Eden; It's Alright, Ma (I'm Only Bleeding); It's All Over Now, Baby Blue.

Highway 61 Revisited, August 1965 (Col. CS 9189, CL 2389)
Side 1: Like a Rolling Stone; Tombstone Blues; It Takes a Lot to Laugh, It Takes a Train to Cry; From a Buick 6; Ballad of a Thin Man.
Side 2: Queen Jane Approximately; Highway 61 Revisited; Just Like Tom Thumb's Blues; Desolation Row.

Blonde on Blonde, May 1966 (Col. C2S 841, C2L 41)
Side 1: Rainy Day Women #12 & 35; Pledging My Time; Visions of Johanna; One of Us Must Know (Sooner or Later).
Side 2: I Want You; Stuck Inside of Mobile with the Memphis Blues Again; Leopard-Skin Pillbox Hat; Just Like a Woman.
Side 3: Most Likely You Go Your Way and I'll Go Mine; Temporary Like Achilles; Absolutely Sweet Marie; Fourth Time Around; Obviously Five Believers.
Side 4: Sad-Eyed Lady of the Lowlands.

Bob Dylan's Greatest Hits, March 1967 (Col. KCS 9463, KCL 2663)
Side 1: Rainy Day Women #12 & 35; Blowin' in the Wind; The Times They Are A-Changin'; It Ain't Me, Babe; Like a Rolling Stone.
Side 2: Mr. Tambourine Man; Subterranean Homesick Blues; I Want You; Positively 4th Street; Just Like a Woman.

John Wesley Harding, December 1967 (Col. CS 9604, CL 2804)
Side 1: John Wesley Harding; As I Went Out One Morning; I Dreamed I Saw St. Augustine; All Along the Watchtower; The Ballad of Frankie Lee and Judas Priest; Drifter's Escape.
Side 2: Dear Landlord; I Am a Lonesome Hobo; I Pity the Poor Immigrant; The Wicked Messenger; Down Along the Cove; I'll Be Your Baby Tonight.

Nashville Skyline, April 1969 (Col. KCS 9825)
Side 1: Girl from the North Country; Nashville Skyline Rag; To Be Alone
    With You; I Threw It All Away; Peggy Day.
Side 2: Lay, Lady, Lay; One More Night; Tell Me That It Isn't True; Country
    Pie; Tonight I'll Be Staying Here With You.

Self Portrait, June 1970 (Col. C2X 30050)
Side 1: All the Tired Horses*; Alberta #1*; I Forgot More Than You'll Ever
    Know; Days of 49; Early Mornin' Rain; In Search of Little Sadie*.
Side 2: Let It Be Me; Little Sadie*; Woogie Boogie*; Belle Isle*; Living
    the Blues*; Like a Rolling Stone**.
Side 3: Copper Kettle; Gotta Travel On; Blue Moon; The Boxer; The Mighty
    Quinn (Quinn the Eskimo)**; Take Me as I Am (Or Let Me Go).
Side 4: Take a Message to Mary; It Hurts Me Too*; Minstrel Boy**; She
    Belongs to Me**; Wigwam*; Alberta #2*.
[*Indicates that Dylan wrote the song; **indicates performance of own song
recorded at the Isle of Wight concert, 31 August 1969.]

New Morning, October 1970 (Col. KC 30290)
Side 1: If Not for You; Day of the Locusts; Time Passes Slowly; Went to
    See the Gypsy; Winterlude; If Dogs Run Free.
Side 2: New Morning; Sign on the Window; One More Weekend; The Man
    in Me; Three Angels; Father of Night.

Bob Dylan's Greatest Hits, Volume 2, November 1971 (Col. KG 31120)
Side 1: Watching the River Flow; Don't Think Twice, It's All Right; Lay,
    Lady, Lay; Stuck Inside of Mobile with the Memphis Blues Again.
Side 2: I'll Be Your Baby Tonight; All I Really Want to Do; My Back
    Pages; Maggie's Farm; Tonight I'll Be Staying Here With You.
Side 3: She Belongs to Me; All Along the Watchtower; The Mighty Quinn
    (Quinn the Eskimo); Just Like Tom Thumb's Blues; A Hard Rain's A-
    Gonna Fall.
Side 4: If Not For You; It's All Over Now, Baby Blue; Tomorrow Is a Long
    Time; When I Paint My Masterpiece; I Shall Be Released; You Ain't
    Goin' Nowhere; Down in the Flood.

Pat Garrett and Billy the Kid, July 1973 (Col. KC 32460)
Soundtrack album from film of the same name.
Side 1: Main Title Theme (Billy); Cantina Theme (Workin' for the Law); Billy 1; Bunkhouse Theme; River Theme.
Side 2: Turkey Chase; Knockin' on Heaven's Door; Final Theme; Billy 4; Billy 7.

Dylan, November 1973 (Col. PC 32747)
Studio outtakes of cover versions.
Side 1: Lily of the West; Can't Help Falling in Love; Sarah Jane; The Ballad of Ira Hayes.
Side 2: Mr. Bojangles; Mary Ann; Big Yellow Taxi; A Fool Such As I; Spanish Is the Loving Tongue.

Planet Waves, January 1974 (Asy. 7E 1003)
Side 1: On a Night Like This; Going Going Gone; Touch Mama; Hazel; Something There is About You; Forever Young.
Side 2: Forever Young; Dirge; You Angel You; Never Say Goodbye; Wedding Song.

Before the Flood, June 1974 (Asy. AB 201)
Concert album, with The Band.
Side 1: Most Likely You Go Your Way (and I'll Go Mine); Lay, Lady, Lay; Rainy Day Women #12 & 35; Knockin' on Heaven's Door; It Ain't Me, Babe; Ballad of a Thin Man.
Side 2: (all tracks performed by The Band alone) Up on Cripple Creek*; I Shall Be Released; Endless Highway*; The Night They Drove Old Dixie Down*; Stage Fright*.
Side 3: (first three tracks by Dylan solo) Don't Think Twice, It's All Right; Just Like a Woman; It's Alright Ma (I'm Only Bleeding); (last three tracks by The Band alone) The Shape I'm In*; When You Awake*; The Weight*.
Side 4: All Along the Watchtower; Highway 61 Revisited; Like a Rolling Stone; Blowin' in the Wind.
[*Written by R. Robertson.]

Blood on the Tracks, January 1975 (Col. PC 33235)
Side 1: Tangled Up in Blue; Simple Twist of Fate; You're a Big Girl Now; Idiot Wind; You're Gonna Make Me Lonesome When You Go.

Side 2: Meet Me in the Morning; Lily, Rosemary and the Jack of Hearts; If You See Her, Say Hello; Shelter from the Storm; Buckets of Rain.

The Basement Tapes, June 1975 (Col. C2 33682)
Practice sessions with The Band, recorded June-October 1967.
Side 1: Odds and Ends; Orange Juice Blues (Blues for Breakfast)*; Million Dollar Bash; Yazoo Street Scandal*; Goin' to Acapulco; Katie's Been Gone*.
Side 2: Lo and Behold!; Bessie Smith*; Clothes Line Saga; Apple Suckling Tree; Please Mrs. Henry; Tears of Rage**.
Side 3: Too Much of Nothing; Yea! Heavy and a Bottle of Bread; Ain't No More Cane*; Crash on the Levee (Down in the Flood); Ruben Remus*; Tiny Montgomery.
Side 4: You Ain't Goin' Nowhere; Don't Ya Tell Henry; Nothing Was Delivered; Open the Door, Homer; Long Distance Operator; This Wheel's on Fire***.
[*Written or arranged by Band members; **by Dylan and R. Manuel; ***by Dylan and R. Danko.]

Desire, January 1976 (Col. PC 33893)
Side 1: Hurricane; Isis; Mozambique; One More Cup of Coffee; Oh, Sister.
Side 2: Joey; Romance in Durango; Black Diamond Bay; Sara.
[All songs except "Coffee" and "Sara" were co-written by Jacques Levy.]

Hard Rain, September 1976 (Col. PC 34349)
Concert album, with the Rolling Thunder Review.
Side 1: Maggie's Farm; One Too Many Mornings; Memphis Blues Again; Oh, Sister; Lay, Lady, Lay.
Side 2: Shelter from the Storm; You're a Big Girl Now; I Threw It All Away; Idiot Wind.

Appendix C

Practical Suggestions for Analysis of Performance

Until technology provides direct recorded sound with every book, and indeed thereafter, readers must trust authors' perceptions and descriptions. Words on paper remain the most effective and permanent medium for analysis. Because a reader's perception differs drastically from a listener's, a reader can slow down, think through, and agree or disagree with written analysis.

Besides words, as a way to convey information about aural perception, a sketch can suggest what music or a voice sounds like. A sketched line can indicate approximate pitch change and can make some distinctions that words cannot (for example, a voice falling in an underhand vs. overhand curve). Such a system is less precise and, therefore, perhaps more true to musical nature than is Western-classical-music notation. Japanese epic singers preserve such a system; and many scholars believe that the three accent marks of Homeric Greek originally guided proper epic singing of words, on pitches that rise (´) or fall (`) or go up then down (⁀).

As you listen to an oral performance over and over, with analytic intentions, you will probably fall naturally into a way of marking pitch changes and other elements (e.g., underlining for loudness), one that makes consistent sense to you. Don't worry too much about the rest of the world, yet. Given constant changes in technology, it will be some time—centuries probably, if ever—before masses of users agree on one system for analysis of oral performance.

In your notes to yourself, use what you know. Don't strain to employ conventions that you're unfamiliar with (e.g., notation, phonetic transcription), for you're likely to forget thereafter what the marks mean. Mark everything that seems important to your own perceptions. You can always go back, relisten, and decide that a particular slur or warble doesn't matter after all. If you hesitate and then mark nothing, however, you'll never go back to the spot.

Take the time, before you start, to type out the text with plenty of space between lines for notations. Faced with a cramped photocopy, you're more likely to leave out or unintelligibly squeeze in your notes. Count on many stops and many repetitions, as you listen and relisten to a passage. Be consistent unto yourself, and be patient.

· As methodological examples, here are two sketches, somewhat formalized from my notes to myself as I listened to each song. For "Isis," I here show only the two instruments that play in between the sung stanzas. At the left I give the number of the stanza and its last few words. At the right I give the length, in measures, of the instrumental break. The solid line shows violin. The broken line shows harmonica. Dashes farther apart indicate a screechier, less melodic harmonica than those spaced closer together. Direction of a line suggests direction of musical pitch. However, I have placed the violin line always higher than the harmonica line, simply to allow an indication of the two playing simultaneously.

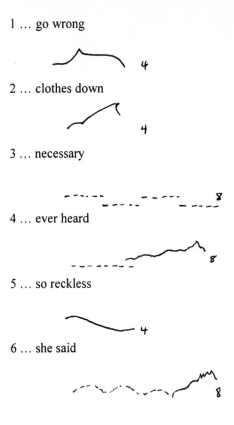

1 ... go wrong

2 ... clothes down

3 ... necessary

4 ... ever heard

5 ... so reckless

6 ... she said

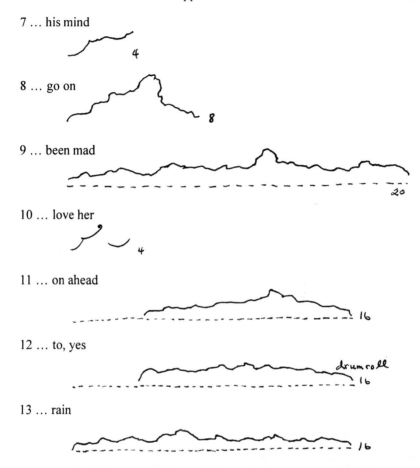

7 ... his mind

8 ... go on

9 ... been mad

10 ... love her

11 ... on ahead

12 ... to, yes

13 ... rain

When you want to separate out and show the interaction of more instruments, as in the following excerpts from the 1974 tour version of "It Ain't Me, Babe," listen several times through for outstanding effects, and then listen for and mark one instrument at a time. It's efficient to mark your own text with different colors of ink. Here I use letters instead: v ⌣ for vocal effects, g ⌢ for lead guitar, k ⌣ for keyboard. Again, direction of a line indicates approximate direction of musical pitch. For percussion, D D D indicates a series of separate drumbeats, and Ddddd, a drumroll.

Go away from my window

Leave at your own chosen speed

I'm not the one you want, Babe

I'm not the one you need D D D

You say you're looking for someone

Never weak but always strong Ddddd

To protect you and defend you Ddddd

Whether you are right or wrong Ddddd

Someone to open each and every dooooor

.... Move lightly from the ledge, Babe

Move lightly on the growound

I'm not the one you want, Babe

I'll only let you down

You say you're looking for someone D D D

Who will promise never to part D D D

Someone to close his eyes for you Ddddd

Someone to close his heart Ddddd

.... Go melt back into the night, Babe

Everything inside here is made of stone

There's nothing in here that's-a moving

And anyway I'm not ay-lone

You say you're looking for someone Ddddd

Who'll pick you up every time you fall Ddddd

Appendix D

Published Reference Sources on Bob Dylan

This bibliography is intended as a guide to bibliographical and discographical resources, not a reiteration of the listed items' contents. I include only books with reference listings, plus articles comprised solely of reference material.

Each entry describes a physically existing item that I have examined. Thus, I can guarantee accuracy of all citations excepting ones marked "not seen." Those "not seen" were not available from U.S. libraries that participate in Interlibrary Loan, as of January 1997. I would like to thank Elizabeth Hart and other librarians at Rutgers/Camden, plus Ken Garson at Drexel, for vital assistance. A researcher wishing to examine as many Dylan books as possible should visit the non-circulating collection at the Minnesota Historical Society, St. Paul. Special Collections at LaSalle University, Philadelphia, also has many non-print and ephemeral items.

I do not attempt to trace publishing history. Many books first published in England were republished in the United States, and vice versa, with differing pagination.

Aaseng, Nathan. *Bob Dylan*: *Spellbinding Songwriter*. Minneapolis: Lerner Publications, 1987. Timeline, pp. 51-56.

Amendt, Günter. *Reunion Sundown*: *Jokerman 84 Revisits Highway 61, eine Robetage über Dylans Europa-Tournee 1984.* Frankfurt am Main, Germany: Zweitausendeins, 1985. Not seen.

Anderson, Dennis. *The Hollow Horn*: *Bob Dylan's Reception in the United States and Germany.* München, Germany: Hobo Press, 1981. Works Consulted, Written in English, pp. 249-63, 272-77; Written in German, pp. 263-72, 278-80.

Antolín Rato, Mariano. *Bob Dylan, 2.* Madrid: Ediciones Júcar, 1975. Discografía oficial, pp. 243-46; Albumes piratas, p. 246; Bibliografía, pp. 247-48; Filmografía, p. 249.

Barth, Mitchell. "Dylan Discography." *Goldmine*, no. 48 (May 1980), 15. Not seen.

Bauldie, John, ed. *Wanted Man: In Search of Bob Dylan*. London: Black Spring Press, 1990. Some Bob Dylan Lists, pp. 203-9.

Blumenstein, Gottfried. *Mr. Tambourine Man: Leben und Musik von Bob Dylan*. Berlin: Henschel Verlag, 1991. Ausserdem verwendete Literatur, pp. 385-86; Diskografie, pp. 387-96.

Cable, Paul. *Bob Dylan: His Unreleased Recordings*. New York: Schirmer Books, 1978. Entire book.

Cartwright, Bert. *The Bible in the Lyrics of Bob Dylan*. Bury, Lanc., U.K.: Wanted Man, 1985. Biblical Annotations, pp. 43-57.

Cesar, Ligia Vieira. *Poesia e política nas canções de Bob Dylan e Chico Buarque*. São Paulo, Brazil: Editora Estação Liberdade, 1993. Referências bibliográficas, pp. 107-10; Obras consultadas, pp. 111-14; Discografia, pp. 115-17.

Cott, Jonathan. *Dylan*. Garden City, N.Y.: Dolphin/Doubleday, 1985. Discography, pp. 242-43.

Day, Aidan. *Jokerman: Reading the Lyrics of Bob Dylan*. Oxford: B. Blackwell, 1988. Chronology of Dylan's Career and Officially Released Recordings, pp. 145-74.

Diddle, Gavin. *Images and Assorted Facts: A Peek Behind the Picture Frame*. Manchester, U.K.: The Print Centre, 1983. Not seen.

Dorman, James E. *Recorded Dylan: A Critical Review and Discography*. Pinedale: Soma Press of California, 1982. Selected Bibliography, p. 123.

Dowley, Tim, and Barry Dunnage. *Bob Dylan: From a Hard Rain to a Slow Train*. Tunbridge Wells, Kent, U.K.: Midas Books; New York: Hippocrene Books, 1982. Discography [subdivided, incl. bibliography], pp. 107-77.

Dreau, Jean-Louis, and Robert Schlockoff. *Hynotist Collectors: An International Illustrated Discography*. Paris: Media Presse Editions, 1989. Not seen.

Ducray, François, Philippe Manœuvre, Hervé Muller, and Jacques Vassal. *Dylan*. Paris: Editions Albin Michel, 1975. Bibliographie, pp. 172-73; Discographie officielle, pp. 174-80; Enregistrements pirates, pp. 181-89; Filmographie, p. 189.

Dundas, Glen. *Tangled Up in Tapes Revisited: A Collector's Guide to the Recordings of Bob Dylan*. Thunder Bay, Ont., Canada: SMA Services, 1990. Not seen.

Dunn, Tim. *"I Just Write 'Em As They Come"*: *An Annotated Guide to the Writings of Bob Dylan*. Painesville, Ohio: Not-A-Ces, 1990. Entire book.

Escudero, Vicente. *Bob Dylan: Hombre, musico, poeta, mito*. Barcelona: Editorial Lumen, 1991. Not seen.

Gans, Terry Alexander. *What's Real and What Is Not: Bob Dylan through 1964, The Myth of Protest*. München, Germany: Hobo Press, 1983. Bibliography, pp. 151-60.

Gray, Michael. *Song and Dance Man: The Art of Bob Dylan*. New York: Dutton, 1972. List of Released Dylan Albums, with Notes, pp. 305-16; Other Officially Released Dylan Recordings, with Notes, pp. 317-21; Recordings Not Officially Released, pp. 322-27. [Rev. New York: St. Martin's Press, 1981, with no reference section.]

Gray, Michael, and John Bauldie, eds. *All Across the Telegraph: A Bob Dylan Handbook*. London: Sidgwick & Jackson, 1987. Reprinted articles, no reference section.

Gray, Michael H. *Popular Music*. New York: R. R. Bowker Co., 1983. Vol. 3 of *Bibliography of Discographies*, 3 vols. to date, 1977- . Items D228-D247, p. 52.

Gross, Michael, with Robert Alexander. *Bob Dylan: An Illustrated History*. New York: Grosset & Dunlap, 1978. Chronology, pp. 139-46; Sources, pp. 148-49.

Hampton, Wayne. *Guerrilla Minstrels: John Lennon, Joe Hill, Woody Guthrie, Bob Dylan*. Knoxville: Univ. of Tennessee Press, 1986. Selected Bibliography, pp. 267-68; Selected Discography, p. 271; Song List, pp. 280-85.

Herdman, John. *Voice Without Restraint: A Study of Bob Dylan's Lyrics and Their Background*. Edinburgh: Paul Harris Publishing, 1982. Selected Bibliography, pp. 155-56; Discography, pp. 156-60.

Hetmann, Frederik. *Bob Dylan: Bericht über einen Songpoeten*. Hamburg, Germany: Rowohlt Taschenbuch Verlag, 1976. Not seen.

Heylin, Clinton. *Bob Dylan: A Life in Stolen Moments Day by Day, 1941-1995*. New York: Schirmer Books, 1996. Entire book.

———. *Bob Dylan: Behind the Shades, A Biography*. New York: Summit Books, 1991. Dramatis Personae, pp. 454-63; Selected Bibliography, pp. 464-66; Bob Dylan Sessionography 1961-90, pp. 467-78.

———. *Bob Dylan: The Recording Sessions, 1960-1994*. New York: St. Martin's Press, 1995. Entire book.

———. *Rain Unravelled Tales: A Rumourography*. Bury, Lanc., U.K.: Wanted Man, 1982. Not seen.

————, ed. *Saved! The Gospel Speeches of Bob Dylan*. Madras, India: Hanuman Books, 1990. Untitled list of venues, pp. 113-15.

————. *To Live Outside the Law: A Guide to Bob Dylan Bootlegs*. Sale, Cheshire, U.K.: Labour of Love Productions, 1989. Not seen.

Hoggard, Stuart, and Jim Shields. *Bob Dylan: An Illustrated Discography*. 2nd edn. Dumbarton, Scotland: Transmedia Express, 1978. Not seen.

Humphries, Patrick. *The Complete Guide to the Music of Bob Dylan*. London and New York: Omnibus Press, 1995. Entire book.

Humphries, Patrick, and John Bauldie. *Absolutely Dylan: An Illustrated Biography*. [British title *Oh No! Not Another Bob Dylan Book*.] New York: Viking Studio Books, 1991. Notes [i.e., subdivided chronology], pp. 169-239.

Imre, Barna. *Bob Dylan: Regény*. Budapest, Hungary: Zenemukiado, 1986. Diszkográfia, pp. 227-29; Irodalom, pp. 229-30.

Krogsgaard, Michael. *Positively Bob Dylan: A Thirty-Year Discography, Concert and Recording Session Guide, 1960-1991*. Ann Arbor, Mich.: Popular Culture, Ink., 1991. Entire book. [Incorporates his earlier publications from Scandinavian Institute for Rock Research.]

Ledbury, John. *Mysteriously Saved: An Astrological Investigation into Bob Dylan's Conversion to American Fundamentalism*. London: Quest Publications, 1981. Not seen.

Lohse, Michael, and Harald Müller, comps. *In the Summertime: A Bibliography of Articles on the Bob Dylan European Concerts, 1981*. München, Germany: Hobo Press, 1981. Not seen.

Marcus, Greil. *Invisible Republic: Bob Dylan's Basement Tapes*. New York: Holt; London: Picador, 1997. Works Cited, pp. 224-31; Discography, pp. 232-72.

Mathias, Pat. *Bob Dylan*. Mankato, Minn.: Creative Education, 1994. Not seen.

McAuliffe, Jon. "The Dylan Collectibles." *Music World and Record Digest Weekly News*, no. 59 (22 August 1979), 10-11; no. 60 (29 August 1979), 12; no. 70 (January 1980), [14-15]. Not seen.

McGregor, Craig, ed. *Bob Dylan: A Retrospective*. New York: William Morrow & Co., 1972. Rpt. New York: Da Capo Press, 1990. Reprinted articles, no reference section.

McKeen, William. *Bob Dylan: A Bio-Bibliography*. Westport, Conn.: Greenwood Press, 1993. Bibliography, pp. 135-79; Performances, pp. 181-284.

Mellers, Wilfrid. *A Darker Shade of Pale: A Backdrop to Bob Dylan*. New

York: Oxford Univ. Press, 1985. Discography, pp. 237-42; Bibliography, pp. 243-44.

Michel, Steve. *The Bob Dylan Concordance*. Grand Junction, Colo.: Rolling Tomes, Inc., 1992. Entire book.

Nogowski, John. *Bob Dylan: A Descriptive, Critical Discography and Filmography, 1961-1993*. Jefferson, N.C.: McFarland & Co., 1995. Entire book.

Ordovás, Jesús. *Bob Dylan*. Madrid: Ediciones Júcar, 1972. Discografía, pp. 103-7.

Price, Dan. "Bibliography of Bob Dylan: Articles and Books, By and About; Albums and Singles Published; and Unreleased Recordings." *Popular Music and Society* 3 (1974), 227-41.

Rémond, Alain. *Les Chemins de Bob Dylan*. Paris: Epi sa Editeurs, 1971. Discographie, pp. 179-82.

Richardson, Susan. *Bob Dylan*. New York: Chelsea House Publishers, 1995. Further Reading, p. 123; Chronology, pp. 124-25.

Riley, Tim. *Hard Rain: A Dylan Commentary*. New York: Alfred A. Knopf, 1992. Discography, pp. 297-323; Selected Bibliography, pp. 325-30.

Rinzler, Alan. *Bob Dylan: The Illustrated Record*. New York: Harmony Books, 1978. Selected Bibliography, p. 120.

Roques, Dominique. *The Great White Answers: The Bob Dylan Bootleg Records*. Salindres, France: Southern Live Oak Productions, 1980. Not seen.

Rowley, Chris. *Blood on the Tracks: The Story of Bob Dylan*. New York: Proteus, 1984. Not seen.

Scaduto, Anthony. *Bob Dylan*. New York: Grosset & Dunlap, 1971. Discography, pp. 275-76.

Schmidt, Mathias R. *Bob Dylans "message songs" der sechziger Jahre und die anglo-amerikanische Tradition des sozialkritischen Liedes*. Frankfurt am Main, Germany: Peter Lang, 1982. Bibliographie, pp. 221-32.

Schmitt [pseud. Liederschmitt], Walter, and Alain Alcot. *Bob Dylan halb und halb und eins*. 3 vols. Trier, Germany: Éditions Trèves, 1981. Not seen.

Scobie, Stephen. *Alias Bob Dylan*. Red Deer, Alberta, Canada: Red Deer College Press, 1991. Works Cited, pp. 191-92.

Shelton, Robert. *No Direction Home: The Life and Music of Bob Dylan*. New York: Beech Tree/Morrow, 1986. Select Bibliography, pp. 511-16; Song Index (by S. J. Estes, ed. and rev. by Roger Ford), pp. 517-45; Discography (by Roger Ford), pp. 547-58.

Spitz, Bob. *Dylan: A Biography.* New York: Norton, 1991. Discography (by Jeff Friedman), pp. 591-646.

Stroop, Jan, and Jan Donkers. *Bob Dylan bij benadering.* Hoorn, Netherlands: Westfriesland, 1973. Bob Dylan in feiten, pp. 158-83; Diskografie, pp. 183-89; Bibliografie, pp. 189-92.

Tang, Jesper. *Bob Dylan smiler!* Kobenhavn, Denmark: Borgens Billigbogs Bibliotek, 1972. Discografi, pp. 227-31; Bibliografi, pp. 232-34; Litteraturliste, pp. 235-36.

Thomson, Elizabeth M., ed. *Conclusions on the Wall: New Essays on Bob Dylan.* Manchester, U.K.: Thin Man, Ltd., 1980. Bibliography, p. 108.

Thomson, Elizabeth, and David Gutman, eds. *The Dylan Companion.* New York: Delta, 1990. Selective Bibliography, pp. 296-315; Discography, pp. 316-24.

Wilcox, Janelle M. "Critical Analyses of Bob Dylan's Poetry: An Annotated Bibliography of Scholarly Criticism from [*sic*] 1965-1988." *Bulletin of Bibliography* 46 (1989), 31-39.

Williams, Don. *Bob Dylan: The Man, the Music, the Message.* Old Tappan, N.J.: Fleming H. Revell Co., 1985. Bibliography, pp. 157-58.

Williams, Paul. *Bob Dylan, Performing Artist: The Middle Years, 1974-1986.* Novato, Calif., and Lancaster, Pa.: Underwood-Miller, 1992. Discography, pp. 309-17; Filmography, pp. 318-20; Bibliography, pp. 321-24.

―――. *Dylan—What Happened?* South Bend, Ind.: and books; Glen Ellen, Calif.: Entwhistle Books, 1979. Recommended Reading, p. 127.

―――. *Dylan—What Happened? One Year Later.* München, Germany: Hobo Press, 1980. Not seen.

―――. *Performing Artist: The Music of Bob Dylan, Volume One, 1960-1973.* Novato, Calif., and Lancaster, Pa.: Underwood-Miller, 1990. Discography, pp. 283-91; Filmography, pp. 293-95; Bibliography, pp. 297-300.

Williams, Richard. *Dylan: A Man Called Alias.* New York: Holt, 1992. Bibliography, p. 190.

Wissolik, Richard David, et al., eds. *Bob Dylan, American Poet and Singer: An Annotated Bibliography and Study Guide of Sources and Background Materials, 1961-1991.* Greensburg, Pa.: Eadmer Press, 1991. Entire book.

Wissolik, Richard David, and Scott McGrath. *Bob Dylan's Words: A Critical Dictionary and Commentary.* Greensburg, Pa.: Eadmer Press, 1994. Bibliography, pp. 233-41.

Wraith, John, and Mike Wyvill. *Down the Highway: 1993 Tourbook*. Bury, Lanc., U.K.: Wanted Man, 1994. Not seen.

————. *From Town to Town: 1994 Tourbook*. Bury, Lanc., U.K.: Wanted Man, 1995. Not seen.

————. *Heading for Another Joint: 1992 Tourbook*. Bury, Lanc., U.K.: Wanted Man, 1993. Not seen.

————. *Still on the Road: 1991 Tourbook*. Bury, Lanc., U.K.: Wanted Man, 1992. Not seen.

Appendix E

A Dylan Chronology, through 1997

This chronology is limited to commercially released albums (i.e., excluding singles, excluding participation in others' recordings), plus significant public appearances, concert tours, and biography relevant to performing art. Concerning the time period covered in this book, also see "Dylan's Albums 1961-1976" (Appendix B).

Outside of this chronology, detailed information on Dylan's life and work is readily available. In "Published Reference Sources on Bob Dylan" (Appendix D), see especially the works by Heylin (1996), Humphries and Bauldie, Krogsgaard, McKeen, Shelton, and Spitz. N.B.: That alphabetical listing implies no endorsement or preference concerning discrepancies in detail that appear in one or another source.

1941   24 May, Robert Allen Zimmerman born to Beatrice and Abraham, Duluth (Minn.).

1947   Zimmerman family moves to Hibbing (Minn.).

1954   Bob's bar mitzvah.

1956-59 Bob plays with high-school dance bands.

1959   Sept., enrolls at University of Minnesota. Performs solo at coffeehouses as Bob Dillon or Dylan.

1960-61 Relocates to New York City [hereafter NYC], encouraged in various ways by Woody Guthrie, Sis Cunningham, Gordon Friesen, Bob and Sid Gleason, Pete Seeger, Robert Shelton, Izzy Young, John Hammond, and others. Performs at cafes and colleges in Conn., upstate N.Y., Minn., and N. J., and at NYC venues including Gerde's Folk City, Carnegie Chapter Hall, Riverside Church (radio broadcast), and recording studios playing backup harmonica for folk and blues artists. 26 Oct., signs first contract with Columbia Records.

1962   19 March, first album *Bob Dylan* released. Performs at cafes, folk clubs, and hootenannies in NYC, upstate N.Y., Mich., Montreal, and London.

1963   27 May, *The Freewheelin' Bob Dylan* released. Performs at folk clubs and folk festivals in London, Rome, Newport (R.I.), Monterey (Calif.), and elsewhere in U.S., and at protest marches in Greenwood (Miss.) and Washington (D.C.). Concerts (some featuring Joan Baez) in Camden (N.J.), NYC, Boston, and elsewhere in U.S. 13 Dec., accepts Tom Paine Award from Emergency Civil Liberties Committee, NYC.

1964   13 Jan., *The Times They Are A-Changin'* released. 8 Aug., *Another Side of Bob Dylan* released. Folk festivals and concerts (some featuring Joan Baez) throughout U.S., plus Toronto and London.

1965   22 March, *Bringing It All Back Home* released. 30 Aug., *Highway 61 Revisited* released. Folk festivals and concerts throughout U.S. and U.K., plus Toronto. After mid-Sept., concerts include Levon and the Hawks, later known as The Band. 22 Nov., marries Sara Lowndes.

1966   16 May, *Blonde on Blonde* released. Concerts throughout U.S., Canada, Australia, U.K., Ireland, and northern Europe. 29 July, motorcycle accident curtails travel.

1967   27 March, *Bob Dylan's Greatest Hits* released. 27 Dec., *John Wesley Harding* released. June-Oct., jam sessions with The Band, often bootlegged and eventually released as "The Basement Tapes."

1968   20 Jan., in first public appearance since 27 May 1966, participates in Woody Guthrie Memorial Concert, NYC.

1969   9 April, *Nashville Skyline* released. 31 Aug., performs at Isle of Wight Festival, U.K.

1970   8 June, *Self Portrait* released. 21 Oct., *New Morning* released. 9 June, accepts honorary D.Mus. from Princeton University.

1971   17 Nov., *Bob Dylan's Greatest Hits Vol. II* released. May, Macmillan publishes his long prose essay *Tarantula*, written mostly before 1966. 1 Aug., participates in benefit Concert for Bangladesh, NYC.

1972   November, travels to Mexico for first role in a film: *Pat Garrett and Billy the Kid*, directed by Sam Peckinpah (released May 1973).

1973   13 July, *Pat Garrett and Billy the Kid* [soundtrack] released. 16 Nov., *Dylan*, containing outtakes from 1969-70 studio sessions, released—reputedly contrary to Dylan's wishes, because he left Columbia for Asylum Records. May, Knopf publishes first authorized collection of song lyrics and related material, *Writings and Drawings by Bob Dylan*.

1974   17 Jan., *Planet Waves* released. 20 June, *Before the Flood* [live concert album] released. Jan.-Feb., much-heralded concert tour with The Band throughout U.S. 9 May, participates in Friends of Chile benefit concert, NYC.

1975   17 Jan., *Blood on the Tracks* released. 26 June, *The Basement Tapes* released. 23 March, participates in SNACK benefit concert for San Francisco public schools. With Howard Alk, at work on his own film *Renaldo and Clara* (released Jan. 1978). Oct.-Dec., Rolling Thunder Review tour of northeastern U.S. and Canada. 27 Dec., annual Modern Language Association conference devotes session to academic analysis of Dylan's work.

1976   16 Jan., *Desire* released. 10 Sept., *Hard Rain* [live] released. 25 Nov., surprise appearance at The Band's farewell concert "The Last Waltz," San Francisco. April-May, Rolling Thunder Review tour of southwestern U.S.

1977   Divorce proceedings and custody battle over five children.

1978   15 June, *Street-Legal* released. Feb.-March, concerts in Japan, Australia, and New Zealand; June-July and Sept.-Dec. in northern Europe, U.K., Canada, and U.S.

1979   23 April, *Bob Dylan at Budokan* [live] released in U.S. (in Japan four months earlier). 18 August, *Slow Train Coming* released. Much-discussed foregrounding of songs advocating Christianity. Nov.-Dec., concerts in western U.S.

1980   20 June, *Saved* released. 27 Feb., accepts Grammy award for Best Male Rock Vocal Performance. May, first annual Bob Dylan Festival Austria (international swap-meet). Jan.-Feb., April-May, and Nov.-Dec., concerts in U.S.

1981   12 Aug., *Shot of Love* released. June-July and Oct.-Nov., concerts in U.S., Canada, U.K., and northern Europe.

1982   15 March, inducted into Songwriters' Hall of Fame, NYC. 6 June, participates in Peace Sunday concert, Pasadena (Calif.). 22 July, first annual Bob Dylan Imitators' Contest, NYC.

1983   1 Nov., *Infidels* released. Sept., much-discussed visit to Jerusalem and apparent interest in Judaism. Accused in three lawsuits of libel, battery, and breach of contract.

1984   29 Nov., *Real Live* [live] released. May-July, concerts (most jointly billed with Santana and Joan Baez) in northern Europe, Spain, Italy, Ireland, and U.K.

1985   8 June, *Empire Burlesque* released. 4 Nov., *Biograph* released. 13 July, participates in Live Aid concert benefitting Ethiopian famine victims, Philadelphia. 25 July, performs in Moscow, sponsored by poet Yevgeny Yevtushenko and the Soviet Writers' Union. 22 Sept., participates in Farm Aid concert benefitting U.S. family farms, Champaign (Ill.). 13 Nov., CBS hosts gala event honoring his 25-year recording career and 35 million records sold, NYC.

1986   8 Aug., *Knocked Out Loaded* released. 20 Jan., participates in tribute concert to Martin Luther King, Washington (D.C.). At work on film *Hearts of Fire*, directed by Richard Marquand (released Oct. 1987). Feb.-March, concerts with Tom Petty and the Heartbreakers in New Zealand, Australia, and Japan; June-Aug. in U.S. and Canada (also some double-billed with Grateful Dead).

1987   20 Oct., *Hearts of Fire* [soundtrack] released. July, concerts with Grateful Dead in U.S. Sept.-Oct., concerts with Tom Petty and the Heartbreakers in Israel, Italy, northern Europe, and U.K.

1988   31 May, *Down in the Groove* released. April-May, jam sessions in his garage studio with George Harrison, Tom Petty, Roy Orbison, and Jeff Lynne (under transparent pseudonyms), released 18 Oct. as *Traveling Wilburys Vol. I.* 20 Jan., inducted into Rock and Roll Hall of Fame, NYC. 4 Dec., participates in Bridge School concert benefitting handicapped children, Oakland (Calif.). June-Sept., concerts in U.S. and Canada. This and subsequent years' concerts come to be called "The Never-Ending Tour."

1989   6 Feb., *Dylan and the Dead* [live] released. 22 Sept., *Oh Mercy* released. 24 Sept., surprise appearance on Chabad Telethon. May-June, concerts in U.K., Ireland, northern Europe, Spain, Italy, Greece, and Turkey; July-Nov. in U.S. and Canada.

1990   11 Sept., *Under the Red Sky* released. 23 Oct., *Traveling Wilburys Vol. III* released. 30 Jan., accepts Commandeur des Arts et des Lettres, France's highest cultural award for foreigners, Paris. 29 Sept., termed one of the twentieth century's "100 Most Influential Americans" by *Life* magazine. Jan.-Feb., concerts in U.S., Brazil, Paris, and London; May-Nov. in U.S., Canada, Iceland, and northern Europe.

1991   20 March, *Bootleg Series Vols. 1-3* released. 20 Feb., accepts Grammy award for Lifetime Achievement. Jan.-March, concerts in northern Europe, U.K., Ireland, U.S., and Mexico; Oct.-Nov. in U.S.

1992   3 Nov., *Good as I Been to You* released. 25-26 Jan., academic conference on Dylan, University of Victoria, B.C., Canada. 16 Oct., tribute concert of others performing Dylan's songs, NYC. June-Nov., concerts in Australia, New Zealand, Canada, U.S., northern Europe, and Italy. [N.B. At this point this chronology will cease listings for The Never-Ending Tour. Full information continues to appear in sources available from the information services named in my "Preface to the Second Edition."]

1993   23 Aug., *Bob Dylan: The 30th Anniversary Concert Celebration* [cover versions live] released. 26 Oct., *World Gone Wrong* released. 17 Jan., surprise appearance at pre-Inaugural concert for incoming President Bill Clinton.

1994   15 Nov., *Bob Dylan's Greatest Hits Vol. III* released. 14 Aug., performs at Woodstock '94 concert, 25 years after avoiding the original. Nov., Random House publishes *Drawn Blank*, Dylan's sketches in pen-and-ink, charcoal, and crayon. 17-18 Nov., does MTV broadcast.

1995   25 April, *Bob Dylan: MTV Unplugged* [adapted soundtrack] released. 19 Nov., participates in concert celebrating Frank Sinatra's 80th birthday, Los Angeles.

1996   Dec., grants first-ever permission to adapt lyrics for a cover version, in support of handgun ban after massacre of children in Dunblane, Scotland.

1997   Jan., nominated for Nobel Prize in Literature. 23 Sept., *Time Out of Mind* released.

Appendix F

The Dylan Exam, F69, UW Madison

As composed by Andy Mirer and Betsy Bowden, this exam has previously been published only in *Kaleidoscope* [Madison, Wis.] 2, no. 2 (14 Jan. 1970), 5, 10.

SIX WEEK EXAM
TIME: 55 MINUTES
THIS EXAMINATION CALLS FOR A CLEARHEADED GRASP OF THE FACTS, NOT FOR VAGUE GENERALIZATIONS. USE YOUR TIME WISELY.

1. *Bringing It All Back Home*, as a whole, has been interpreted both as a glorification of the drug culture and as a vindication of it. Discuss this important critical question with reference to "Mr. Tambourine Man," "Subterranean Homesick Blues," and at least one other song.

2. Analyze two of the following:
   a. Courtly-love conventions in "She Belongs to Me."
   b. Fertility goddess and/or Fisher King imagery in "Maggie's Farm."
   c. The "ubi sunt" theme in "It's All Over Now, Baby Blue."
   d. The tradition of the Gothic novel in "Love Minus Zero."

3. Can "Bob Dylan's 115th Dream" be classified as a Menippean satire? If not, what is its raison d'être?

4. Compare and contrast style and thematic import of "Gates of Eden" and John Milton's *Paradise Lost*.

5. Trace the development of Dylan's concept of illusion and reality in "On the Road Again" and "Gates of Eden." How does this concept

essentially differ from the fantasy worlds of "Mr. Tambourine Man" and "115th Dream"?

6. "The pump don't work 'cause the vandals took the handle." What archetypal myths does this line bring to mind? Discuss.

7. Discuss the theme of fatalism in "It's Alright Ma." Is the overall impact of the song affirmed or denied by the final stanza? How?

8. Relate *Bringing It All Back Home* to the whole of Western literature. Be specific.

Notes

Overview

1. Bob Dylan, interviewed by Nat Hentoff, *Playboy*, March 1966; rpt. in *Bob Dylan: A Retrospective*, ed. Craig McGregor (New York: Morrow, 1972), p. 139. Cited throughout this study as *Retrospective*, this compilation is essential for futher reference on Dylan because many items included in it—especially those from early issues of rock periodicals like *Creem* and *Crawdaddy!*—cannot be found in libraries. Therefore, I give page references only for the *Retrospective* reprint in each case.
2. See bibliographies throughout Barre Toelken, *The Dynamics of Folklore* (Boston: Houghton Mifflin, 1979).
3. As examples of theoretical gun-jumping see most (not all) essays in Richard Bauman et al., *Verbal Art as Performance* (Prospect Heights, Ill.: Waveland Press, 1977), and in Dan Ben-Amos and Kenneth S. Goldstein, eds., *Folklore: Performance and Communication* (The Hague: Mouton, 1975).
4. Michael Benamou and Charles Caramello, eds., *Performance in Postmodern Culture* (Madison and Milwaukee: Coda Press and Center for Twentieth-Century Studies, 1977).

Chapter I. Protests

1. Bob Dylan, interviewed by Hubert Saal, *Newsweek*, 26 Feb. 1968; rpt. in *Retrospective*, cited in n. 1 to Overview, p. 245.
2. Anthony Scaduto, *Bob Dylan* (New York: Grosset & Dunlap, 1971), pp. 10-12.
3. Partly because of this same McCarthyite climate, only a few booklength studies of the history of protest songs in the U. S. have been completed: R. Serge Denisoff's right-leaning *Great Day Coming: Folk Music and the American Left* (Urbana: Univ. of Illinois Press, 1971); Josh Dunson's left-leaning *Freedom in the Air* (New York: International Publishers, 1965); Richard Reuss's unpublished *American Folklore and Left-Wing Politics* (Ph.D. diss., Indiana Univ., 1971); and David King Dunaway's *How Can I Keep from Singing: Pete*

Seeger (New York: McGraw-Hill, 1981). For articles see David Dunaway, "Protest Song in the United States: A Selected Bibliography," *Folklore Forum* [Indiana Univ.] 10 (Fall 1977), 8-25.

4. On the situation see Scaduto, cited in n. 2, pp. 139-41. Throughout this study, a date given with a song title is its copyright date, which for a released song usually coincides with the release date of its studio album. (See album discography, Appendix B.) As noted below, the unreleased "John Birch" song first appeared in print, with variant title and lyrics, eight years before Dylan recopyrighted it with Warner Bros.

   Bibliographical reference for printed texts of songs is spotty, although most can be found in one of two books. The lyrics of most released and unreleased songs before 1973 are in Bob Dylan, *Writings and Drawings* (New York: Knopf, 1973). The lyrics and sheet music to most songs copyrighted between 1966 and 1975 are in *The Songs of Bob Dylan from 1966 through 1975* (New York: Knopf, 1976). For words and sheet music of songs copyrighted before 1966 or after 1975, however, the reader needs one or more of the songbooks put out by New York record companies (ASCAP), usually with no publication date. Larger early collections include *Bob Dylan* (Warner Bros.), *Bob Dylan: The Original* (Warner Bros.-Seven Arts Music), *Bob Dylan Song Book* (M. Witmark), and *Bob Dylan: A Retrospective* (Warner Bros.). Songs have also been copyrighted by Duchess Music, Bob Dylan Words and Music Co., Dwarf Music, Big Sky Music, Ram's Horn Music, and Special Rider Music.

5. Back issues of *Broadside*, an important sociohistorical document for this period, can still be ordered from its original editors, Sis Cunningham and Gordon Friesen, 215 W. 98th St., no. 4D, New York, NY 10025.

6. See, for example, obituaries in *Rolling Stone*, no. 213 (20 May 1976), pp. 12, 15; *Village Voice* 21 (19 April 1976), 87; and *Open Road* [Detroit], Summer 1976, pp. 27, 31.

7. Appendix A also provides texts of all other songs closely analyzed in this study, and recording information for each performance. Ochs's song has not been recorded.

   As precedent to my methdology see Scaduto, cited in n. 2, p. 136. He compares Ochs's "Ballad of Medgar Evers" (*Broadside*, no. 29, July 1963) to Dylan's "Only a Pawn in Their Game" (*Broadside*, no. 33, 12 Oct. 1963). Also see Ochs's "Davey Moore" (*Broadside*, no. 25, late April 1963) and Dylan's "Who Killed Davey Moore?" (*Broadside*, no. 29, July 1963).

8. See *Woody Guthrie Folk Songs* (New York: Ludlow Music, 1963), pp. 94-95 for "Union Maid" and p. 7 for "This Land Is Your Land." Concerning Dylan's relationship with Guthrie, see Scaduto, cited in n. 2, pp. 39-59 and passim; Dylan's poem "Last Thoughts on Woody Guthrie" in *Writings and Drawings*, cited in n. 4, pp. 52-56; and Dylan interviewed by Nat Hentoff, *New Yorker*, 24 Oct. 1964, rpt. in *Retrospective*, p. 58.

9. "The Times They Are A-Changin'" appears in *Broadside*, no. 39 (7 Feb. 1964) and on Dylan's album of the same name (Col. KCS 8905). Its title has been collected several times in the California Folklore Archives, functioning as both a straightforward and an ironic proverb.

10. Quoted by Dunson, cited in n. 3, pp. 105-6.

11. Bryan Ferry, a British art-school student in 1970, as lead singer and songwriter helped form the precedent-setting "glitter rock" band Roxy Music. His solo career began in 1973. See *The Illustrated New Music Express Encyclopedia of Rock*, comp. Nick Logan and Bob Woffinden (London: Hamlyn, 1976), s.v. Roxy Music.

12. Thanks to Evelyn Hammer for this formulation, and to any other students at Penn State or Rutgers/Camden whose ideas have encouraged my analyses.

13. Quoted from *The Norton Anthology of Poetry*, shorter edition, rev., ed. Alexander W. Allison et al. (New York: Norton, 1975), p. 33. A "Child ballad" is one of the 306 traditional narrative songs included, with variants from manuscript and print sources, in Francis James Child's *English and Scottish Popular Ballads*, 5 vols. (Boston: Houghton Mifflin, 1882-98). According to the cover notes of *Freewheelin'*, Dylan had recently been listening to Martin Carthy perform Child ballads.

14. A convenient summary of Child-ballad characteristics appears in Albert B. Friedman's introduction to *The Viking Book of Folk Ballads of the English-Speaking World* (1956; rpt. New York: Penguin, 1976).

Chapter II. Developments

1. Bob Dylan, interviewed by Ron Rosenbaum, *Playboy* 25 (March 1978), 72.

2. On early British influence see Anthony Scaduto, *Bob Dylan* (New York: Grosset & Dunlap, 1971), p. 176 and passim. Dylan's first gospel-sound albums are *Street-Legal* (June 1978, Col. JC 35453) and *Slow Train Coming* (August 1979, Col. FC 36120).

3. In the *New York Times*, on 2 Aug. 1976, p. 22, Alan C. Rothfeld claims that Carter had reversed the meaning of "He's not busy being born, he's busy dying," from "It's Alright, Ma" (1965). On 16 Aug. 1976, p. 30, Patrick Anderson cites three sources of evidence to prove that the line is "He not busy being born is busy dying" and Carter's paraphrase "therefore true to Dylan's meaning."

4. "John Lennon's Realpolitik," *Newsday*, July 1972; rpt. in Robert Christgau, *Any Old Way You Choose It* (Baltimore: Penguin, 1973), p. 279.

5. The key work is Homer G. Barnett, *Innovation: The Basis of Cultural Change* (New York: McGraw-Hill, 1953).

6. For a count of Dylan's song topics, see George H. Lewis, "The Pop Artist and His Product: Mixed-Up Confusion," *Journal of Popular Culture* 4 (1970), 327-38.

7. Interviewed by Nat Hentoff, *Playboy*, March 1966; rpt. in *Retrospective*, cited

in n. 1 to Overview, p. 133.

8. See Appendix A for texts and recording information for these four studio performances.

9. For discussion and bibliography of "worldview" studies, see Barre Toelken, *The Dynamics of Folklore* (Boston: Houghton Mifflin, 1979), pp. 225-61.

10. Frank Kermode [and Stephen Spender], "Bob Dylan: The Metaphor at the End of the Tunnel," *Esquire* 77 (May 1972), 118. Wilfrid Mellers's fullest discussion is "Bob Dylan: Freedom and Responsibility," orig. in *Retrospective*, pp. 398-407. [Note to second edition: See Appendix D for Mellers's 1985 book on Dylan.] Some of the academic and journalistic overviews described in Chapter VII share this trait of linear schematization.

11. Jon Landau, "John Wesley Harding," *Crawdaddy!* May 1968; rpt. in *Retrospective*, p. 257.

12. Quoted by Paul Oliver, *The Meaning of the Blues* (1960; rpt. New York: Collier/ Macmillan, 1963), pp. 106-7.

13. Ibid., p. 105.

14. See Samuel Charters, *Robert Johnson* (New York: Oak, 1973), pp. 38, 86.

15. "You're the Nearest Thing to Heaven," by Johnny Cash, Hoyt Johnson, and Chet Atkins (BMI, Hi-Low Music, and E. & M. Pubs., n.d.), and "You Were Meant for Me," by Arthur Freed and Nacio Herb Brown (ASCAP, Robbins Music, 1929); quoted by S. I. Hayakawa in an early recognition of the power and artistry of blues lyrics, "Popular Songs vs. the Facts of Life," *Etc.* 12, no. 2 (1955), 85.

16. LeRoy "Satchel" Paige, *Maybe I'll Pitch Forever*, as told to David Lipman (Garden City, N.Y.: Doubleday, 1962), p. 227. The item often appears as filler in sports sections of newspapers.

17. Listen, for example, to his performance of "Milkcow Blues Boogie," recorded in 1954 and rereleased on *Elvis: The Sun Sessions* (1976, RCA APMI-1675).

18. That is, Sandy Gant's computerized discography of unreleased Dylan performances lists no bootleg version, 1960-1976. [Note to second edition: Information documented in Appendix D confirms that Dylan never performed "Sad-Eyed Lady" in any public venue through 1995.]

19. As examples see Edmund R. Leach, "Genesis as Myth" (1962) and Claude Lévi-Strauss, "Four Winnebago Myths: A Structural Sketch" (1960), rpt. of both in *Myth and Cosmos: Readings in Mythology and Symbolism*, ed. John Middleton (Garden City, N.Y.: Natural History Press, 1967), pp. 1-26. As introduction to the interdisciplinary subject see Jean Piaget, *Structuralism*, ed. and transl. Chaninah Maschler (New York: Basic Books, 1970).

20. *Playboy* interview, cited in n. 1, pp. 70, 69.

21. As examples see motifs J2324 and D1741.8 in Stith Thompson, *Motif-Index of Folk Literature*, 6 vols. (Bloomington: Indiana Univ. Press, 1955-58).

22. Joseph Campbell, *The Masks of God*, vol. 3, *Occidental Mythology* (New York: Viking, 1964), p. 21. It should be noted that Campbell publishes speculation,

not scholarship.

23. Roland Barthes, *Elements of Semiology*, transl. A. Lavers and C. Smith (New York: Hill & Wang, 1968), p. 74.
24. Personal communication with Greil Marcus, 1 November 1977.
25. Ibid.
26. This point is made succinctly by Leonard B. Meyer, *Emotion and Meaning in Music* (Chicago: Univ. of Chicago Press, 1956), p. 257: "For example, the image of a triumphal procession might within a given culture be relevant to the character of a piece of music; but the association might for private reasons arouse feelings of humiliation or defeat."

Chapter III. Performances

1. Bob Dylan, interviewed by Jann Wenner, *Rolling Stone*, 29 Nov. 1969; rpt. in *Retrospective*, cited in n. 1 to Overview, p. 346.
2. The term is Ellen Willis's, in a pithy account of the early sociohistorical and musical context: "Dylan," *Cheetah*, ca. 1968; rpt. in *Retrospective*, pp. 218-39. Most of this article first appeared in *Commentary* 44 (Nov. 1967), 71-78, as "The Sound of Bob Dylan."
3. Quotations come from, respectively, "Talkin' World War III Blues" (1963), "Lay, Lady, Lay" (1969), "Tangled Up in Blue" (1974), and "You're a Big Girl Now" (1974).
4. The essential subjectivity of literary judgment is defended by F. R. Leavis in *The Living Principle* (New York: Oxford Univ. Press, 1975), pp. 16-69. Another possible interpretation of "Just Like a Woman" is offered by Ron Loewinsohn. He understands the major conflict in the song as that between the ribbons-bows-curls Baby and the fog-amphetamine-pearls Baby, who are "two embodiments of the same thing, a complex figure that might be taken in either of two ways: 1) a change in time in which a straight middle-class Shirley Temple or Barbie Doll type slides into the subterranean drug culture 'like all the rest,' but where she retains, even in that costume, all the negative attributes she had when she lived in the suburbs; 2) a composite 'Baby' who can be found in Suburbia and in the East Village, and who has to be rejected, like the Sirens, wherever she is found. In this latter case, 'Baby' is a figure for America, a siren with many avatars" (personal communication, 20 Jan. 1978).
5. Michael Gray, *Song and Dance Man* (New York: Dutton, 1972), pp. 196-97.
6. Bear image from *McCall's* magazine, quoted by Gil Turner in "Bob Dylan—A New Voice Singing New Songs," *Sing Out!* Oct.-Nov. 1962; rpt. in *Retrospective*, p. 25. Dog image from Mitch Jayne of the Dillards, quoted by Nat Hentoff in "The Crackin', Shakin', Breakin' Sounds," *New Yorker*, 24 Oct. 1964; rpt. in *Retrospective*, p. 55.
7. Richard Middleton, *Pop Music and the Blues* (London: V. Gollancz, 1972), p. 47.

Chapter IV. Causes

1. Bob Dylan, interviewed by Ron Rosenbaum, *Playboy* 25 (March 1978), 70.

2. Michael Owen Jones, "Aesthetic Attitude, Judgment, and Response: Definitions and Distinctions," paper read at American Folklore Society meeting, 17 Oct. 1980.

3. ˙For discussion and bibliography see Barre Toelken, *The Dynamics of Folklore* (Boston: Houghton Mifflin, 1979), for aesthetics esp. pp. 181-97, for audience interaction esp. pp. 106-21. A key article is Ilhan Başgöz, "The Tale Singer and His Audience," in *Folklore: Performance and Communication*, ed. Dan Ben-Amos and Kenneth S. Goldstein (The Hague: Mouton, 1975), pp. 143-203. Başgöz compares two texts of a Turkish *hikaye* as performed among his subject's coffeehouse companions and then on stage at a government-sponsored "folk festival," finding the former much richer and more elaborated. He discusses only textual variants, however.

4. Among interviews to this effect see *Ramparts* (1966) and *Rolling Stone* (1969), both rpt. in *Retrospective*, cited in n. 1 to Overview, pp. 187, 347; *Knockin' on Dylan's Door: On the Road in '74*, ed. editors of *Rolling Stone* (New York: Pocket Books, 1974), p. 104; and *Playboy*, cited in n. 1, p. 82. Dylan described his composition of the song—which began as a ten-page "rhythm thing on paper all about my steady hatred directed at some point that was honest" and then acquired music "like swimming in lava"—for *Saturday Evening Post*, 1966; rpt. in *Retrospective*, p. 158.

5. Similarly, see Roger Sessions, *The Musical Experience* (Princeton: Princeton Univ. Press, 1950), p. 97: "The really 'understanding' listener takes the music into his consciousness and remakes it actually or in his imagination, for his own uses."

6. For accounts of a number of the concerts and related material, see *Knockin' on Dylan's Door*, cited in n. 4. For a summary see Greil Marcus, "Heavy Breathing," *Creem*, May 1974, p. 37 ff.

7. Al Kooper with Ben Edmonds, *Backstage Passes: Rock 'n' Roll Life in the Sixties* (New York: Stein & Day, 1977), pp. 55-56. [Note to second edition: Clinton Heylin questions this account in *Bob Dylan: The Recording Sessions 1960-1994* (New York: St. Martin's Press, 1995), pp. 40-41.]

8. As examples, see accounts of the Forest Hills concert on 28 Aug. 1965 in Anthony Scaduto, *Bob Dylan* (New York: Grosset & Dunlap, 1971), p. 217, and in Kooper, cited in n. 7, pp. 64-66. For widely varying accounts of the incident at Newport '65, see Kooper, p. 60; Scaduto, quoting Ric von Schmidt, pp. 214-15; and in *Retrospective* Irwin Silber pp. 71-72, Paul Nelson pp. 73-76, and Dylan interviewed by Nat Hentoff pp. 130-31.

9. Quotations, starting from "your debutante just knows," are from "Stuck Inside of Mobile" (1966), "It's All Over Now, Baby Blue" (1965), "Absolutely Sweet Marie" (1966), "George Jackson" (1971), and "Dear Landlord" (1968). See

the chapters on proverbs and riddles in *Folkore and Folklife: An Introduction,* ed. Richard M. Dorson (Chicago: Univ. of Chicago Press, 1972), pp. 117-43. Also see Robert A. Rothstein, "The Poetics of Proverbs," in *Studies Presented to Professor Roman Jakobson by His Students,* ed. Charles E. Gribble (Cambridge, Mass.: Slavica, 1968), pp. 265-74.

A whole related topic, besides the proverbial function of newly created rock lines, would explore a major means of oral survival nowadays for traditional proverbs: in so-called "shaggy dog jokes," with endings such as "People who live in grass houses shouldn't stow thrones" and "A Benny shaved is a Benny urned." Another practice preserves traditional proverbs in parody form, e.g., "When the going gets weird, the weird turn pro," attributed to Hunter Thompson. The wisdom of the ages does not slip out of human memory without a good fight, apparently.

10. Charlie Gillett, *The Sound of the City* (New York: Outerbridge & Dienstfrey, 1970), p. 1.

11. Robbins Burling, *Man's Many Voices* (New York: Holt, 1970), p. 137.

12. See Roger D. Abrahams, *Deep Down in the Jungle: Negro Narrative Folklore from the Streets of Philadelphia* (Hatboro, Pa.: Folklore Associates, 1964), esp. pp. 52-53; Thomas Kochman, "Toward an Ethnography of Black American Speech Behavior," in *Afro-American Anthropology,* ed. Norman E. Whitten, Jr. and John F. Szwed (New York: Free Press, 1970), pp. 145-62; and Jerry W. Leach, Alan Dundes, and Bora Özkök, "The Strategy of Turkish Boys' Verbal Dueling Rhymes," in *Directions in Sociolinguistics,* ed. John J. Gumperz and Dell Hymes (New York: Holt, 1972), pp. 130-60. For a literary perspective on rhyme see W. K. Wimsatt, "One Relation of Rhyme to Reason: Alexander Pope," *Modern Language Quarterly* 5 (1944), 323-38.

13. Harold Wentworth and Stuart Berg Flexner, comps., *Dictionary of American Slang,* 2nd supp. edition (New York: Crowell, 1975), s.v. "hang out."

14. Michael Gray, *Song and Dance Man* (New York: Dutton, 1972), pp. 182-83.

15. Personal communications with Marcus, Gant, and Ford respectively, all January 1978; Scaduto, cited in n. 8, p. 240.

16. This is the title of one of Dylan's songs (1964). Perhaps the comment functions as a hostile equivalent of the kind of teasing at other concerts, wherewith the musicians trick the audience into believing it is about to hear a different song.

17. Roger Ford reports that in fact a new drummer, Mickey Jones, had replaced Levon Helm for the 1966 world tour (personal communication, 11 Jan. 1978).

18. Kooper, cited in n. 7, p. 60.

19. See esp. the conflicting accounts of the concert in *Sing Out!* Nov. 1965, by Irwin Silber and Paul Nelson; rpt. in *Retrospective,* pp. 71-76.

Chapter V. Effects

1. Bob Dylan, interviewed by Ron Rosenbaum, *Playboy* 25 (March 1978), 80.

2. Tom Wilson quoted by Nat Hentoff in "The Crackin', Shakin', Breakin' Sounds," *New Yorker*, 24 October 1964; rpt. in *Retrospective*, cited in n. 1 to Overview, p. 46.

3. I can propose no quasi-scientific method for measuring a song's continuing popularity among amateur musicans and listeners to already-purchased albums. As a rough measure of continuing popularity, the young British readership of *New Musical Express*, 17 Dec. 1977, pp. 28-29, voted Dylan the ninth best male singer and second best songwriter of 1977, despite his having released no material in 1977.

4. Tristram Coffin, "Mary Hamilton and the Anglo-American Ballad as an Art Form," *Journal of American Folklore* 70 (1957), 209.

5. All songs on *Another Side* were cut during the same evening session, according to Hentoff, cited in n. 2, pp. 44-61. "All I Really Want To Do" makes for a good comparison because its narrator, too, is rejecting Baby's romantic expectations of him—but with the gleeful aid of howling and swooping vocal inflections.

6. Bob Neuwirth is singing harmony with Dylan, according to Roger Ford (personal communication, 11 Jan. 1978). Any other singers are barely audible after the first refrain, on my copy of this tape.

7. The musicians are probably Family Dog, according to Sandy Gant, or the Bonzo Dog Doo-Dah Band, according to Wayne Bernhardson; both bands fl. late 1960s.

8. Sandy Gant's computerized discography lists six early performances as follows: Joan Baez concert, Forest Hills, 8 Aug. 1964; Los Angeles Civic Auditorium, April 1965; London Albert Hall, 9-10 May 1965; BBC, recorded 8 June, broadcast 12 June 1965; Forest Hills, 28 Aug. 1965; Isle of Wight, 31 Aug. 1969. [Note to second edition: See Appendix D for published sources of similar information.]

9. See *Top 10's and Trivia of Rock & Roll and Rhythm & Blues, 1950-1973*, comp. Joseph Edwards, arranged chronologically from *Billboard* listings (St. Louis: Blueberry Hill, 1974). In Dylan's career, except for "Like a Rolling Stone," only "Rainy Day Women #12 & 35" in May 1966 and "Lay, Lady, Lay" in Sept. 1969 became Top Ten radio singles.

Chapter VI. Improvements

1. Bob Dylan, interviewed by Jonathan Cott, *Rolling Stone*, no. 257 (26 Jan. 1978), p. 44.

2. Note to second edition: Information documented in Appendix D now confirms that Dylan never performed "Subterranean Homesick Blues" in concert until 7 June 1988. He then used it as opening number at most concerts through 1989. Would he re-memorize the lyrics just before coming onstage?

3. These cue cards were drawn by Joan Baez, Donovan, Alan Price, and director

D. A. Pennebaker, according to Pennebaker (personal communication, 8 March 1978).

4. Interviewed by Ron Rosenbaum, *Playboy* 25 (1978), 70.

5. Alexander Pope, *An Essay on Criticism*, 1711, line 298; quoted from *Eighteenth-Century English Literature*, ed. Geoffrey Tillotson et al. (New York: Harcourt, Brace & World, 1969), p. 558.

6. He unfortunately rhymes this line with "You were always responded [*sic*] when I needed your help," in "Sara" (1975). Wayne Bernhardson, as what Alan Dundes would term "folk commentary," offers the following gloss (personal communication, May 1977):

> The beach was deserted except for some sand
> You were always right there when I needed a hand
> The beach was deserted except for sandpipers
> You were always right there to change the kids' diapers
> The beach was deserted except for a whale
> You were always right there with your mop and your pail
> The beach was deserted except for a porpoise
> You were never *delicti* when I needed a *corpus*
> The beach was deserted except for a seahorse
> You were always right there—now you want a divorce?

7. Quotations from "The Times They Are A-Changin'" (1963) and "Gates of Eden" (1965).

8. Note to second edition: See Appendix D for sources of information on numerous outtakes now available.

9. *Playboy* interview, cited in n. 4, p. 82.

10. See K2213.1, T231, and related references in Stith Thompson, *Motif-Index of Folk Literature*, 6 vols. (Bloomington: Indiana Univ. Press, 1955-58). Chaucer uses the theme in the Wife of Bath's Prologue, line 587 ff., and Shakespeare in *Richard III*, act 1, scene 2.

11. Harold Wentworth and Stuart Berg Flexner, comps., *Dictionary of American Slang*, 2nd supp. edition (New York: Crowell, 1975), s.v. "where it's at" (in Supplement).

12. See the first two chapters of Paul Oliver, *The Meaning of the Blues* (1960; rpt. New York: Collier/Macmillan, 1963).

13. Bob Dylan, "Last Thoughts on Woody Guthrie," in his *Writings and Drawings* (New York: Knopf, 1973), p. 56.

14. See Anthony Scaduto, *Bob Dylan* (New York: Grosset & Dunlap, 1971), pp. 39-51 and passim, concerning Woody Guthrie's *Bound for Glory* (New York: Dutton, 1943).

15. Personal communication with Marjorie Guthrie, Jan. 1977.

16. In some folklores, menstruation directly symbolizes the difference between male and female, e.g., *The Tain*, transl. Thomas Kinsella (Oxford: Oxford Univ. Press, 1970), p. 250. Elsewhere the monthly cycles of moon and woman have combined into many cultures' moon goddesses.

17. For "Grand Coulee Dam" see *Woody Guthrie Folk Songs* (New York: Ludlow Music, 1963), pp. 8-9. In 1968 Dylan and others recorded it in concert for *A Tribute to Woody Guthrie, Part One* (Col. KC 31171).

18. The late-1960s song "Chestnut Mare" was co-written by Roger (Jim) McGuinn, who played in many Rolling Thunder Review concerts excluding the one recorded for *Hard Rain*, and Jacques Levy, who co-wrote with Dylan most of the songs on *Desire*. Make of that what you will.

19. Plate 29 of *Milton*, 1804; rpt. in *The Complete Poetry and Prose of William Blake*, ed. David V. Erdman, rev. edition (Berkeley: Univ. of California Press, 1982), p. 127.

20. Annotations to *The Works of Sir Joshua Reynolds*, after 1798; reprod. in Blake, cited in n. 19, p. 641.

21. As examples John Lennon and Harry Nilsson sing it on *Pussy Cats* (RCA CPL 1-0570); and Michael Stanley makes it strophic, with "Look out kid" as the refrain, on *Michael Stanley* (Tumbleweed TWS 106).

Chapter VII. Aesthetics

1. Bob Dylan, interviewed by Happy Traum and John Cohen, *Sing Out!* Oct.-Nov. 1968; rpt. in *Retrospective*, cited in n. 1 to Overview, p. 286.

2. See esp. Eric A. Havelock, "The Preliteracy of the Greeks," *New Literary History* 8 (1976-77), 369-91.

3. Charles Keil, *Urban Blues* (Chicago: Univ. of Chicago Press, 1966), p. 205. For the possibility that musicologists, like literary critics, will someday agree upon terminology, see Jacques Barzun, "Music into Words," orig. 1951, in *Lectures on the History and Art of Music: The Louis Charles Elson Memorial Lectures at the Library of Congress, 1946-1963* (New York: Da Capo, 1968), p. 92. On the difficulty of using words to describe what music means, see Charles Seeger, "Music as a Tradition of Communication, Discipline and Play," *Ethnomusicology* 6 (1962), 156-63; and Leonard B. Meyer, *Emotion and Meaning in Music* (Chicago: Univ. of Chicago Press, 1956). See also Keil's criticism that Meyer's analysis applies only to composed, repeatable music in a culture that puts value on delayed gratification, in "Motion and Feeling through Music," *Journal of Aesthetics and Art Criticism* 24 (1966), 337-49.

4. Paul Oliver, *Aspects of the Blues Tradition* (1968; rpt. New York: Oak, 1970), pp. 2-3.

5. Brownie McGhee and Elvin Bishop both quoted by Robert Neff and Anthony Connor, *Blues* (Boston: Godine, 1975), pp. 25, 34; Dylan from "Pledging My Time" (1966).

6. An alphabetized list of these sources follows, with the two anonymous reviews first. In my discussion I refer to each article by the author's name and periodical title only. I provide page references to the reprint (not the original) of any article longer than three pages.

"Basic Dylan," *Time* 91 (12 Jan. 1968), 50.

"Dylan, Back on Pop Scene, Gets Instant Gold Disk," *Variety* 249 (17 Jan. 1968), 1, 54.

Aronowitz, Alfred G., "Dylan's Big Nonelectric Comeback," *Life* 64 (9 Feb. 1968), 12.

Christgau, Robert, "Secular Music," *Esquire*, May 1968; rpt. in Christgau's *Any Old Way You Choose It* (Baltimore: Penguin, 1973), pp. 50-61 (52-55 on *JWH*).

Fager, Charles E. "Cryptic Simplicity," *Christian Century* 85 (19 June 1968), 821.

Gleason, Ralph J., "Country Music Station Plays Soft," *Rolling Stone*, no. 5 (10 Feb. 1968), p. 10.

Goldberg, Steven, "Bob Dylan and the Poetry of Salvation," *Saturday Review of Literature*, 30 May 1970; rpt. in *Retrospective*, pp. 364-77.

Goldstein, Richard, "Dylan: Nothing Is Revealed," *Village Voice* 13 (1 Feb. 1968), 1, 41.

Landau, Jon, "John Wesley Harding," *Crawdaddy!* May 1968; rpt. in *Retrospective*, pp. 248-64.

March, Michael, "The 'I Wanna Be with You if You Wanna Be with Me' Fiction Interview," *Fusion*, 31 Oct. 1969; rpt. in *Retrospective*, pp. 306-8.

Mills, Gordon, "*John Wesley Harding*, Bob Dylan (Columbia CS 9604)," *Rolling Stone*, 24 Feb. 1968; rpt. in *The Rolling Stone Record Review*, ed. editors of *Rolling Stone* (New York: Pocket Books, 1971), pp. 508-11.

Nelson, Paul, "Bob Dylan's Latest," *Sing Out!* 18 (March-April 1968), 34-35.

Scaduto, Anthony, "1968: I'll Be Your Baby Tonight," in his *Bob Dylan* (New York: Grosset & Dunlap, 1971), pp. 249-57.

Shelton, Robert, "Dylan Sings of Lovers, Losers," *New York Times*, 14 Jan. 1968, sec. 4, p. 22.

Weberman, Alan, "John Wesley Harding Is Bob Dylan," *Broadside* [New York], no. 93 (July-Aug. 1968), pp. 5-10.

Williams, Paul, "God Bless America," *Crawdaddy!* Jan. 1968; rpt. in his *Outlaw Blues* (New York: Dutton, 1969), pp. 71-78.

Willis, Ellen, "Dylan," *Cheetah*, ca. 1968; rpt. in *Retrospective*, pp. 218-39 (236-39 on *JWH*).

Wood, Michael, "Bob Dylan: Wicked Messenger," *New Society*, no. 283 (29 Feb. 1968), pp. 314-15.

7. Greil Marcus, "Heavy Breathing," *Creem*, May 1974, pp. 38-39.

8. Weberman, cited in n. 6, pp. 8-9.

9. Michael Gray, *Song and Dance Man* (New York: Dutton, 1972), p. 73. For a representative critique see Greil Marcus, "Self Portrait No. 25," *Rolling Stone*, 23 July 1970; rpt. in *Rolling Stone Record Review*, cited in n. 6 (s.v. Mills), pp. 529-30. The *JWH* comments are excerpted from Marcus's "Let the Record Play Itself," *San Francisco Express-Times*, 10 Feb. 1969, p. 7.

10. Goldberg, cited in n. 6, p. 374.
11. Scaduto, cited in n. 6, p. 249.
12. Ibid.
13. Scaduto, cited in n. 6, p. 253.
14. This paragraph refers to *Rolling Stone*, no. 26 (1 Feb. 1969), p. 17; Landau, cited in n. 6, p. 262; and Gray, cited in n. 9, pp. 225-28.
15. Quotations in this paragraph all come from Mills, cited in n. 6. Dylan had in fact been reading at least Rimbaud, according to the *Rolling Stone* interview, 29 Nov. 1969; rpt. in *Retrospective*, p. 334.
16. Quotations in this paragraph all come from Gleason, cited in n. 6. William Butler Yeats's "The Tower" meditates on the inevitable coming of old age and death, a theme shared by other poems in *The Tower* (1928), such as "Among School Children" and "Sailing to Byzantium." The denizens of Dylan's watchtower are trapped inside cyclical time, doomed to watch forever for the approach of something inevitable; and the song shares in its album's themes of fear, death, time, and possible redemption.
17. Gleason, cited in n. 6, adapting lines from Dylan's "It Takes a Lot to Laugh, It Takes a Train to Cry" (1965) and "Rainy Day Women #12 & 35" (1966).
18. By 1980 the following six theses had been filed: Betsy Bowden, "Performed Literature: Words and Music by Bob Dylan," Ph.D., Univ. of California at Berkeley, 1978; Lawrence D. Medcalf, "The Rhetoric of Bob Dylan, 1963-66," Ph.D., Indiana Univ., 1978; Bill King, "Bob Dylan: The Artist in the Marketplace," Ph.D., Univ. of North Carolina, 1975; Carolyn Bliss, "Younger Now: Bob Dylan's Changing World and Vision," M.A., Univ. of Utah, 1972; John William McDonough, "Bob Dylan: The Romantic Sensibility in the Modern Cauldron," M.A., Univ. of North Carolina, 1968; and Carolyn Ball, "Bob Dylan: Contemporary Minstrel," M.A., Univ. of Maryland, 1967. For the Modern Language Association session on "The Artistry of Bob Dylan," see *PMLA* 90 (1975), 1015.
19. Landau, cited in n. 6, pp. 261-64.
20. Willis, cited in n. 6, p. 239.
21. Williams, *Outlaw Blues*, cited in n. 6, overleaf to title page.
22. Quotations in this paragraph all come from Williams, "God Bless America," cited in n. 6, pp. 72-76.
23. *Sing Out!* interview, cited in n. 1, p. 277.
24. "How Rock Communicates," rpt. in Williams's *Outlaw Blues*, cited in n. 6, pp. 171-88.
25. "Tom Paine Himself: Understanding Dylan," rpt. in Williams's *Outlaw Blues*, cited in n. 6, pp. 66, 62.
26. Susan Sontag, *Against Interpretation and Other Essays* (New York: Delta, 1966), p. 14.
27. "Tom Paine Himself," rpt. in Williams's *Outlaw Blues*, cited in n. 6, pp. 64-65. [Note to second edition: For other reprints see Williams's *Bob Dylan: Watching*

the River Flow, Observations on His Art-in-Progress 1966-1995 (London and New York: Omnibus Press, 1996).]

28. Weberman's Dylan Archives allegedly contained a computerized Dylan Concordance, one printout of which is said to have been purchased by the Duke University library system. Librarians and patrons found it not useful, however, on account on its bulk, its idiosyncratic system of reference, and its inclusion of not only the whole of *Tarantula* but also a number of songs by other people (e.g., Robbie Robertson) that Weberman believed were actually written by Dylan.

29. Gray, cited in n. 9, pp. 55-103. Setting out in this chapter to discover Dylan's "literary background from the evidence not of the man but of his work," Gray finds echoes of many writers including John Bunyan, D. H. Lawrence, John Donne, William Blake, Robert Browning, and T. S. Eliot. Most parallels seem coincidental, however, and Gray never says what these possible influences have to do with the rest of his analysis.

30. Gray, cited in n. 9, p. 172.

31. Ibid., pp. 262-63.

32. Carl Belz, *The Story of Rock*, 2nd edition (New York: Oxford Univ. Press, 1972), pp. 3, 167. The book expands his article "Popular Music and the Folk Tradition," *Journal of American Folklore* 80 (1967), 130-42.

33. Belz, cited in n. 32, pp. 232-43.

34. Richard Meltzer, *The Aesthetics of Rock* (New York: Something Else Press, 1970), p. 7.

35. Ibid., pp. 11-12.

36. As examples see Susanne K. Langer, *Problems of Art* (New York: Scribner's, 1957), p. 85; Barzun, cited in n. 3, p. 83; and Roger Sessions, *Questions about Music* (Cambridge: Harvard Univ. Press, 1970), pp. 102-3. For a statement of the opposite extreme, that words always swallow music, see Edward T. Cone, "Words into Music: The Composer's Approach to the Text," in *Sound and Poetry*, ed. Northrup Frye (New York: Columbia Univ. Press, 1957), pp. 3-15.

37. Wilfrid Mellers, *Twilight of the Gods* (New York: Viking/Schirmer, 1974), p. 15.

38. Ibid., p. 163.

39. Wilfrid Mellers, "Bob Dylan: Freedom and Responsibility," orig. in *Retrospective*, pp. 398-407. [Note to second edition: See Appendix D for Mellers's 1985 book on Dylan.]

40. Richard Middleton, *Pop Music and the Blues* (London: V. Gollancz, 1972), p. 34.

41. Ibid., pp. 174-83.

42. Robert Jerome Smith, "The Structure of Esthetic Response," *Journal of American Folklore* 84 (1971), 68-79. For overview and bibliography see Barre Toelken, *The Dynamics of Folklore* (Boston: Houghton Mifflin, 1979), pp. 151-97. Case studies include Michael Owen Jones, *The Hand Made Object*

and Its Maker (Berkeley: Univ. of California Press, 1975), and Henry Glassie, *Pattern in the Material Folk Culture of the Eastern United States* (Philadelphia: Univ. of Pennsylvania Press, 1968).

43. Meyer, cited in n. 3, p. 5. Also see Steven Feld's equally acerbic survey article, "Linguistic Models in Ethnomusicology," *Ethnomusicology* 18 (1974), 197-217.

44. Abraham Kaplan, "The Aesthetics of the Popular Arts," *Journal of Aesthetics and Art Criticism* 24 (1966), 351-64.

45. John G. Cawelti, "Notes Toward an Aesthetic of Popular Culture," *Journal of Popular Culture* 5 (1971), 267.

46. Herbert J. Gans, *Popular Culture and High Culture* (New York: Basic Books, 1974), p. 127.

47. Ibid., p. 116.

48. Ibid., p. 150.

Bibliography

The following works provided background and methodology for this book's first edition in 1982. For works specifically on Bob Dylan, see Appendix D.

Words and Music

Barzun, Jacques. "Music into Words." Orig. 1951. In *Lectures on the History and Art of Music: The Louis Charles Elson Memorial Lectures at the Library of Congress, 1946-1963*. New York: Da Capo, 1968. Pp. 67-93.

Boswell, George. "Reciprocal Controls Exerted by Ballad Texts and Tunes." *Journal of American Folklore* 80 (1967), 169-74.

————. "Stanza Form and Music-Imposed Scansion in Southern Ballads." *Southern Folklore Quarterly* 31 (1967), 320-31.

Bright, William. "Language and Music: Areas for Cooperation." *Ethnomusicology* 7 (1963), 26-32.

Bronson, Bertrand Harris. "The Interdependence of Ballad Tunes and Texts." Orig. 1944. "On the Union of Words and Music in the 'Child' Ballads." Orig. 1952. Both in his *The Ballad as Song*. Berkeley: Univ. of California Press, 1969. Pp. 37-63, 112-32.

Brown, Calvin S. *Music and Literature: A Comparison of the Arts*. Athens: Univ. of Georgia Press, 1948.

Davison, Archibald T. "Words and Music." Orig. 1953. In *Lectures on the History and Art of Music*, q.v. Barzun. Pp. 95-120.

Einstein, Alfred. "Words and Music." In his *Essays on Music*. New York: Norton, 1956. Pp. 90-118.

Feld, Steven. "Linguistic Models in Ethnomusicology." *Ethnomusicology* 18 (1974), 197-217.

Frye, Northrup, ed. *Sound and Poetry: English Institute Essays, 1956*. New York: Columbia Univ. Press, 1957.

Herzog, George. "Speech-Melody and Primitive Music." *Musical Quarterly* 20 (1934), 452-66.

Lanier, Sidney. *The Science of English Verse*. New York: Scribner's, 1880.

List, George. "The Boundaries of Speech and Song." *Ethnomusicology* 7 (1963), 1-16.

————. "An Ideal Marriage of Ballad Text and Tune." *Midwest Folklore* 7 (1957), 95-112.

Lomax, Alan. "Special Features of the Sung Communication." In *Essays on the Verbal and Visual Arts*, ed. June Helm [MacNeish]. Seattle: Univ. of Washington Press, for American Ethnological Society, 1967. Pp. 109-27.

Mellers, Wilfrid. *Twilight of the Gods: The Music of the Beatles*. New York: Viking/ Schirmer, 1974.

Roberts, Helen H. "A Study of Folk Song Variants Based on Field Work in Jamaica." *Journal of American Folklore* 38 (1925), 149-216.

Schwadron, Abraham A. "On Words and Music: Toward an Aesthetic Conciliation." *Journal of Aesthetic Education* 5.3 (1971), 91-108.

Performance

Alcheringa/Ethnopoetics. Journal, from 1970.

Baüml, Franz H. "Varieties and Consequences of Medieval Literacy and Illiteracy." *Speculum* 55 (1980), 237-65.

Ben-Amos, Dan, and Kenneth S. Goldstein, eds. *Folklore: Performance and Communication*. The Hague: Mouton, 1975.

Crosby, Ruth. "Oral Delivery in the Middle Ages." *Speculum* 11 (1936), 88-110.

Crystal, David. *The English Tone of Voice: Essays in Intonation, Prosody and Paralanguage*. New York: St. Martin's Press, 1976.

Dundes, Alan. "Texture, Text, and Context." *Southern Folklore Quarterly* 28 (1964), 251-65.

Finnegan, Ruth. *Oral Poetry: Its Nature, Significance and Social Context*. Cambridge: Cambridge Univ. Press, 1977.

Havelock, Eric A. *Preface to Plato*. Cambridge: Harvard Univ. Press, 1963.

Keil, Charles. *Urban Blues*. Chicago: Univ. of Chicago Press, 1966.

Literature in Performance. Journal, from 1980.

New Literary History 8 (Spring 1977), 335-535. Issue on oral poetics.

Okpewho, Isidore. *The Epic in Africa: Toward a Poetics of the Oral Performance*. New York: Columbia Univ. Press, 1975.

Shattuck, Roger. "How to Rescue Literature." *New York Review of Books* 27 (17 April 1980), 29-35.

Toelken, Barre. *The Dynamics of Folklore*. Boston: Houghton Mifflin, 1979.

Rock and Its Roots

Baggelaar, Kristin, and Donald Milton. *Folk Music: More Than a Song*. New York: Crowell, 1976.

Belz, Carl. *The Story of Rock*. 2nd edn. New York: Oxford Univ. Press, 1972.

Castleman, Harry, and Walter J. Podrazik. *All Together Now: The First Complete Beatles Discography, 1961-1975*. Ann Arbor, Mich.: Pierian, 1976.

Christgau, Robert. *Any Old Way You Choose It: Rock and Other Pop Music, 1967-1973*. Baltimore: Penguin, 1973.

Denisoff, R. Serge. *Solid Gold: The Popular Record Industry*. New Brunswick, N.J.: Transaction Books, 1975.

Dimmick, Mary Laverne. *The Rolling Stones: An Annotated Bibliography*. Pittsburgh: Univ. of Pittsburgh Graduate School of Library and Information Sciences, 1972.

Dunaway, David King. *How Can I Keep from Singing: Pete Seeger*. New York: McGraw-Hill, 1981.

Ewen, David. *All the Years of American Popular Music*. Englewood Cliffs, N.J.: Prentice-Hall, 1977.

Ferris, William. *Blues from the Delta*. Garden City, N.Y.: Doubleday, 1978.

Garon, Paul. *Blues and the Poetic Spirit*. London: Eddison, 1975.

Gillett, Charlie. *The Sound of the City: The Rise of Rock 'n' Roll*. New York: Outerbridge & Dienstfrey, 1970.

Guthrie, Woody. *Woody Guthrie Folk Songs: A Collection of Songs by America's Foremost Balladeer*. New York: Ludlow Music, 1963.

Harmon, James E. "Meaning in Rock Music: Notes Toward a Theory of Communication." *Popular Music and Society* 2 (1972), 18-32.

Havlice, Patricia Pate. *Popular Song Index*. Metuchen, N.J.: Scarecrow Press, 1975.

Hirsch, Paul M. "Sociological Approaches to the Pop Music Phenomenon." *American Behavioral Scientist* 14 (1971), 371-88.

Laing, Dave, Karl Dallas, Robin Denselow, and Robert Shelton. *The Electric Muse: The Story of Folk into Rock*. London: Methuen, 1975.

Lloyd, A. L. *Folk Song in England*. New York: International Publishers, 1967.

Logan, Nick, and Bob Woffinden. *The Illustrated New Musical Express Encyclopedia of Rock*. London: Hamlyn, 1976.

Malone, Bill C. *Country Music U.S.A.: A Fifty-Year History*. Austin: Univ. of Texas Press, 1968.

Marsh, Dave, with John Swenson, eds. *The Rolling Stone Record Guide*. New York: Random House, 1979.

Middleton, Richard. *Pop Music and the Blues: A Study of the Relationship and Its Significance*. London: V. Gollancz, 1972.

Oliver, Paul. *Aspects of the Blues Tradition*. [British title, *Screening the Blues*, 1968.] New York: Oak, 1970.

———. *The Meaning of the Blues*. [British title, *Blues Fell This Morning*, 1960.] New York: Collier/Macmillan, 1963.

Rolling Stone editors, eds. *The Rolling Stone Record Review*. New York: Pocket Books, 1971.

Sandberg, Larry, and Dick Weissman. *The Folk Music Sourcebook*. New York: Knopf, 1976.

Schicke, Charles A. *Revolution in Sound: A Biography of the Recording Industry*. Boston: Little Brown, 1974.

Tobler, John, and Pete Frame. *Rock 'n' Roll: The First 25 Years*. New York: Exeter, 1980.

Williams, Paul. *Outlaw Blues: A Book of Rock Music*. New York: Dutton, 1969.

Miscellaneous

Bayard, Samuel P. "Prolegomena to a Study of the Principal Melodic Families of British-American Folk Song." *Journal of American Folklore* 63 (1950), 1-44.

Burling, Robbins. *Man's Many Voices: Language in Its Cultural Context*. New York: Holt, 1970.

Dorson, Richard M., ed. *Folklore and Folklife: An Introduction*. Chicago: Univ. of Chicago Press, 1972.

Freeman, Donald C., ed. *Linguistics and Literary Style*. New York: Holt, 1970.

Gans, Herbert J. *Popular Culture and High Culture: An Analysis and Evaluation of Taste*. New York: Basic Books, 1974.

Langer, Susanne K. *Problems of Art: Ten Philosophical Lectures*. New York: Scribner's, 1957.

Meyer, Leonard B. *Emotion and Meaning in Music*. Chicago: Univ. of Chicago Press, 1956.

Seeger, Charles. "Music as a Tradition of Communication, Discipline and Play." *Ethnomusicology* 6 (1962), 156-63.

Sessions, Roger. *The Musical Experience of Composer, Performer, Listener*. Princeton: Princeton Univ. Press, 1950.

———. *Questions About Music*. Cambridge: Harvard Univ. Press, 1970.

Sontag, Susan. *Against Interpretation and Other Essays*. New York: Delta, 1966.

Index

Included here are substantive endnotes as well as the body of the text, but not appendices or bibliography. This index has five subdivisions, as follows: personal names, other names, song titles, other titles, and general index. Brackets indicate information added to the text.

Index of Personal Names

Index of Other Names

Index of Song Titles
(by Dylan unless specified otherwise)

Index of Other Titles
(dates for released Dylan albums only)

General Index

(including academic disciplines
and musical styles)